P9-DEO-873

HONDA
CONQUERORS OF THE TRACK

Also by Christopher Hilton

Nigel Mansell
Conquest of Formula 1
Ayrton Senna: The Hard Edge of Genius

Patrick Stephens Limited, part of Thorsons, a division of the Collins Publishing Group, has published authoritative, quality books for enthusiasts for more than twenty years. During that time the company has established a reputation as one of the world's leading publishers of books on aviation, maritime, military, model-making, motor cycling, motoring, motor racing, railway and railway modelling subjects. Readers or authors with suggestions for books they would like to see published are invited to write to: The Editorial Director, Patrick Stephens Limited, Thorsons Publishing Group, Wellingborough, Northants, NN8 2RQ

HONDA
CONQUERORS OF THE TRACK

CHRISTOPHER HILTON

Foreword by Wayne Gardner

Patrick Stephens Limited

British Library Cataloguing in Publication Data

Hilton, Christopher *1944-*
   Honda. Conquerors of the track
   1.   Honda Motorcycles, history
   I.   Title
   629.2275

   ISBN 1-85260-371-2

Patrick Stephens Limited is part of the Thorsons Publishing Group, Wellingborough, Northamptonshire NN8 2RQ, England

Typeset by Trintype, Wellingborough, Northamptonshire
Printed in Great Britain by The Bath Press, Bath, Avon

10 9 8 7 6 5 4 3 2 1

Contents

Foreword
by Wayne Gardner

Honda—that word means many things to many people. To millions around the world it stands for the best motorcycles, to others it means superb cars, and even lawnmowers and generators. To me that one word means above all a great motor racing company—a company totally committed to competitive excellence.

It is a great feeling to be part of that commitment which pervades the whole company, a feeling instilled in everyone who works with Honda by the man who started it all, Mr Soichiro Honda himself. He loves racing.

I have been a Honda rider since 1982—virtually my entire professional career—and I have been proud to lead the factory 500 cc squad since 1987, the year I won the World Championship. I was following some great names who have won championships for Honda, including the immortal Mike Hailwood, Jim Redman, another Australian Tom Phillis, Toni Mang, Sito Pons and Freddie Spencer. I found their stories—and the story of Honda—fascinating and I am delighted to have been asked to write this foreword.

ONE

The Time Machine

O N a hot September afternoon in 1989 Eddie Lawson was a couple of laps away from the World 500 cc motor bike championship at Goiania, Brazil, when a backmarker tumbled down directly in his path at the chicane. 'No, no,' Lawson thought, but his reflexes and control—sharpened and smoothed over twenty-four years of racing—were enough to let him hold a safe line, go through, and finish in second place. For several reasons this was enough to bestow immortality on him, quite apart from bestowing on Honda, manufacturers of the bike which had taken him there, a natural climax to a thunderous season. Honda had also taken the 250 cc championship, the World TT Formula One championship, the FIM World Endurance championship, the World 500 cc and 250 cc Moto-Cross championships; and yet nothing fundamental had changed across three decades.

On a June afternoon in 1959 a strong man called Naomi Taniguchi, on a bike with a fraction of Lawson's power, twisted through a place called Governor's Bridge on the Isle of Man, landed, held the bike steady, accel-

Lawson, the master of control and self-control, moving towards the World Championship in 1989.

Lawson's beautiful bike had famous ancestors. Kunimitsu Takahashi on the grid for the 1961 West German 250 race, which he won.

Wheeling the bikes onto the grid for the Spanish Grand Prix in the early 1960s.

Teisuka Tanaka on the 250 in Malaysia.

Mechanics contemplating the bike of Ulsterman Tommy Robb.

erated through an anonymous stone-clad village, flowed on to where an elderly official waved a black and white flag, and took for himself a sixth place after ten taut, tricky laps. This was the end of Honda's first major race and, almost precisely, the beginning of an epoch that would grow, falter, and grow again all the way to Lawson. As it did so, it drew to itself many different men and would bestow upon each a kind of nobility.

On a June afternoon three years after Taniguchi a strong, sure man called Derek Minter moved like a flood tide round Keppel Gate on another part of the Isle of Man, flicked through the right hander at Creg-ny-Baa, through the left-hander at Brandish Corner, twisted through the same Governor's Bridge, held the bike steady, and accelerated towards a different finishing line. He knew he'd lost, although that scarcely mattered because he had expected to lose. He wasn't even a works rider, and besides he'd been discreetly asked not to win. When he had passed the line he slowed the bike—it took over 300 yards, gently does it—and wheeled it onto the rough path towards scrutineering. So I lost, he thought very calmly, so what?

He was wrong.

Weeks later a rugged-looking much-loved Scot called Bob McIntyre was working on his bike—specifically, changing the sprockets—amid the bustle of the paddock at Oulton Park. An Ulsterman, Tommy Robb wandered up to him and couldn't help seeing how busy McIntyre was. 'I'll see you later, Tommy,' McIntyre said affably as Robb moved away so as not to interfere with the work in hand. But Robb never did see him again.

On a September afternoon in 1967 an impossibly rich and handsome Englishman called Mike Hailwood had a lead of seventeen seconds with a mere two laps of the Nations Grand Prix at Monza left to run. Honda would have a World 500 cc champion. They'd won everything else and now, as a vast Italian crowd watched bitterly, the final, exultant trophy for the big cabinet was at hand. Then the crankshaft buckled. A man equally as handsome as Hailwood, Giacomo Agostini, on an Italian MV bike went effortlessly by and took the trophy for himself. Many wept and Hailwood himself was close to tears. By another bitter irony Hailwood would not live to see Honda have a 500 cc champion, would not live to see a deeply-religious American called Frederick Burdette Spencer from Shreveport, Louisiana, crank his big Honda over to flow through the staccato left-right at Imola, move into the finishing straight and take that particular black and white flag. Spencer was second and, like Lawson, it didn't matter. Spencer had 144 points and it was enough. The big trophy was in the cabinet now, although it had taken more than two of the three decades of the epoch to put it there; but this does not alter the original premise that nothing fundamental changed because it was, and is, all uniquely about men and the machines they were on. Minter got £250 for his win, Wayne Gardner has enough to live in Monte Carlo but the fundamentals are too deeply rooted and they always lead back to the same equation: the man and his machine.

There are hard edges to this story as well as the triumphs. Wreathed among the winners are the ultimate losers: those who died. In that sense, at least, it is not always make for comfortable reading. Here too you will find post-war resentment, one blatant example of attempted bribery —nothing whatsoever to do with Honda, but nevertheless a strand in the

Freddie Spencer wins the 250 race at the Dutch Grand Prix in 1985 on his way to the double.

Soichiro Honda in Spain, 1985, still curious about details …

story of three men within the book—and the extraordinary vision of Soichiro Honda fulfilled. He pledged a near-bankrupt company, who had scarcely ventured out of Japan, that they would beat the world, and he did it. There were anxious moments during the passage of time when even he thought he'd pledged too much, and that's another strand in the story.

Along the way motor bike racing was to be enriched and made respectable, and yet it remained undiluted (although by summer 1990 this was being questioned). Supporters still chat happily to riders as riders, not demi-gods. Autographs still get signed. The many millions of yen, lira, pounds, dollars, and D-marks expended by Honda and others have not dehumanized it, although it is necessary to say that many fear it will become like Grand Prix motor racing where even the mediocre make their own millions and aren't necessarily available for interviews, never mind informal chats with fans.

It is demonstrably true that bike and car racing share the same basic impulses—men being propelled round circuits (often the same circuits)—and in both cases there will be one winner and the rest will be losers; but somehow a car is a capsule, a car is what you take your family out in, a car is constructed to shield and protect. A bike leaves you out in the open, the rider is essentially unshielded, unprotected save by his own ability to stay on it. Perhaps that's why the bike rider is closer in attitude to other human beings and will remain so: because, constantly exposed, he is closer to the elements of wind and rain, life and death. Mother Earth is always just there under his feet. Well, Mother Tarmacadam, anyway.

I am indebted to many people, some of whom are riders, some not. Murray Walker, almost a cult figure as a BBC motor sport commentator, explained the ground rules with touching patience and read the manuscript with corresponding care; that said, the mistakes are mine, not his. Others opened their treasure-chest of memories, helped, advised, and encouraged. They were (in no particular order) Vera Armstrong, Brian Webb, Kikue Carran, Arthur Carran, Agnes Carlier, Dickie Attwood, Nobby Clark (who took the trouble to send me 3,000

... all the details.

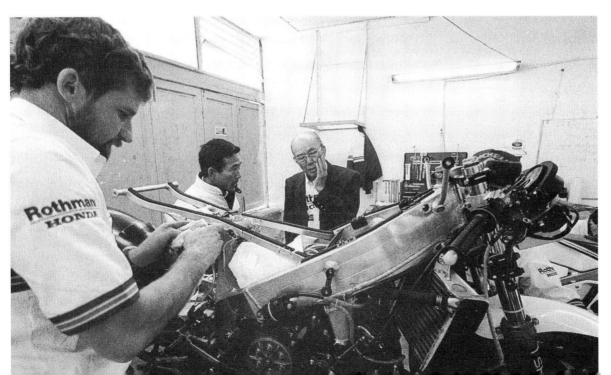

words in careful longhand), Shirley Robinson, Eoin Young, Tommy Robb, Bill Smith, Ralph Bryans, Derek Minter, Jim Redman, John Dee, Willie Stevenson, Peter Johnson, Harris Barnett, Wayne Gardner, Lonnie G. Hardy, Nick Harris, Toni and Collette Mang, Dawne Lemon, Mick Grant, Stuart Hall, Graham Sanderson, Kenny Roberts and Ted Macauley. In any other context it is an unlikely group and they are united only by Honda and the story.

Stuart Graham checked and added to the chapter 'A Mountain to Climb'; Ken Sprayson lent private photographs and his Mike Hailwood correspondence; Luigi and Tildi Taveri fed and watered me and lent their private photographs; Shiela Radburne of Castrol UK became an enthusiast and spent many hours combing their picture library. The results are here.

In any story of this scope you need reference books, magazines, and newspapers. *Motorcycle News* and *The Motor Cycle* were invaluable, and so was the Isle of Man *Daily Times*. The Isle of Man Tourist Board produced a map of the Island at a scale of 1:60,000 which helped to take me round. Castrol were generous in giving me permission to reproduce the Murray Walker-Hailwood interview from their 1967 video. I used the *Marlboro Grand Prix Guide* and the *Rothmans Grand Prix Motorcycle Year Book* as life-supports.

The magnificent, opulent *Motocourse* (Hazelton) was a delight to handle as well as consult. Peter Carrick has written two notable studies, *The Story of Honda* (Patrick Stephens) and *Great Motor Cycle Riders* (Robert Hale). Robb kindly gave me a copy of his book *From TT to Tokyo* (Courier-Herald), which was gratefully received, as was permission to quote extensively from it. I have also quoted—with kind permission—from: *Wheels of Fortune* by Jim Redman (Century Hutchinson), *The Languages of Britain* by Glanville Price (Arnold), *Hailwood* by Ted Macauley (Cassell), and *Fast Freddie* by Nick Harris and Peter Clifford (MRP).

I have drawn background from the *Directory of Classic Motorcycles* by Brian Woolley (Aston), *Honda Motor* by Tetsuo Sakiya, *The Race for Leadership* (Motor Sport Land Ltd., Tokyo), *Freddie Spencer* and *Honda Team Guide* by Michael Scott (Kimberleys), *The Story of the TT* by G.S. Davison (The TT special), *The Wayne Gardner Story* by Nick Hartgerink (Fairfax Magazines). And now that we are in to the video era, thanks to Rothmans for a tape of the 1987 season as well as their sincere co-operation. They also allowed me to comb their photographic library and the bulk of the pictures in the book are courtesy of them or Honda, who provided a magnificent selection of the early days.

Two other tapes, *TT Tribute* and *The Golden Mountain* from Duke Marketing, brought it alive. The races shown are by definition period pieces and can't escape the logistical nightmare of trying to cover everything over 37.75 miles of the Isle of Man; but they do get the full flavour, the sheer, stark speed, those ragged dry-stone walls ready to caress your elbow or tear it off, and in one case they got a very self-confident young lady spectator clutching both her unadorned assets in both hands in a most provocative way.

So while this may not be a definitive story of men and machines it is, I hope, readable by all. The technical history of Honda's engines has been written several times and is a subject for specialists anyway. This is a

Wayne Gardner at San Marino in 1986 ...

... leaning at Assen in 1987 ...

... and at full tilt at Assen, too.

story of riders rather than sprockets and to illustrate this, one of the videos contains a contradiction so absurd and yet so delightful that it seems to represent life itself.

The scene: somewhere on the Isle of Man.

The location: a normal British high street with terraced houses strung along both sides.

The dramatis personae: two ladies sitting on a bench taking their ease with nothing between them and a rider contesting the TT just a few feet away.

The action: the rider going by risking the wrath of the Gods if he loses control but holding his head down hard in the tuck position behind the fairing to get himself everlasting fame if he wins the race. As he passes the ladies wave to him in precisely the way elderly, becalmed, benevolent ladies do when they sit on benches.

The dialogue—inevitably it is the commentary of Murray Walker: 'The rider didn't exactly have time to wave back at a hundred and twenty miles an hour.'

He didn't. None of them ever did.

Nothing fundamental changed.

TWO

In the Nursery

T HE big van turned off the main road in Onchan Village on the Isle of Man and crawled slowly up the long, curved drive. Lawns and woods stretched away to either side, arranged as the British insist on arranging them by bringing order to nature and yet—here is the trick—leaving it looking natural.

A young, pretty, rather apprehensive woman stood by the front door of the Nursery Hotel and the people in the van could see it for what it was, a pebble-dash building with all the wooden window frames painted black in the old fashioned way. She was called Vera Armstrong and she was not long married. With her father, Brian Webb, she had just taken the place over. It was an ancient farm converted long before into a public house-cum-hotel. She was apprehensive because the occupants of the van were her very first guests and, to compound it, they were Japanese. It was raining.

The van stopped and a tall 30-year-old American with fair, curly-floppy hair hopped out. Bill Hunt, something of an amateur motor bike rider, introduced himself to Vera Armstrong as leader of the Honda team. Then the van disgorged the Japanese, a dozen of them, four other riders, mechanics, a doctor, and a cook. Methodically, quietly, deftly they began to unload many metal containers from the rear of the van. Vera Armstrong was very impressed.

Early May 1959 on the outskirts of Douglas, main town of the Isle of Man—an outcrop of land 38 miles long in the Irish Sea between England and Northern Island. The Island had a rocky backbone but it was lush as the forty shades of green of Ireland down in the pastureland below the backbone. It was much favoured by the English for both trips and holidays. It was only four hours on the ferry from Liverpool and you could go for the day if you wanted. Thousands did. In truth the Isle of Man was, and is, a jagged jigsaw piece on a storm-tossed sea and in any other context but motor cycle racing just another off-shore island.

As the van was being unloaded nobody knew, nobody even suspected that an epoch was poised to begin. They had no reason. Why should any-

Blessed, innocent days in the Nursery. Everyone's looking.

one have suspected? As a nation the Japanese were conclusively regarded as people who copied what other people had invented and, to broaden that impression, 1959 was the last epoch before mass travel, an era when Japan was even further from the Isle of Man than it is today, an impossible, unattainable, undreamed of distance for ordinary folk like the residents of Onchan village.

Nor was it as simple as geography. Traditional European and American manufacturers bestrode the world in virtually everything and this was perfectly illustrated by the Tourist Trophy races on the Island. These

Blessed, innocent days. Everybody's talking.

races, first run in 1907, had belonged to Norton, Velocette, Matchless, AJS, MV Augusta, and Gilera. That was the way the world was, and that was the way the world would surely always be. Only one Japanese had ever ridden on the Island, a man called Kenza Tada in 1930, and he'd finished fifteenth on a Velocette. Somehow that locked itself into history, one Japanese fifteenth 29 years before riding a British bike.

It is also true that memories of the Second World War were still vivid, resentment still lingered, and it is necessary to say that the Japanese would encounter this very quickly; in the saloon bar of the Nursery Hotel, in fact.

To understand why Honda arrived that May day it is necessary to travel back to 1954. Soichiro Honda, founder of the company which bore his name, sensed intuitively that they had to look and move outwards. That year they dispatched a rider called Mikio Omura to Sao Paulo, Brazil to ride a 90 cc bike in a race there. The race was to celebrate the 400th anniversary of the city. This was Honda's first attempt to measure one of their bikes against the outside world. Twenty two riders competed and Omura finished thirteenth. It was not, let us say, a triumphant opening; rather it was evidence of how good Honda were not. At this particular moment, too, Honda were in financial difficulties—bankruptcy was mentioned—but instead Mr Honda issued a proclamation, dated 20 March 1954:

Since Honda Motor Co. was established in 1948 we have achieved incredible progress owing to the tremendous enthusiasm of each of our employees. My childhood dream was to be a champion of motor racing with a machine built by myself. However, before becoming world champion, it is strongly required to establish a stable corporate structure, provided with precise production facilities and superior product design. From this point of view we have been concentrating on providing high quality products to meet Japanese domestic consumer demand and we have not had enough time to pour our efforts into motor cycle racing until now.

I have gained more details of the present situation of European and American companies through the report of the International race in Sao Paulo. Although I have always tried to turn my eyes to the countries of the world I realize that I paid too much attention to the Japanese domestic situation. Today world technological development is progressing very fast.

However my confidence was suddenly aroused and I feel sure I can win if I utilize my accumulative experience and unique conception. My spirit of challenge will not permit our present situation.

Today we have accomplished a production system in which we have full confidence and the chance has come to compete. I have decided to participate in the TT race next year!

This aim is definitely a difficult one but we have to achieve it to test the viability of Japanese industrial technology and demonstrate it to the world. Our mission is the enlightenment of Japanese industry.

I here avow my intention that I will participate in the TT race and I proclaim with my fellow employees that I will pour all my energy and creative powers in to winning.

Three months later Mr Honda travelled to the Isle of Man to have a look for himself. It was not a happy visit. He met resentment and did not care to be called a 'Jap'. But the Isle of Man races made a profound impression on him. TT week was the great motor cycle racing centrepiece of the year attended by pilgrims from all over Britain and Europe. It drew, sometimes willingly, sometimes unwillingly, all the great men and machines, and their deeds on the extraordinary 37.75-mile circuit were deeply woven into the folklore of the sport. As Mr Honda watched TT week unfold, as he watched the Gileras and Nortons and MV Augustas and NSUs flow past the pits, he was frankly 'shocked'. He reflected privately: 'How little I knew about the outside world' and sensed he might have been 'too audacious' in making his declaration.

Honda's first bike, the 98 cc Dream, had appeared in 1949. It effectively launched the company and in 1953 new factories opened at Shirako and Yamoto, to be joined by Aoi in this year of 1954. But the 13 horsepower Dream only revved up to 7,000 and some of the bikes that flowed by had 36 horsepower and 10,000 revs. His eyes missed no detail. These teams seemed so professionally organized, their equipment was so refined. The tyres and chains were superior. He took with him back to Tokyo a Reynolds chain and an Avon tyre 'like the professionals used'.

The declaration to compete in 1955 was not realized. It is hardly surprising. Instead Honda competed domestically and in 1955 contested the All-Japan Endurance Road Race at Mount Asama, winning the 350 and 500 classes but not the 125 or 250. Two years later—the second time the races were run—they took the 350 but again not the 125 or 250. Mr Honda reflected quietly as he had done on the Isle of Man: 'We should never imitate foreign technology, although a certain manufacturer here imitated it and won. We must win the Tourist Trophy races through our own technology however hard it is to develop.'

The days of copying were about to end.

Honda came to the Island discreetly in the late 1950s to watch, learn, and absorb. They were not yet ready for more and this timing was not a question of fine-tuning. You only went on to the big public stage when you had rehearsed enough and could play your part properly. If you were seen to be bad it would actively damage your reputation.

Murray Walker was a commentator and the essential enthusiast. His voice still vibrates with enthusiasm. Given his background he could scarcely have been anything but the person he is. 'My father, Graham, was a professional motor cycle rider from the 1920s and he was a tuner of engines as well. He became a commentator and journalist. I was born in 1923 and I grew up in a racing environment. Racing was what dad did and it seemed the most natural thing to me. I suppose when I was small I assumed that that was what every dad did. I'm told I first visited the Island in 1925 when I was two and a half. We stayed at the Castle Mona Hotel and in those days riders came down to breakfast in their leathers, had their breakfast, went out and raced in the TT and came back again. I used to sit in the grandstand and read my comics. I didn't realize how lucky I was . . . ' He still regrets the feast spread before him at which he didn't sup.

'I suppose the TT was a bit amateurish in the late 1950s—by present standards, anyway. The most professional British team from the 1930s onwards was Norton but they and the others were nothing like as professional or as highly-funded as today's Japanese teams.' Walker, shrewd, as detached as a journalist ought to be, watched as Honda arrived to observe.

These Japanese were going round the paddock in brown raincoats and homburg hats taking photographs of everything. Don't forget this was a time when they were still regarded as a nation of copyists. So they were going round the paddock taking photographs of brake drums and gearboxes and tyres and saddles and bikes—everything—and nobody had seen anything like this before. People thought: we'd better go and talk to them to see what they're up to. A sample conversation would be (adopting the traditional British attitude of speaking slower and more loudly to foreigners):

'Where are you from?'
'Honda Motor Company.'
'Where?'
'Honda Motor Company.'
'Honda, never heard of Honda, what do they do?'
'Make motor cycles.'
'I see. What kind?'
'Small motor cycles, four-stroke motor cycles.'
'And why are you here?'
'Because we're coming to race!'

The truth of it was, as Walker freely confesses, 'we were taking the mickey out of these blokes a bit. They told us they were coming back with 125 cc machines next year and with our certainty that they were copyists we envisaged a sort of 500 cc Norton—big, bulky bikes—with a small hole in the single cylinder to allow a 125 piston. And what did they really turn up with?' All will be revealed in good time.

Tommy Robb was a rider and, like Walker, a familiar figure in and around the paddock. 'They'd been taking their photographs for the previous three years, one or two Japanese, and quietly. I remember seeing them because an Irishman can walk around and not be recognized until he speaks but a Japanese can't because, obviously, he looks different.' Robb noted that whatever Honda were and whoever Honda were, their people were very thorough indeed.

Honda had had the sort of problems you might expect. Chief amongst

Tommy Robb (right) *with Luigi Taveri. Whoever Honda were, Robb thought, they are very thorough indeed.*

them was how to increase engine speed without destroying the motor when you took the 7,000 revs up to 10,000. To compound the problem, people who'd bought the Sports Club complained that if they revved it to its limit the flywheel cracked. Tests proved it. Fragments of the flywheel broke the engine housing and hit the ceiling. The head of the sales division, Mr Fujisawa, was naturally alarmed at any chance of a customer being injured. Mr Honda himself solved the problem. With infinite care he examined a flywheel and saw it was fractionally too large and needed grinding and hardening. Moreover, this was the Super Club, successor to the Dream, which any vulnerable, non-heroic member of the public could buy.

The point about racing is that, of necessity, each part of the machine is stressed more, and this is why you can learn so much from it. What you are doing is taking a machine to its structural limits and the lessons, when transferred to ordinary commercial bikes, are invaluable. They ought to be. They cost a fortune to learn in racing. This is why in January 1959 Bill Hunt, who worked for Honda in America, came to London with Ichioo Niitsuma, head of Honda's Research and Design team, to talk to the governing body for the sport, the Autocycle Union. Then they moved to the Island itself for a few days to have a look. They were warmly welcomed (the Island naturally liked publicity) and were driven regally round both courses, the Mountain and the Clypse. It was raining.

In April the Honda entry forms for the 125 race arrived at the Autocycle Union. The pace had quickened.

On 5 May the four Japanese riders landed at Heathrow Airport and stood posing for photographs on the stairway down from the aeroplane. They were all waving. They wore neat suits, white shirts—everybody did then—and ties. They looked exactly like a phalanx of young business executives, and in a powerful sense that was exactly what they were. They were called Naomi Taniguchi, who was 23, Teisuka Tanaka, 22, Junzo Suzuki, 28, and Giichi Suzuki, also 28 and no relation. The bikes were already in place. Peter Carrick has written these significant words:

Members of that very first foray. From left to right Teisuka Tanaka, Giichi Suzuki, and two who would come later, Takahashi and Sadao Shimazaki.

'The last bike . . . was said to be fitted with a top-secret modification and it arrived with special tools and equipment which enabled the Honda mechanics to carry out similar modifications to the rest of the machines. Hunt, establishing the pattern of inscrutability which was to be a Honda characteristic . . . would only say that the modification was the result of recent intensive research which had produced results sooner than expected.'

And now the van had come up the drive to the Nursery Hotel, now the containers were being unloaded, now Mrs Vera Armstrong was fussing to make her guests feel at home. 'They brought their own cook and their own food and he prepared it in the kitchen. He made big rice cakes which were brown round the edges and dried fish which they sometimes fed to our cats as well. The cats liked the dried fish.

'The Japanese all slept on the floor of the bedrooms facing one way (for religious reasons), two to a room although the rooms were large. They didn't want to sleep on beds so we took the bedsteads out and they slept on the mattresses on the floor. I had to make the beds on my hands and knees! But, you know, under the pillow of each they left 6d (a small sum but worth having. You could buy a bar of chocolate for 1d) to say thank you to me for making the beds.' Mrs Armstrong still treasures this little kindness three decades later.

'They were young but nice, polite, so polite, quiet. They were good fun. There was some resentment among the older people in the saloon bar but that soon went. Everything they did was very ordered. They were forever taking baths (cultural note: in 1959 baths were still, perhaps, something of a luxury in Britain) and we only had a small tank to heat the water so we had to install a larger tank.' This is reinforced by her father: 'The Tourist Board had come and asked us if we'd fix the team up. When Honda arrived there must have been about twelve of them. Hunt was a typical American. The Japanese are tolerant and we had no trouble although it was difficult because they wanted a bath every morning. They paid for the new tank. The bill for their accommodation was cheap, very cheap indeed, 23 shillings [£1.15] per person full board.' But the real fun, and it's not a disrespectful word at all, was about to begin.

Honda took over the courtyard at the back of the hotel and started serious work. A lot of people were very curious indeed. A vast number arrived to see what was going on, as Mrs Armstrong remembers: 'The Japanese were quite happy, they didn't object but we had to stop the people going in.'

So much for secrecy and inscrutability.

Her father both confirms this and expands on it: 'In the end we had to get the police to control it. Because the Japanese were young and loved to kick a ball they played football in the grounds with some of the kids who had come to look at them. They'd brought Honda hats and all sorts of things to give away, badges, portable wireless sets. One container was full of it all. The Customs and Excise heard about it and a man in plain clothes arrived. "You can't distribute this," he said, "you didn't declare it when you came through customs." He made them lock the container . . . '

Kikue Carran opened her morning paper and was very surprised indeed. She had met her husband, a British serviceman, and married him in

Tokyo and had lived on the Isle of Man since 1953. She had not returned to Japan nor met a Japanese since. 'I read that they were staying at the Nursery Hotel. I went because I just wanted to speak to them. I didn't know anything about motor bikes. When I got there some of them were walking about and I said "good afternoon" in Japanese. They were very surprised. The next day I returned with Japanese food. I made rice cakes with English rice and soup—spring onions, scrambled eggs, fish—and everybody had a cup of it.' (Aside from her son Arthur: 'I remember my mother making a rice and seaweed concoction as well.')

There is a lovely innocence about all this, but do not be deceived. The future was already weaving itself into our story. Among the curious who journeyed to the Nursery Hotel and stood watching anonymously were several men who would become important. One was Tommy Robb: 'The first thing I noticed was that all the mechanics were in uniform, immaculate overalls, freshly-laundered. They wore white woollen gloves and I could never figure out how they could change parts with them on. The cook brought their food out on trays, each dish foil-wrapped and with a name on it—at least that's what I assumed they were because I couldn't read Japanese at all.

'There was an awful lot of anti-Japanese feeling because people remembered the war but they were so impeccably polite they won the people over. I got the strong impression that Honda meant business right from the first half hour of looking at them.' Today Tommy Robb sells Honda motor cycles.

Luigi Taveri was interested because he had never seen a Japanese bike before: 'Carlo Ubbiali [another rider] and I went to see. The bikes were not the same as our bikes but watching what Honda were doing I felt they already had the potential to make a very good bike quickly.'

Ken Sprayson was an expert welder employed by a British firm called Reynolds—they made tubes—and he repaired bikes which had had mishaps on the Island. He was kept very busy. He, too, journeyed to the Nursery Hotel to have a look and took some photographs (reproduced here). 'The team were a curiosity in themselves. Everyone kept gazing at them and they looked quite fearsome! But the motor cycle fraternity is a very friendly one; they were soon accepted and everybody became friends. However, that first year they were a nine-day-wonder and as a result they were the centre of a lot of attention!'

Bill Smith, also a rider and until recently a Honda cycle dealer, went 'out of curiosity. There was a guy there called Kawashima, who subsequently became President of Honda Motor Company, and he was in charge. I was intrigued by the 125s because they were twin-cylinder 12,000 and 13,000 revs left-hand gear change with a seven-speed gearbox. I asked if there was any chance of borrowing one for the races . . . '

Others were equally impressed, including a certain Derek Minter, who liked what he saw. 'Everybody said they'd be no trouble to us.' Minter wasn't so sure. Neither was the newspaper *TT Special*. 'It was the workshops that caught our eye, with various white sheets on which, written in blue and red Japanese, were the names and numbers of all the other runners in the 125 lightweight event, race signals, course markings and other information useful to the newcomer rider. Complete with compressors, electrics, tools and racks—all brought from Japan—this is indeed a self-contained unit.'

Ken Sprayson, welder and construction expert, at work. He came to the Nursery to have a look.

Legend insists that Honda knew so little about racing that the bikes were shod with 'nobbly' tyres of the kind used in scrambling events, but this is not so. The engine was 125 cc twin-cylinder with measurements of 44 by 41 mm and vertical alloy cylinders. The gearbox had six speeds and the frame has been described as 'sturdy'. The bike had been designed from scratch by Tadashi Kume (later President of Honda) and Kimio Shimmura, two young engineers who had been given a blank piece of paper and also given their head. They had just joined the company. Kume describes this assignment as being both 'interesting' and 'exciting'. The engine was assembled by Design Section Chief Kiyoshi Kawashima—whom Bill Smith would meet at the Nursery. There were problems. The rod connecting the piston to the crankshaft and the bearings kept breaking under stress and Mr Honda himself decreed that, rather than endlessly strengthening it, the rod should be lighter and smaller, and so should the bearings. Moreover, the number of bearings were reduced. The theory was based on a Japanese proverb which says that 'a large tree can be blown down by high winds but the slender and flexible bamboo cannot'. It worked. The project had taken two years.

The riders went round for a couple of weeks before official practice watching and learning. They covered, according to one source, two thousand miles on the Clypse circuit where the 125 race would be run. They also came upon a cultural problem of their own, of which Mrs Armstrong is one of few remaining witnesses: 'They wouldn't overtake Hunt on a point of honour!' Her father reinforces this: 'The four Japanese riders were better than Hunt but they would always set off after him and follow him. He'd go to one side of the road and wave them through but they wouldn't do it. But he was the boss and he told them to and they soon got over their inhibitions.'

During official practice the Japanese discovered—it was hardly surprising—that Europeans were going faster. Mr Webb again: 'Soon enough they wanted British food and they gave all their own food away. They wanted steak because they saw that they people going faster ate steak, so every day I ordered thirty or forty steaks from the local butcher.'

So the arrival, modest and scrupulously well conducted, is in place and now it is time to examine the Clypse circuit, 10.79 miles long and which, by coincidence, passed directly in front of the Nursery Hotel. The Clypse has gone into memory and is not to be confused with the full-blown Mountain circuit. Their only point of intersection was that they both used some of the same stretches of road.

On the Clypse the riders began at the TT start and went down Bray Hill, turned right at a crossroads, went up a steep hill and along past a cemetery; the road twisted and turned, eventually joining the Mountain circuit but going in the opposite direction; it then turned off through high banks into Onchan Village and back to the start. The Clypse had some haunting, evocative Gaelic place names, just as the Mountain circuit did, and some plain Anglo-Saxon ones, too: Parkfield, Willaston, Edge's Corner, Hillberry, Brandish Corner, Creg-ny-Baa, Ballacarrooing, Ballacoar, Cronk-ny-Garroo, Morney Bends, Half Corner, Whitebridge, Manx Arms, Signpost Corner, Governor's Bridge.

'It was,' Robb says as he gazes back across the decades, 'one of the trickiest circuits I can remember. The road surface was really rough—tarmacadam with granite chippings in it.' To this Taveri adds with a feeling which still lives vividly: 'I crashed twice on the Clypse. The first time was in 1956 or 1957 when I was on an MV, I pushed too hard on the first lap, I hit a wall—it was all walls!—and went completely over it. I broke my shoulder. It was raining.' The Clypse was a hell of a place to begin and there was only one worse, the Mountain, and Honda would be on that next year . . .

Official practice began on Saturday 23 May but for the 500s. The Isle of Man *Daily Times* reported that 'watching from the grandstand were Bill Hunt and the Japanese contingent who were deeply interested in the dispatch of the riders.' Oh yes, watch closely and learn. Honda took their turn on the Monday and were not in the top six. The next morning the same newspaper carried a front page headline. LAST NIGHT . . . JAPANESE ON THE CLYPSE COURSE as if it had been at best a curiosity, at worst an invasion.

'In perfect weather it was the performance of Taniguchi which gave food for thought. Taniguchi, in his first appearance outside Japan on his first "closed road" practice—and with a machine that has never been on a Continental or TT circuit—recorded a time of 9 minutes 59.2 seconds—61 seconds slower than Ubbiali.' (Ubbiali, an Italian, had been riding since 1950 and at this point had won the world 125 title four times. He was on an MV Augusta and now did 8 minutes 58.6 seconds, an average speed of 72.12 miles an hour. Someone called Hailwood was fifth fastest on a Ducati.)

'Competitors were warned of wet tar at Signpost Corner before

Taniguchi got away, closely followed by Ubbiali, Provini, Ken Tully (Ducati), and Hunt, who crouched over his tank as he made for Parkfield. Hunt got as far as Morney Three where his engine gave up.'

During the Tuesday session 'Hunt with his space man visor'—it was an amazing shape, curving down over his chin—'was a noticeable figure and he managed to complete two laps. On his previous practice the front brakes of his Honda seized and the machine reared, giving him some anxious moments. He was forced to take on the role of spectator. Taniguchi speeded up, knocking 12 seconds off his best lap on Monday, but it was 20 seconds behind the sixth fastest man. G. Suzuki came off at Parkfield, but was not hurt.'

At the end of the week, after daily sessions from Monday through to Friday, Honda were still not in the top six and some people were so intrigued they ruminated aloud that Honda may have been keeping a great deal in reserve. One report wondered if the Japanese were 'foxing'—because Honda's fastest man, Taniguchi, had only done 9 minutes 59.2 seconds. It added that the 124 cc Honda double-o.h.c. twins created intense interest. The camshaft drive was on the left, offset from the cylinder axis towards the front of the machine. The same report judged that Hunt's 'space travel head gear' resembled an 'astronaut's helmet'.

The Isle of Man *Daily Times*, previewing the race on Tuesday 2 June,

Taveri and Mike Hailwood. Both were in the very first race.

fuelled it with an extremely ambitious heading. JAPAN'S BID FOR TT HONOURS. It spoke of the 'impressive features of the riders and mechanics. There is a strong suspicion Hunt has been "foxing" during the past week and the riders have been riding to a schedule—giving nothing away.'

The Japanese riders were now a familiar presence. Each day they took a 'spin' on the ordinary road bikes they had brought with them, circling the Clypse course again and again. It simply didn't matter what journalists wrote. The Honda team had no thoughts of winning anything individually. They hoped for the team prize and that, of course, was for reliability. The idea was to get a lot of finishers as high up as they could manage.

And so they came to the race. It was 12:30 and banks of cloud built across to the west of the island but not enough to swallow glorious sunshine in Douglas. The wind of early morning had died. Thirty-three riders arranged themselves for a mass start—not the lock-step of two-by-two at timed intervals which the Mountain circuit was so famous for. This must have been why one reporter, as highly charged as any of the riders, wrote this in notebook: 'A deafening bellow marked the riders' fantastic departure—to use a mild term.' We must be thankful he didn't feel impelled to go searching for stronger terms.

Hailwood, in only his third season as a racer, got away first but was soon engulfed by the older, more seasoned men, Taveri, Ubbiali, Tarquinio Provini, the East German Ernst Degner; and that was the order as they completed lap one. Hailwood was fifth, Robb on a Ducati eleventh. The clouds were still gathering and the crowds leant over the stone walls and Taveri stayed in the lead. The Hondas were off the pace and clearly hadn't been foxing. They were going as fast as they could. And there went Taveri, tucked so neatly onto his famous MZ. Who could have guessed, as he moved into Parkfield to begin lap two, that, in the years to come, he would win twenty 125cc races on a Honda? And here is Hailwood, so firmly locked onto the famous Ducati, holding fifth. He would become a legendary man on a Honda. And here is Robb on another Ducati, sandwiched between Taniguchi and Junzo Suzuki. In the years to come he would win on a Honda, but a 250, not a 125 . . .

Because this was Honda's very first lap, and because so many of the names carry their own portents of the decades I set it out fully:

L. Taveri (MZ)	8:57.2
C. Ubbiali (MV)	8:58.6
T. Provini (MV)	9:00.6
E. Degner (MZ)	9:02.8
M. Hailwood (Ducati)	9:05.2
B. Spaggiari (Ducati)	9:14.0
H. Fugner (MZ)	9:21.4
D. Chadwick (MV)	9:34.4
F. Villa (Ducati)	9:50.6
N. Taniguchi (Honda)	9:52.2

T. Robb (Ducati)	9:53.0
J. Suzuki (Honda)	9:55.6

Hunt had the 'first reported accident'. He came off at Ballacoar but was unhurt. As they crossed the line to complete lap three Taniguchi had moved up to ninth and a lap later to eighth. At the end of lap seven Junzo Suzuki had come into the pits to have his brakes adjusted and that would cost him dear. Giichi Suzuki was working his way up from fourteenth on lap one to tenth on lap eight. Tanaka got past Robb.

Interesting, Robb thought, as he saw confirmation of what he had anticipated at the Nursery actually happening, but he kept his head down and went for it. As with any rider, the future was a long way away and you were a dangerous fool if you thought beyond the next bend. He never imagined he'd live beyond thirty years of age anyway, a conscious judgement of the life he had chosen.

One race report said that Taniguchi was riding 'superbly' behind the Chadwick-Villa duo and when they fell on lap nine he found himself in a 'lonely' sixth place. He wasn't lonely for long because Ubbiali caught him. Ubbiali had battled to fifth after restarting ninth following an oil pipe problem. Provini overtook Taveri on the eighth lap and won. It had taken him 1 hour 27 minutes 25.2 seconds, an average speed of 74.06 miles an hour. Taniguchi had taken 1 hour 34 minutes 08 seconds (68.29 mph). That was the direct comparison and, on the strictly individual basis, marked out the chasm between where Honda were and where they would have to be. But as their riders came in things were looking better and better. Giichi Suzuki seventh . . . Tanaka eighth . . . Jenzo Suzuki eleventh. They had won the team prize, and no one had ever done that before first time out on the Island.

The top twelve finishers demand, like the first lap, to be set out in full: Provini, Taveri, Hailwood, Fugner, Ubbiali, Taniguchi, G. Suzuki, Tanaka, Robb, Purslow (Ducati), J. Suzuki, Porter (MV). Taveri, incidentally, set a new record of 74.99 miles an hour on lap three. 'What I remember,' he says, 'is that the Honda riders were the same as tourists. They

Giichi Suzuki in an early race (though not here on the Isle of Man. Malaysia?)

lacked experience. They went very nicely and the bikes went very nicely
. . . but like tourists.'

Hunt was openly delighted with the team prize, and so was the 32-year-
old designer Kiyoshi Kawashima. 'We came to the TT for our first big
international effort and the team prize is most encouraging,' he said
softly. It was not understatement. It was the truth.

Whoever wrote the short anonymous guide to that year's TT (published by British Petroleum) judged that Honda had made 'a useful
debut'. That, also, was neither understatement nor overstatement; simply
the truth.

Tommy Robb offers a reflection: 'Those original bikes didn't steer all
that well and they were a bit flexible. The fact that they had finished—and
just off the leaderboard, as it were—meant that they were going to
become a force if they maintained the intensity with which they had
come to the Island.'

At the very instant when you might have expected the Honda mechanics to catch the bus into Douglas and indulge in some celebrating they
had their woollen gloves on again and were busy in their own neat,
methodical way removing the engines from the bikes, which had now
been brought back to the courtyard. The engines were to be air-freighted
to Japan to contest the National Road Race championships there. That in
part was a direct and conclusive answer to Robb's point about maintain-
ing the intensity. The intensity was already evident and to confirm it here
are three postscripts:

(1) A few weeks later Soichiro Honda made a second proclamation
although this one was not put up on notice boards. It was: we will go back
in 1960.

(2) Peter Carrick would write: 'It didn't take long to work out that five
riders and a team of mechanics travelling to the Isle of Man by air, five
racing machines and four practice bikes, spares and tools sufficient to set
up a completely self-contained workshop on the Island, altogether would
probably have cost in excess of £10,000 (at 1959 values!)—more than
many factories would then be spending on racing development in a whole
year.'

(3) Bill Smith, who'd wanted to borrow a 125, was not a man to be
deterred. In August 1959 Honda sent two bikes to England so that, as he
says, 'I could compete in the British Championships at Oulton Park. I
rode the first Honda factory bike ever to reach the United Kingdom.
(The Isle of Man enjoys a separate status.) At Oulton the other one was
ridden by a local chap called Alan Diggdale. I finished second to
Hailwood, who was on a factory Ducati.'

Hailwood, only nineteen, already had pedigree. In the British
Championships the year before he had taken the 125, 250, and 350
classes; now, in a great imperious sweep, he did it again and added the
500; and finishing second to him was in no sense a disgrace. 'The Honda
was very difficult to ride,' Smith says, 'because of the left-hand gear
change, and none of us had ever raced with those before. They didn't
have rev counters, they had spark indicators—which were
transistors—and they gave you spark revolutions! But I remained so
impressed that I wrote to Honda and asked if I could import them commercially and they came and saw me . . . '

And that was 1959. Those who had watched, and who had known what

Mike Hailwood at the start on the Glencrutchery Road.

to look for, had seen. Ralph Bryans had seen all right—each nut on the bike was 'wire-locked'. 'The Honda philosophy was that nobody in their right mind was going to wire lock a nut unless they had already checked if the nut was tight or not. If it was wire locked it must have been tightened. There is a small hole in the nut and what happens is that once you've tightened the nut you thread a piece of wire through the hole, twist it and anchor it somewhere and once you've done that everybody knows the nut is tight. When you have a lot of personnel working on a bike this is a quick and efficient way of doing it. (The wire had no other function except as an aide-memoire.) It meant that a mechanic did not have to go round with a spanner, all he had to do was look at the wire-locks to see. In all the years I raced for Honda I never had anything fall off.' Bryans' gentle, warming, lilting Ulster accent mingles, as he reminisces, with that of Robb, also an Ulsterman. Attention to detail? As Robb has already said and it's worth repeating: 'The first thing I noticed was all the mechanics in uniform, immaculate overalls, freshly-laundered . . .'

THREE

A Mountain to Climb

No man is an Island, entire of itself;
Any man's death diminishes me,
Because I am involved in mankind;
And therefore never send to know for whom the bell tolls;
It tolls for thee.

John Donne (1571–1631)

Luigi Taveri on the Island. 'You see, it was very dangerous.'

'ONE minute. Riders nervously meddle with their petrol taps. Push their goggles on and off. Wipe smudges that aren't there. Fix helmet straps that are already fixed. They test the brakes. Twist the throttle. Pull in the clutch, slip the machine into gear . . . they settle, crouched two abreast. The eyes don't flit now. They are fixed steadily on the man with the starter's flag. The seconds drag and you think: Come on . . . come on . . . come on . . . drop that bloody flag. But you daren't blink an eye in case you miss it . . .'

The words are those of Jim Redman, although they might have been written by any of the thousands who have faced just this moment across the decades on the Isle of Man. The backdrop was deceptively ordinary: a broad, level stretch of everyday road called Glencrutchery. It was flanked by the pits, which were backed by a grandstand that always seemed to be full. Officials, statuesque in the era of blazers with gold insignias on the breast pockets, moved about doing their business, photographers milled, mechanics nursed their own anxieties. The road itself had a white line bisecting it to mark exactly the start and finish. The riders went off two-by-two at intervals; when one pair had been launched, the next came forward from the second row to take their places.

Some riders were frightened, more were just apprehensive. 'When I had to go to the TT I was always unhappy.' Taveri says. 'You see it was very dangerous. Once you had understood that, you had respect for it. When I won a race there it gave me the most satisfaction because it was so dangerous.' Many, many other racing circuits were alarming. The Nürburgring, used by racing cars as well as racing bikes, was a wild roller-coaster ride through the Eifel Mountains of Germany; but that was a purpose-built circuit and by definition could never be as raw as the Island. Daytona allowed supreme speed but it was mostly banking, not the same thing as the Island at all. Assen in Holland was the only circuit purpose-built for bikes, and the 200,000 who came to make the race a festival could intimidate by their sheer numbers. Monza was notorious for theft, chaos, and unhelpful, inflexible officials. Le Mans was really for sports cars—the bikes used the shorter Bugatti circuit—and those sports cars reached 240 miles an hour on the Mulsanne Straight. Spa in Belgium was a tamer version of the Nürburgring but prey to meteorological mischiefs, driving rain on one part of it, perfectly dry on another; and when it rained, Spa was alarming. Redman himself would be fortunate to survive a crash on his 500 Honda there. Imatra, Finland, was a log-forest; Brno in Czechoslovakia had two dangerous villages; and so it went on; nowhere was utterly safe.

But there was nothing like the Island. God made the circuit and man merely added roads that faithfully followed the natural contours. Man also added stone walls, telegraph poles, kerbs, lamp-posts, sign-posts, hump-back bridges, and roads contorted so hard that they bucked and kicked. In his wisdom, man had decreed that part of the circuit would go up the Mountain, nearly 1400 feet above sea level. When the corners weren't bucking you, the road surface was.

One cannot begin to appreciate—never mind savour—the magnitude of Honda's achievements without close examination of the Island. In the late 1950s and early 1960s the Island was central to everything in bike racing. Commercially, for example, 'the races there were the ones to win because that meant you could advertise all the year round all over the world'. The words are those of a mechanic, Nobby Clark, whom we'll be meeting again in a moment.

It had started in 1907 when, evidently, British motor racing wasn't doing well and some enthusiasts met to see what could be done about it. A man with the amazing and delightful name of the Marquis de Mouzilly St Mars provided a trophy, but Britain had a nationwide speed limit of twenty miles an hour and, just as important, Britain had no laws to allow roads to be closed for a race. The Isle of Man was different. I quote from *The Languages of Britain* by Glanville Price. 'The Island has never been absorbed administratively into England, nor, indeed, is it part of the United Kingdom (it has never been represented in the House of Commons) and under the present constitution, which in its essentials dates from 1866, it enjoys a considerable degree of self-government.'

It meant that the Island could close whatever roads it wished and, moreover, it had no speed limits. This is how the Tourist Trophy—known as the TT—began. There were twenty-five riders in 1907 and nearly half finished a course of 15 miles 1430 yards. The winner, incidentally, averaged 38.25 miles an hour on a bike that did 94.5 miles to the gallon.

The TT grew into an occasion and then *the* occasion. Geography helped because it was not far from a major British port, Liverpool, while Fleetwood was further up the coast and Ardrossan served Glasgow. You could catch a boat from Belfast and Dublin, too. Nor were prices prohibitive and the bike magazines were full of advertisements for ways of getting you there. In 1959 it cost £2. 15s. 0d. first class from Liverpool or Fleetwood (£2.75p), £2. 5s. 0d. second class (£2.25p); from Ardrossan

£3. 8*s*. 0*d*. first (£3.40p), £2. 11*s*. 0*d*. second (£2.55p), and the motor bikes themselves £1. 10*s*. 0*d* (£1.50p).

John Dee was a typical spectator: 'I used to travel over from Liverpool on a boat we called the cow shed because it was so packed with people and bikes. The Irish Sea could get very, very rough indeed and the four hours between Liverpool and Douglas was a long time if it did.' Each year a flood tide of people like Dee were disgorged by these ferries. Some slept in tents—forests of them sprung up all over the place—some stayed in hotels, some, like Dee, in boarding houses.

TT week became governed by a self-generating tradition itself. People instinctively stayed in the same hotel, the same boarding house each year, pitched their tents in the same spot. They drank in the same pubs, which became their temporary 'locals'. Friendships were struck which existed for the week alone but endured for decades. No one truly knows how many spectators came because the only place they could be charged for admission was the grandstand at the start-finish line. The rest simply went where they fancied—lolled on a grassy bank, leant over a wall, stood in a village square and watched as much or as little as they wished.

Taken together, it gave the Island a strange intimacy and a delightful informality, a distinctive mingling of business and pleasure, and it fashioned itself into one of the great sporting occasions, quite unlike any other. Mechanics worked on bikes in the garages of hotels while inside the hotels themselves total strangers chatted amicably with the riders and, as Redman attests, young bucks pretended to be riders to improve their chances with the girls (and doubtless, some of the girls knew better; some didn't).

'There was great camaraderie, as you might say. I stayed in a boarding house and there were various regular pubs which people drank in,' Dee says. 'We used the Dog's Home in Douglas. I went over one year on a Norton, fell off and damaged it [just riding around, you understand; Dee was a spectator] and a lad I knew vaguely but hadn't seen for a couple of years suddenly arrived and helped me to repair it. The Island was like that. I often watched at the Gooseneck. I'd go out there on my bike and a lot of other people did, too, because you could get there using roads away from the circuit. Once you got inside the circuit you could watch at Ballaugh and then go up to the Bungalow, go on to Milntown. And Milntown was hairy. They'd be doing a ton in mid-air. They'd be coming out of Sulby and you could hear them coming. There was a bit of a bounce in the road, a bit of a bump and as they landed you could hear the wheels go thump. One rider used to angle his bike in mid-air, actually leaning it with the wheels completely off the ground to be in the right position when he did land. A chap was killed there—he hit the kerb—and a rider I travelled over with one year, a friend, got skinned there, all his face torn.'

But the mobility of the spectator who'd brought his own bike—there was a web of smaller roads inside and outside, the circuit—gave the Island another unique characteristic. Just as the famous English diarist of the seventeenth century, Samuel Pepys, enjoyed moving from church to church in London to taste the sermons, so the spectator on the Island could taste the bikes from several vantage points. Don't forget that we are talking of six laps of 37.75 miles and the 500 cc race in 1960 would last $2^1/_2$ hours, so there was time, ample time for a spectator to move around.

'Occasionally,' Dee says, 'I'd go and watch at the hairpin at Ramsey and you could stand there and hear the BMWs the other side of Sulby four miles away, this buzzing as if an aeroplane was flying towards you. Then there was Mad Sunday, which the police eventually stopped. It was the Sunday before race week began and you could get on an ordinary road bike—you know, like the Norton I went over with—and go round the Mountain circuit, because of course it was on ordinary roads and they were open when the racing wasn't on. But because the roads were subject to ordinary law the traffic was going both ways, just like traffic normally does. Kids went out on the circuit and it got so bad that the police had to be placed at strategic points to wave them to slow down. You'd go round some of the bends, like the one at Creg-ny-Baa, and there would be a great big grandstand full or people watching the kids come round—waiting for somebody to come off, and they did . . . '

That did not affect the general atmosphere of the week. Pilfering and vandalism—we are talking about 1960s, not the 1980s—were all but unknown. Willie Stevenson, who was a bit of a mechanic and a bit of a rider and a friend of Derek Minter, captures this precisely: 'We'd leave our van open with all the stuff inside and nobody ever stole a thing. It never occurred to us that anybody would.'

It was also an age of financial innocence. Works riders, as well as privateers, paid their own fare to get there, settled their own hotel bills, and the start money was so modest that even if they won they might be out of pocket. So why did they go at all? The Island was too important for them to miss, and nobody knew that better than the organizers themselves.

In late May 1960 Honda arrived for their second year. They had a larger team and would contest both the 125 and 250 cc classes—and they brought, as Walker attests, 'not just ordinary 250s but four-cylinder 250s! This was at a time when British enthusiasts, accustomed to the single-cylinder Nortons which had dominated their beloved TT for so long, were still marvelling at the 500 cc Italian Gileras and MVs. Japanese technology was frighteningly showing the way.' The 125 had been completely redesigned and the 'camel-backed tank' gone.

It didn't matter that Taniguchi, Giichi Suzuki, and Tanaka knew the Clypse course because they'd have to start learning all over again. The Clypse, used between 1954 and 1959 by the 125s and only the 125s, was already a memory and would not be used again. This time Honda faced the Mountain.

'Practice started at 4.30 in the morning,' Walker says, 'and the roads were closed at first light. Practice went on until about 6.30 and then all the riders went to the Cadbury's tent in the paddock [Cadbury's were an early sponsor] and everybody had cups of cocoa.'

A celebrated rider, Ralph Bryans, stayed in a boarding-house in Douglas. 'The alarm clock would go off in the darkness—there was no such thing as an early morning call—and I'd make my own way down to the kitchen, get myself a cup of tea and off I'd go. It would still be dark. We didn't drink alcohol the night before but even if we had we'd have woken up fast by the time we were going down Bray Hill.'

John Dee: 'After a few years in the boarding-house I moved into a flat. Before dawn I'd look out of the window and see an MV mechanic riding the race bike up towards the pits. I'm not sure where their garage was

Hailwood on the Island on the 125 cc Honda.

because nobody was allowed near that. After the race, you'd see him riding it back.'

Nobby Clark: 'When I was with Honda we were always offered a bonus of 100 dollars if we won all solo classes at the Island (or any other Grand Prix). On the Island we worked really long hours. Most days we got up at four o'clock for the early morning practice. When that was over we headed back to the garage, unloaded the vans and worked for about an hour, had breakfast, and slept for an hour or two. Then it was all go again until everything was finished for the next practice . . . there would be brake shoes which needed new linings, there were always tyres which needed to be changed. We used to try and get everything done as soon as possible. Most of us had girlfriends and after a week on the Island we really enjoyed their company—it got us away from the day-to-day hard work. We got one day a month off . . .'

John Dee adds further pertinent observations: 'Some riders slept in tents and some of them probably had their bikes in there with them! The tents were at the back of the paddock or sometimes they'd find a quieter spot. In many ways it was informal. A friend went over with a Norton and raced it in the 250 and 350. He'd practise for the 350, whip that engine out, put the 250 in, practise with that, whip it out, put the 350 back for the race, whip it out, put the 250 back . . . '

Walker says:

'It really was a wonderful atmosphere. They had a fantastic scoreboard opposite the grandstand and on it each rider had a number. Underneath the number was a clockface and a hand which could be moved round it. A Boy Scout operated this. He wore a pair of earphones and when a rider passed certain points on the circuit a message was relayed back and the clock hand adjusted.

There was an enormous amount of tension because don't forget it was all a race against time. Seeding didn't exist in those days. Number two to go could be an ace rider and so could number thirty-seven and what was important—because

they went at intervals—was their actual time rather than who was physically leading on the circuit. Hence the tension. We all had to wait for the Boy Scout to
adjust the time of one rider on the clockface and then wait for it to be done with
another rider so we could compare the times and see if one was gaining on—or
losing to—the other.

When the rider crossed the line to begin another lap the Boy Scout tore off a
number under the rider's racing number (corresponding to the number of laps
the rider had done) so it was possible to know where all the riders were, and if
you listen to the old broadcasts made by my father they were very exciting
because when a rider reached Governor's Bridge—which was almost within
sight of the line—a light came on over the rider's number on the scoreboard and
my father used to say: 'Here he comes . . . here he comes . . . he's approaching us
from Governor's Bridge . . . '

Lovely, innocent days. It would all be on television now; Longines
would have instantaneous quartz figures on the screen displaying all
manner of statistics, and you'd see it all again in slo-mo, probably from a
different angle. In 1960 some messages to the Boy Scout were relayed by a
system of wires stretched across the back of the scoreboard. The messages—folded pieces of paper—were held on by clips and travelled along
the wires until they stopped at an aperture. The Boy Scout, standing at
the front of the scoreboard, reached through, took the piece of paper,
read it, and adjusted the clockface accordingly.

'The pits were a little bit of wall about four feet high with small stone
squares in front of it (the work area!) and, behind the wall, a walkway
with wooden railing behind that,' Walker says. 'Each pit had a big post on
to which were fixed the petrol fillers because they worked by gravity
feed. Roofs? No, if it rained you got wet. The really advanced people, like
Mike Hailwood's father, Stan, actually had his own telephone screwed to
the wall in the walkway and he'd ring strategic points round the circuit to
see what was happening. One of these places was called Stella Maris on
the approach to Ramsey hairpin; it was a house. I'm not sure if Stan
'phoned the house or if someone was in it to watch and ran down to a public box to take the call.'

Pit signals were as direct and rudimentary as they had always been: a
board on a pole, the message chalked on the board. But this innocence
co-existed with stark reality. When a rider had covered thirty miles from
Douglas and he was approaching a place called Stone Bridge he couldn't
help seeing a futuristic shelter on the right-hand side of the road. The
Graham Memorial, erected in honour of Les Graham, World 500 cc
Champion in 1949, killed on the Island in 1953. This did not deter his son
Stuart from racing there, sometimes on a Honda, and passing the
Memorial, I suppose, several hundred times. Many would die on the
Island and I use the Graham Memorial, with respect, to honour them all.

When the chilled dawn practices were already forgotten and the pilgrims had settled into their self-appointed vantage points, the riders
would come to that line bisecting Glencrutchery Road and they'd hear a
crisp, educated, firm English voice pronounce: 'One minute . . . '

And now it's June, high summer in the Irish Sea, which is a diplomatic
way of saying that the weather could be anything—stormy, windy, foggy,
misty, drizzle, lashing rain, even sunshine—and all on the same day. But
the mist—you'd leave Douglas on a bright, fine morning and it would be
wreathed like a shroud around the Mountain.

To move inside a rider's mind, particularly once the flag has fallen, is a delicate and frustrating matter. Most riders are articulate but, as Minter says, 'the circuit is simply too long for you to be able to recall it in detail. On the morning of a race I'd do a complete lap in a van to convince myself that I knew my way round. I never rode a bike when I did that because if you ride a bike you get carried away, even if it's only an ordinary road bike your hand will be on the throttle, you'll have the throttle wide open. What I needed was a refresher course to see if there were any marks on the road I could use as braking points from the last time I went round.

'I believe that so many riders get killed there because they don't weigh it up enough. I would go round in my van, stop, and walk all the corners—I did this for years—because the 37.75 miles is so much to try and memorize and so many corners look the same but you've got to take this one at a hundred miles an hour and the next one, seemingly so similar, down to eighty miles an hour. And this is where I say a lot of people get killed—because they run out of road.'

Nor did the journey in the van guarantee immunity from the caprices of the Mountain circuit. Minter again:

'One year it was so hot it melted the tarmacadam at one place and the next lap I decided to miss that. I went out wide, I hit the kerb, the front wheel mounted the kerb, the back wheel didn't, and I finished up in a big heap.

The 250 cc Honda had six speeds on it and you were changing from fifth to sixth or keeping it in sixth most of the time. You were unaware of speed. You were aware of the rev counter because once it dropped below a certain point you'd not got the power so you had to knock it down a cog [gear] to get the power back on. The idea was to keep it between twelve and fourteen thousand revs.

Really and truly your mind was one step ahead of your body. You're in this corner but your mind is actually in the next corner so you know what part of the road you need to be on when you get there. You never think of anything else. If you did, you'd crash. I looked for markers at the side of the road, maybe a kerb, maybe a drain to give me my braking point. When I went back to the Island in 1987 after twenty years I was rushing from Creg-ny-Baa to Brandish Corner [a mile-long straight on the Mountain descent to a left hander] and there should have been three little bushes over to the right. That had always been my braking point. But now there were only two bushes. Subconsciously I'd anticipated the three and I was so disconcerted that I arrived at the corner much too quickly. Somebody could have cut the third one down during the years in between, it could have had a disease . . . but that third bush wasn't there any more.

The delicacy of moving inside the rider's mind is compounded by several contradictions. Here is one, explained by Stuart Graham: 'I didn't use markers as braking points at all. My braking points were the places where it felt right to brake.'

Ah, the Mountain. Ah, the misty legends. Ah, the moments of madness that no man could anticipate. A rider, Tommy Robb: 'I was in one of the early morning practices doing about 130 miles an hour when I saw a seagull in the middle of the road about three or four hundred yards ahead. I put the brakes on and rose from the saddle. The bird flapped its wings and took off in flight towards me. It hit me full in the goggles, pressing them and the aluminium frame back into my face and this seagull disintegrated all over me. I was still about a hundred yards from the corner so I was able to get round it. But if you take my speed as 130 and the bird's speed as 30, the impact speed was 160. I felt the sort of blow you'd get from a bloke like Mike Tyson. When I got back to the pits my

Taveri at Quarter Bridge.

face was covered in feathers and seagull blood—and worse . . . '

So here we are on the Island in 1960. Fasten your seat belt, as they say, listen for that English voice, and watch out for everything, seagulls included.

The flag.

You push the bike hard from the front row. Running alongside it and blipping the throttle, you vault on to it side-saddle as the acceleration is gathering, uncoil your body across the saddle, mould yourself to the bike, and watch the trees along the Glencrutchery Road flick by. Already the grandstand is gone, already you've covered 250 yards, already you're over a crossroads and onto Bray Hill, a fast descent to the left with neat, detached houses on either side and the road surface a bumpy patchwork of differing colours where it has been repaired so many times. It is flanked by threatening curbs, with an alarming dip near the bottom which forces your chest down onto the fuel tank.

Quarter Bridge is a mile and a bit out, a sharp right-hander at the bottom of a hill hemmed on the nearside by a stone wall, and as you drift urgently into the corner the side of a building rises like a cliff face with a mound of protective sacks at its base. Many would crash here, misjudging their speed after the sustained, full bore descent from the start.

More stone walls stretch like a funnel towards Braddan Bridge a mile further on. Braddan is a descent with a kink, almost a protrusion, in the stone wall and it's suddenly there at your elbow. A dense crowd is spread up the hillside but you don't watch them watching you because you're still hearing the clipped tones of Derek Minter above the torment of your engine: 'If you do, you crash.'

The bridge at Braddan is a stone arch far, far below—so far that the road that passes above it is level. To you it's only a bridge in name, only another landmark isolated in the rush and surge of impressions.

Going through it you need to make a fluid flick-left-flick-right, the bike shifting its centre of gravity as fast as you can control it to accommodate the change of direction. The masters—Geoff Duke, Hailwood, Redman and company—make it an extraordinary moment, a smooth majestic

Takahashi on one of the tight, tight hairpins: Governor's Bridge.

sweep as if, simultaneously, they are raising mere movement to a form of art. You have other thoughts. A policeman wearing a distinctive white helmet stands alone, hands locked behind his back in the classic position, stands on the rim of the road.

Miss him, miss him.

Union Mills is a mile further on. Union Mills is a hamlet down a descent that angles to the right, a pavement on one side, a wall on the other. A church spire peers quizzically over peaceful tree tops and the road is dragging you down towards it and you're in the hamlet. You have covered two and a half miles.

Now whole places flick by and you're straining not to ease off the throttle: the crossroads at Crosby, the Highlander pub where you take off over a bump, Greeba—just a tiny cluster of houses encamped at the roadside, already seen and forgotten.

Stuart Graham: 'Precision was vital here.'

Greeba Bridge, just beyond them, is a twisting left-hander—you can use the pavement if you want—and now you're running full towards the far coast of the island. You've done 6½ miles. If you're Hailwood, it has been 4 minutes. But you don't go on to the coast; you turn north well before it at Ballacraine. That's down a tree-lined dip and deep within the right-hand corner—where your lines pitches you—more protective sacks are heaped against a building. The instant you're through, and the bike is vertical again, the trees are taller, their branches interlocking high above to form a ceiling. The road is carpeted with deceptive shadows and the crowd cranes to see you as you accelerate the couple of hundred yards to a left-hander and move out of their sight.

Minter: 'The worst bit was the right turn at Ballacraine towards Laurel Bank a mile away. The camber of the road was shocking. You had to ride over the camber and if it was even a little bit wet you were into wheelslide.'

Now you have begun to climb. Ballacraine is 200 feet above sea level, Doran's Bend and Laurel Bank further up although—paradoxically—

Laurel Bank itself is a long descent to a right-hander, the bike flung hard over to position it for the corner hugging the far kerbing as you feel for the line. Glimpsed: more protective sacks against a wall.

Miss them, miss them.

Stuart Graham: 'Laurel Bank and its approach from Doran's Bend was very, very bumpy, it was nasty, it was dangerous—a fast left and then a right-hander with a stone wall on the outside. Coming out once on the Honda-six I must have overdone it because the back end jumped away. I was pitched against the wall and the sole of my riding boot was torn off. I bounced away from the wall across the road into the wall at the other side, bounced off that all the way back—amazingly I was still on the bike but sitting on the fuel tank—and I regained control. Christ, I thought. Then I kept on going.'

You're climbing again, towards Glen Helen at 500 feet above sea level—it's a long left-right—and this is the highest point before you move down to sea level again. Glen Helen is 9 1/2 miles out. If you're Hailwood, that 5 1/2 minutes. Now a sharp, bumpy uphill section to Sarah's Cottage. The descent is through Cronk-y-Voddy—another crossroads—and then a long, long straight with the road undulating in front of you past Handley's Cottage onto the descent to Barregarrow.

Graham: 'This was all nearly flat out and you left your stomach behind.' Now you are virtually within sight of the coast because the road north loops out towards the sea and you've reached another hamlet, Kirk Michael. In the distance you can see—but don't look, don't look—a couple of hillcocks smoothed by the ages as a timeless backdrop. The road narrows in Kirk Michael and you're in a right-hander, a telegraph pole looming ominously on one side, a stone wall on the other, and you're dipping helter-skelter into a cluster of wind-raked houses. You're in a normal high street and you flick right as the road threads between the shops, skimming the kerbs on each side, flick right again for the rush to Bishop's Court a mile and a half further on.

Minter: 'I did the first hundred mile an hour lap on a Norton in 1960 but next lap the oil tank split at Kirk Michael. I went round it at seventy or eighty miles an hour like a speedway rider. I had a full left-lock in the right-hander and I thought: "Dear oh dear, that was a bit naughty." I looked down at the rear tyre and it was shining with oil.'

Graham: 'It was tricky from here to Ballaugh, it was fast under trees, but the sun could dazzle you in the afternoon.'

At Ballaugh you're 17 miles out, nearly at sea level. Ballaugh is a bridge which, at the speed you're approaching it, is sharply hump-backed; so steep that as you approach it the houses beyond seem partially submerged because you can only see the top floors. You're airborne, you travel ten feet with metal railing coursing along beside you, you're trying not to land front wheel first, and when you do land the whole bike lurches on impact. Now you're moving inland on the mile to Quarry Bends and that's nineteen miles out. Just over half way . . .

Hailwood was here in 11 1/2 minutes.

Sulby is a glorious hammer-hammer straight but bumpy, then a sharp right-hander at Sulby Bridge, then a fast left-hander at Ginger Hall. Walker: 'Lift your head to prevent your brains being beaten out against the telegraph pole.' Ginger Hall feeds you out onto a long descent with banking on one side, a stone wall on the other and you're over a rise in

Hailwood on the Mountain.

the road and the crowd can't see you anymore. Through Churchtown and Milntown you're rushing towards the town of Ramsey, on the east of the Island. Ramsey is a quaint town and along Lezayre Road you're into Parliament Square, a market place where people are standing ten deep restrained by only a simple wooden barrier, chest high—men, women, children.

Miss them, miss them.

Graham: 'The engine always fell out of the power band here and you had to coax the power back on.'

Flick right as you cross the square but watch the pavement, which is snaking out towards you as if it wanted to trip you; go round it, flick left into Queen's Pier, a broad, suburban road decorated by trees set at regular intervals, get the power back on because you can feel it now: the big climb up the Mountain has begun. That's 24 miles, 14½ minutes. But the climb is not constant. You've gone through another square, along May Hill, you're into the Ramsey Hairpin—where John Dee might be watching among so many others—and the hairpin is a tortuous switchback

Taveri, and those stone walls ready to caress your elbow—or tear it off.

taken upwards at as low as 10 miles an hour and you're kicking the gears down, slipping the clutch. The climb is on through Waterworks. The Gooseneck, a mile further on, is reached by a contorted road. The Gooseneck is 600 feet above sea level, a right-hander with scrubland within its arc and canvas advertisements draped over the wall outside it. Look down over your right shoulder and there, far below, is the Waterworks you were peering up at a mile ago. The crowd is large here, and they're clutching stopwatches, wielding binoculars, scribbling times into notepads.

The road climbs steeply, straightens towards the Guthrie Memorial and that's 1000 feet above sea level. Guthrie is a long gentle descent to a left-right-left snake, a white wall and white posts glimpsed and the climb begins again into the bleak, barren, rock-strewn landscape. This is the mountain Mile, strangely one of the fastest stretches of the whole lap.

At East Mountain Gate you're 28 miles out, it's 1200 feet, it's bleak, it's windswept, and you're near the top of the Mountain. Along the Veranda watch the deep ditches at the edge of the road. The Graham Memorial is coming at you fast. Stuart Graham: 'It's a mountain shelter, a stone building with a very modern-looking roof. We were surprised that they built that rather than a conventional monument, but in retrospect it was nice because it could be used by marshals during the races and, in bad weather in winter, by anybody else. It was supposed to be one of my father's favourite parts of the circuit. He wasn't killed there, no, he was killed on Bray Hill . . . '

The Bungalow is at 31 miles—it was an hotel with a sloping tiled roof and the words 'Fully Licensed' in tall lettering along the top of that. The Snaefell Mountain Railway crosses the road here, and brightly-painted carriages wait nearby to take spectators back down.

Minter: 'It was a funny atmosphere up there because you had so few buildings, no trees, all you had was a big open space and on one side a big

Taveri and Hailwood at Creg-ny-Baa.

Tom Phillis at Governor's Bridge.

drop. I used to think: Christ, what would happen if you go through the fence here? It was just wire with posts. You'd have gone two or three hundred yards before you stopped and in some places you would have gone further than that—half a mile or more.'

Through Brandywell at the 32nd Milestone the big, final descent began. Bryans: 'As Bob McIntyre once said, you go up the Mountain as fast as you can and come down the Mountain as fast you dare. That just about sums it up.' (If you want to be pedantic, the highest point is 250 yards beyond the Bungalow and Hailwood was here in 18 minutes.)

Windy Corner is deep into the descent, a right-hander in open country-side, Windy Corner is 1200 feet. Graham: 'I was actually blown off the road here by the wind on a lightweight machine in practice. The wind blew straight up the valley and across the corner.'

At the 33rd Milestone you're in a double sweeping left with more fallen rock spreading back. Keppel Gate is a left-hander and in the early days there really was a gate which was opened for the races. Kate's Cottage is glimpsed and forgotten, and the descent seems steeper on the short, sharp rush to Creg-ny-Baa. As you approach you see two high signposts like sentries on either side of the road providing a graphic warning: You are approaching a geometrically perfect right-hand turn. The signposts don't tell you how far away it is. You're expected to know.

Creg, at 1000 feet, is another cluster of houses and the corner is in front of the Keppel Hotel with grandstands arranged round it. The rush is taking you to Brandish Corner, a left-hander flanked by elegant, curved, white railings. That's 34¹/₂ miles. There's usually a speed-trap between Creg and Brandish and Graham was timed at 150 mph on a 250 Honda-Six in 1966.

Then Hillberry at 400 feet, a long gully of road and a very fast right-hander with the crowds all along it to a bouncy left-hander at Cronk-ny-Mona, then Signpost Corner, a stinging right-hander with a wall on the nearside topped by ragged rocks set into it, and suddenly, as the fury of the descent is gathering and gathering, a vista of ordered fields up a hillside, each divided by high hedgerows.

Signpost Corner flings you through Bedstead Corner towards The Nook and Governor's Bridge half a mile away and that's a left with two more soldiers guarding you from it; but the pictures this time are showing you an impossibly cramped right-hand hairpin—not geometrical at all but writhing like a python in pain. Governor's Bridge: a wall on the right which runs down into the apex of the hairpin like an outcrop of rock and the spectators positioned behind it could almost reach out and touch you. The surface of the road is scarred by the criss-crossing of scalded rubber at a chaos of angles helplessly laid by those riders before you who braked too damned hard when they found themselves locked into the hairpin. The racing lines are all different. And after so many miles of sustained speed you have to move down the gears mentally to judge it. The hairpin is slow, slow, slow.

And now your light is on next to your name on the big scoreboard and Graham Walker is calling into his microphone: 'Here he comes . . . here he comes . . . he's approaching us now . . . '

You cross the line and there is Bray Hill again falling away from you, and you're at full bore. Redman: 'On my first visit I was not looking too carefully at where I was going or what I was doing. Instead of aiming to miss the dicey kerb at the bottom of the dip I looked at my rev counter and when I looked up again I was heading straight for the pavement edge. The force of the impact took about a foot out of the kerb . . . I went out of Bray sideways with the front wheel on full lock.'

Tom Phillis, seen here in 1961.

Tommy Robb: 'I saw a rope dangling down with a noose in it...'

This lap, from the line on Glencrutchery Road and back: in 1967 on a Honda 500 Hailwood would do it at an average speed of 108.77 miles an hour. That's 20 minutes and 82 seconds. Like inter-stellar distances, you need a special kind of mind to be able to imagine it at all.

Soichiro Honda put the situation in 1960 succinctly and pragmatically. 'To race at the Isle of Man we paid foreigners five or six million yen each, which was a lot of money at the time. Those riders were so eager to win that they made many demands, telling us for example that the machine wobbled or the brakes were not effective enough and such demands raised our own technical standards. Japanese riders were not like that. They wouldn't tell us anything. Some of them would even damage the machines. In other countries people had been used to riding at 100 kph since they were babies. The Japanese certainly did not get accustomed to such speed in their childhood.'

Honda signed two Australians—Tom Phillis, who became their first team captain, and Bob Brown, who joined only four days before the TT. Both were firm, quiet chaps, exactly the right stuff to construct a team around. Brown had been racing 250 NSUs since 1956 and this would be immediately useful in that class on the Island. The full Honda entry: S. Shimazaki, G. Suzuki, T. Tanaka, T. Phillis, M. Kitano, and N. Taniguchi in the 125; Phillis, Brown, Suzuki, Taniguchu, Shimazaki, and Tanaka in the 250.

'Honda went up a step at a time,' says Murray Walker. 'They'd come in with the 125 twin in 1959, then in 1960 they brought in the four-cylinder 250. In those days it was like Ford producing a car with a rocket engine which worked and was reliable and went fast. We had just absorbed the concept of a four-cylinder 500 cc bike—the MVs and Gileras—but the thought of bringing it down to 250, that was like throwing a bucket of cold water in our faces.' (Honda would claim that the 125 had 18 horsepower and the 250 had 35 horsepower.) 'Later,', Walker adds. 'Honda even had a five-cylinder 125!'

On the first day of practice Tommy Robb, soon to become a Honda rider, set off at 4.45 on a Matchless 500: 'I remember leaving the start line and they held out a little chalk board which said: Mist on the Mountain. I thought oh hell, I've forgotten to de-mist my goggles. It was a pleasant enough morning in Douglas, you see. I can still remember turning right in Parliament Square, Ramsey, but my goggles steamed up at Windy Corner and I crashed in the fog. I should have turned right but apparently I tried to demolish the wall straight ahead. The next thing I saw was a bright light above my head and a voice saying: "His neck's broken." I must have passed out again in fright. When I came round I was in hospital and I saw a rope dangling down with a noose in it and I thought: Bloody hell, they're going to hang me! It turned out, of course, that the rope and noose were only for patients to haul themselves up. In the next bed was Ernst Degner, and the bed next to that the great world champion Eric Oliver [a side-car man], and the bed next to that Mitsuoh Itoh. I discovered later that he found his way out of the hospital squirming out of a window despite his broken leg and he cut the plaster from his leg with garden shears.' In fact Tommy Robb would discover most things about 1960 later. "That year is obliterated from my memory.'

A journalist, watching Honda closely, had no doubts about the progress they had made. Even with a 'cursory glance' at the new Honda models he saw that the lessons of 1959 had been learnt. The 125 twin had been extensively modified. The 125s had had 'questionable handling and lightness at the front end'. To get over this the engine had been angled forward to 45 degrees shifting the weight distribution and lowering the centre of gravity. The new transverse-four 250 used the same frame as the 125 and the engine was virtually the same but doubled. He added these significant words: 'Scrupulous attention to detail is evident everywhere; the mechanics are by far the best turned out in the Island and the race camp at the Nursery Hotel, Onchan is a perfect example of quiet, methodical organization.' He also added that the 250s had shaken everyone, they were fast and although road holding problems had not been completely solved, at Union Mills Tom Phillis was every bit as impressive as the master, John Surtees.

In practice on Saturday 4 June Phillis was actually second quickest behind Provini, Taniguchi fifth in the 125, Shimazaki was fourth, Suzuki fifth, Tanaka sixth. Ah, blessed, innocent days. On the Tuesday the riders had no cocoa—twenty gallons of milk had gone sour.

The 125 race was run in a vicious gale force wind which raked the Mountain and, exactly as in 1959, the Hondas were extremely reliable: Taniguchi sixth, Suzuki seventh, Shimazaka eighth, Tanaka ninth, Phillis—who had had a misfire and been into the pits for new plugs—tenth. The breakthrough, and I do not use the word in any sense carelessly, was the 250. Although the Honda was not yet fast enough to threaten the leaders and Phillis retired on lap four, Brown brought it home fourth, Kitano fifth, Taniguchi sixth. Immediately afterwards Brown said crisply: 'The bikes are very good and I think they will be a real challenge to the Italians once they have sorted out some trouble with the carburation.' That result in full:

G. Hocking (MV)	2 hours 00.53
C. Ubbiali (MV)	2 hours 01.33
T. Provini (Morini)	2 hours 01.44
B. Brown (Honda)	2 hours 06.53
M. Kitano (Honda)	2 hours 18.11
N. Taniguchi (Honda)	2 hours 20. 41

A Honda team spokesman said it was 'rather satisfactory. We will certainly be back next year', and the understatement would have done credit to the British themselves.

A week later Honda were at Assen for the Dutch Grand Prix. They had taken a decision which, in its way, was another breakthrough. They would contest the rest of the season and at Assen they would be devastated by injuries in practice to both Phillis and Taniguchi. They would find from nowhere a replacement quite literally on the doorstep of their caravan. He was seen by some of his fellow riders as a born loser. They had misjudged him. He was a gem.

FOUR

The Prince of Adventure

The man who was a gem: the serious face of Jim Redman (No. 38).

THE man meandered round the paddock at Assen. He had no ride and no immediate prospect of one. He'd been born in England, moved to Rhodesia (now Zimbabwe) in order—his word—to 'skip' National Service in the British Army. He had a family to support and didn't consider service wages adequate for that. He returned to Europe in 1958 to try and become a rider, stayed for 1959, failed and had simply gone back to Rhodesia, disconsolate. Of him, Minter would say sharply that 'he rode Nortons when he first came and to be honest he was bloody hopeless. He raced at Brands Hatch and we blew him off—just like that'. Mind you,

Brands is no easy circuit and Minter, whose local track it was, had become the master of it. Never mind.

The man would judge himself at this time and say he must have been 'a fearsome sight'. He was called Jim Redman and in 1960 he resolved to have a last lunge at Europe. If he failed again he definitely wouldn't be coming back. Now, in late June, the East German MZ team seemed interested but—maddeningly—wouldn't make a final decision. So he meandered round the paddock. At this stage in the season there was virtually nothing else he could do except board a plane for Salisbury and kiss it all goodbye, whatever 'it' had or had not been.

In practice Phillis was 'a shade too enthusiastic' crashed heavily, destroying his 250 and breaking his collar bone. Taniguchi broke his right wrist, too. Redman knew Phillis and went to see how he was. Other riders, seeing a chance, were milling outside the caravan. Inside Phillis scarcely needed to say that he couldn't compete, and at that moment his 125 bike was vacant too. His 250 ride was gone because he'd eliminated the bike in the crash. Phillis said he would recommend Redman to team manager Kawashima, Phillis rose and walked awkwardly across the paddock to where Kawashima stood. There was a brief conversation.

It was on.

The next day in the final 45-minute practice session Redman clambered onto the Honda 125 which he had never ridden before. He was deeply conscious that Phillis had already gone fast on it and he could not escape the direct comparison of his time against that of Phillis. Kawashima was an extremely sensible and sensitive man and he knew what would be going through Redman's mind. Quietly he explained it: You are not expected to go faster than Phillis and we will be extremely happy if you get to within two or three seconds of him. Redman completed a couple of laps, drew into the pits and contemplated the whole circuit clinically as if he had laid out a mental map of it and was riding it in the abstract. For a man desperately short of time on the bike it was a brave decision. With time ticking by to the end of the session it would have been understandable simply to plough on, do your best, and see what happened. When he had composed himself he twisted the throttle towards the right-hander at De Strubben, and went for it. Crossing the line he was ten seconds quicker than Phillis . . .

Redman will never forget that 'a rumour that the time-keepers were wrong flashed round the paddock and officials walked round shaking their heads in . . . disbelief'. In its context this must rank as one of the great laps. But fate had only begun its gentle games with Jim Redman. A rider called John Hartle ought to have ridden the other 250 bike but he was contracted to Mobil and Honda were contracted to Castrol so Hartle was out of it. Honda turned to Brown who had, after all, been in that fourth place on the Island. But the Assen organizers stipulated (correctly) that because he had not taken part in practice at all he could not compete. Would, Kawashima ruminated aloud, Redman like to have a go in the 250 as well? Redman would—and could because he'd been in the practice, albeit on the 125. The problem was that there was no further practice. Redman faced the 250 totally untried. As he noted cryptically himself, the full and complete extent of his exploration of the bike was getting it from the paddock to the start.

He finished seventh.

He rode the 125, as he would remember, 'over the limit' and 'nearly fell off half a dozen times trying too hard'. A contemporary account puts it in more sober perspective: 'Redman dropped back to keep a wary eye on the leaders.' Ubbiali, who had won the 250, now added the 125 and Redman was fourth. He was as delighted as Honda. They kept him for Spa in early July and he and Brown rode the 125s. (The 250s had been so punished by the 'wear and tear' of Assen and spares were in such short supply that they weren't entered.)

Three weeks later they were at Solitude, a 7.1 mile track just off the Stuttgart-Karlsruhe autobahn and a distant memory now. First used in 1952, it would go from the calendar in 1964. At Solitude a dilemma was born. What would happen when Phillis recovered? Two bikes, three riders—Phillis, Brown, Redman. It solved itself in the most savage way. In practice Brown crashed on the 250 Honda. Witnesses said the awkward three-mile rear section of the track was dangerous because a film of dust lay on the surface from dried mud. Brown died shortly afterwards in hospital.

In the race Gary Hocking, a highly-talented Rhodesian, won followed by the ubiquitous Ubbiali (who had won a race on a 125 as long ago as 1950, his first world title as long ago as 1951). Tanaka was third, Takahashi sixth.

At the Ulster Grand Prix at Dundrod in August, with mist on the high ground, there was Ubbiali out in front on his 250 MV, Phillis second, Redman third; but with a handful of laps left the crowd began to 'seethe' because the Hondas were starting to catch the leader. Ubbiali responded immediately and opened the gap to eleven seconds. Three laps from the end Phillis attacked again and hacked the gap down to five seconds. Ubbiali held it there and going into the last lap it was four seconds. Still Phillis came and as they crossed the line Ubbiali had won by a mere two seconds, Redman, wielding the bike like a hungry man, a mere 1.2 seconds after that. And, as a sort of bonus, Takahashi was fifth. In the 125 Tanaka fell and broke his right ankle.

The big point had been made—and decisively made. On the Island, Brown had been fourth but never a direct challenger to the MVs. The Honda wasn't, as we have seen, that quick. It was now at Monza and to emphasize it Redman 'shocked the cynics', as Peter Carrick says, by slicing a path up through the field after a bad start, taking Degner and Takahashi on the last lap and finishing behind Ubbiali. It was the last race of the season and gave Redman a total of ten points, fourth in the championship table while Honda (19) were second to MV (48 but only 32 counting.) But that didn't matter at all. They could now stay with the MVs even if they hadn't yet beaten them. As the bikes were loaded up on the evening of 11 September 1960 and the vans nosed their way out of the paddock at Monza a great many people wondered what would happen in 1961.

Among them was a diminutive Swiss we have met before, Luigi Taveri. Born of an Italian father and a Swiss mother he'd become fascinated by bikes when his elder brother began racing them. 'My first race was in 1947 at Berne. By this time my bother was competing in side-cars and I was his passenger. I wasn't frightened. I was so young then. My first solo race was a year later, a grass track meeting. I finished third. I started to compete on bigger bikes and when I first won the Swiss Championship it was on a 350. My first contract with MV Augusta was for a 500 but then Count Augusta gave me a smaller bike—the 125—and in my first or second race I won. That was the Spanish Grand Prix in 1955.' Count Augusta had made an inspired decision. Although Taveri stands only 5 ft 2 in and weighs only 8 st 9 lb he never had a problem controlling the big bikes; but 'I found the 125 was the best for me. In the spring of 1961 I didn't have good bikes. I had ridden many different works machines but some of the Italian teams were stopping, I didn't seem to have many chances and I considered stopping myself. I judged Honda to be the bike of the future. I wrote to Japan and they told me to contact their service operation in Holland. I flew to Rotterdam and met Mr Kawashima and Mr Idah in an hotel. Mr Kawashima was the team manager and Mr Idah was also very important. I said I would like to ride their bikes. They said it was very difficult because the team was already organized for the season and they added that they didn't have enough bikes. But Mr Kawashima did make me an offer: we can give you last year's model for the first three races and then see if you are happy and we are happy. I went home and talked it over with my wife. I felt I had no chance with an old bike.'

The first race of the season was Barcelona and Taveri didn't compete there. The second was Hockenheim: 'I thought, OK Hockenheim is not so far to travel, OK so I'll go to Hockenheim.'

But before that we must pause to look at Barcelona. The new bikes weren't ready and both Phillis and Redman were on the models Taveri had been promised, vintage 1960; and because of what were called 'geographical problems' no Honda personnel were able to reach the meeting. In this unpromising situation Phillis made a direct challenge to Hailwood (EMC) but towards the end of lap fourteen was still about 38 seconds behind. Then Hailwood's engine started to let go and on lap twenty-three Phillis was through. Redman finished third. In the 250, Phillis was only 22 seconds behind the winner, Hocking. Now Hockenheim. Enter Taveri.

'In the 125 I was the leading Honda rider because they had problems with the new bike [he was fifth, Shimazaki sixth, Redman seventh] and

Here is Hailwood on the Honda 125 his father bought. He wrote his own caption: Thank you, Mr Honda.

A glimpse of the 125 race in France before the Island. Number 3 is Takahashi, 17 is Hailwood, 9 is Ernst Degner.

that was a good result.' In the 250 Takahashi had an epic result after an epic race. Hocking set off in the lead but Takahashi and Redman overtook him on the second lap and at one stage four riders were locked in a frantic bunch—Takahashi, Redman, Hocking and Provini (Morini). Redman was in the lead, Provini was in the lead, Hocking was in the lead—before his engine blew—and on the last lap it was Redman then Takahashi. As they came furiously towards the line Takahashi slipped out and crossed the line first. The difference: 0.4 seconds. No Japanese had won a Grand Prix before.

Clermont Ferrand must be seen in retrospect as the beginning of the domination. Phillis won the 125, Redman third, Taveri fifth, while in the 250 Phillis won, Hailwood second, Takahashi third—a clean sweep for Honda. Taveri says: 'It was another good result for me and the team said: OK, you can have a new bike for the Isle of Man.' He was already beginning to enjoy himself. 'The Japanese mechanics didn't speak good English and I spoke very bad English but for the races, for the technical

The 125 cc race on the Island. Redman (3) leads Phillis (18) and Degner.

matters, we could communicate. I felt good with them. They always did their best. I had had experience of Italian mechanics, I knew their mentality and I was not happy. They were always a little bit, you know, never straight. What they said was not always what they were thinking. When you are good, when you are very special then you have all the possibilities but when you are not the best you have a very, very difficult time in an Italian factory. When I came to Honda I felt comfortable because I quickly saw that it made no difference if it was a Japanese rider or a European rider—the bikes were prepared exactly the same, one was not a little better than another.'

All this was but a prelude. Hailwood was poised for immortality and within the space of three days would elevate himself up and over the boundaries of bike racing to become an international sporting presence. It was what his father Stan had always intended and here it was. Stan had already negotiated a Honda 250 bike for his son, and would soon do some hard bargaining.

Hailwood himself would later say cryptically, that when he journeyed to the Island in June 1961 he had no particular expectations of winning anything. By mid-week Hailwood hysteria had spread to the mainland and every ferry was bringing more and more people who sensed that this was a chance they simply dared not miss.

It's almost ridiculously ironic that when Hailwood approached Honda for a 125 bike they solemnly informed him that he couldn't have one. They didn't have enough. Hailwood accepted that. He was facing enough of a mountain in the 250, 350, and 500 races and regarded himself as physically too big for the 125s anyway. But Stan Hailwood did not accept it. Stan Hailwood betook his formidable presence to the Nursery Hotel and, and we must assume, made an extreme nuisance of himself. Stan Hailwood also pulled a familiar masterstroke, and it went like this: you give my son a 125 and I will sell your bikes through my extensive dealer-

Bob McIntyre shatters the 250 cc lap record.

ships in Britain (Kings of Oxford). It worked. It was never going to fail.

On the last day before practice Honda handed Taveri's practice machine to Stan Hailwood, who promptly hoisted it into a van and vanished. When Mike tried it he found it was both 'terrible' and 'clapped out'. The mechanics worked on it and Hailwood took it to the race. Redman—did he sense the threat from Hailwood the privateer?—was first away. He didn't use the side-saddle technique; instead he made a straight vault on to the rear of the saddle and, as the acceleration began to bite, slid his body into position. The crowd in the grandstand saw his bright blue crash helmet bob-bob-bobbing as he fed more and more power into his Honda and was gone down Bray Hill.

Already a rider called Alan Shepherd (MZ) and Taniguchi had wheeled their bikes up to the front row and now they set off. You could see immediately the advantage of a strong, muscular, athletic shove. Shepherd took exactly twelve strides before he had reached what airplane pilots call the critical speed for take-off, used the side-saddle technique, and was gone down Bray Hill after Redman. He already had a hundred-yard lead over Taniguchi, still pushing towards his critical speed.

Then Hailwood on the practice bike.

By Sulby—half way round, remember—Taveri and Hailwood had caught Redman; at the Guthrie Memorial they were past him and now it became a straight duel, the old master against the new, Taveri squeezing everything to shake Hailwood off. At Signpost Corner Taveri had pulled out a hundred yards and at the right-hander there Taveri flung the bike furiously, tilting it hard over the kerbing. An instant later Hailwood did the same.

At Governor's Bridge Hailwood was gaining and was ahead on time

Phillis on his way to second place behind Hailwood.

anyway because Taveri had started 10 seconds before him. But, as is the way of it with racers, once they see each other the racing really begins. All their tribal instincts take over, the juices are flowing as fast as the bikes, and who cares about times?

If you did care about times you'd have savoured the tannoy announcement that Hailwood, in reaching Taveri, had broken the lap record by two miles an hour. As they crossed the line the length of a bike separated them and on that second lap Hailwood overtook Taveri and broke the lap record again. But . . . Taveri was an old master and up there on the Mountain he retook Hailwood who responded by re-taking him.

We can never know now what Hailwood was thinking as he moved down the Mountain, Taveri snapping at his heels. We do know he questioned whether the bike would last. We do know he won by seven seconds. We do know this was Honda's first TT victory.

'Mike became a good friend, he stayed at my house many times between races and for me I always say Mike was the best,' Taveri says. 'I looked up to him. He was a natural rider, he could go fast on anything, he could win when he didn't have the best bike.' As he had just proved in the 125.

Hailwood	Honda	1 hour 16:58.6
Taveri	Honda	1 hour 17:06.0
Phillis	Honda	1 hour 17:49.0
Redman	Honda	1 hour 20:04.2
Schimazaki	Honda	1 hour 20:06.0
Rensen	Bultaco	1 hour 21:35.2

This was the morning of 12 June. The 250 race was in the afternoon.

Phillis and Hailwood in the 125 cc race at Assen.

Hailwood's Honda had been overheating but Stan devised an ingenious solution. He'd noticed that some aeroplanes had air-vents in their wings and promptly had one cut under the crankshaft. McIntyre on a factory Honda took the lead and hammered the lap record, pushing it up to 99.58 miles an hour and would subsequently claim he'd have gone through the hundred mile an hour barrier 'if it had been necessary'. But on the last lap his engine seized (an oil leak), this engine which—again subsequently—McIntyre would claim could do 145 miles an hour, 'only ten miles an hour slower than an MV 500'.

Hailwood in second place took the lead, although he was less than pleased with the suspicion that Stan was deducting precious seconds from his time as the pit boards were waved to make him go faster.

Hailwood	Honda	1 hour 55:03.6
Phillis	Honda	1 hour 57:14.2
Redman	Honda	2 hours 01:36.2
Takahashi	Honda	2 hours 02:43.2
Taniguchi	Honda	2 hours 07:20.0
Ito	Yamaha	2 hours 08:49.0

This does not, of course, include Bob McIntyre. It does include, however, some instructive facts. No Japanese manufacturer had won both the 125 and 250 before; more than that, Honda had taken the first three places in the 125 as well.

By Wednesday the boats were bringing more people into Douglas and they all wanted to see if Hailwood could do the Hat Trick. He was on an AJS for this and, as he would recount, the day began badly because the van with all the kit in it ran out of petrol as it was making its way towards

Below *Another, almost panoramic, view of the same race. Phillis is 26, Hailwood 22.*

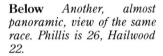

Below right *Spa. Taveri is 12, Redman 26.*

Taveri and Honda team member Happy-San at Spa.

the circuit with no petrol station in sight. 'A young fellow on his motor bike saw we were in trouble and siphoned off all the fuel from his tank into the van. He refused to give us his name or even accept any payment from us.' Ah, blessed, innocent days.

In the race Hocking took the lead but was hampered by mechanical problems and Hailwood not only took it for himself but built it up until it was comfortable. A mere 13 miles from the finishing line a gudgeon pin ended it all and Hailwood stood impotent as first Phil Read then Hocking went by. At the moment the gudgeon pin went Hailwood's lead was in the order of 2 minutes . . .

That left the 500, and although neither it nor the 350 are strictly part of the Honda story—Hailwood was on a Norton for the 500—they demand inclusion if only because of what Hailwood would subsequently do in both classes on a Honda. At Ballaugh, McIntyre (Norton—this was a Norton event) was in the lead, but Hailwood was behind him and attacking, Hocking behind Hailwood and attacking. At Ramsey, Hocking had

McIntyre on the 250 at Ulster and on his way to victory from Hailwood.

overtaken them both. At Windy Corner, Hailwood had overtaken McIntyre for second place. At the end of lap one Hocking had stretched it out to 15 seconds and Hailwood couldn't catch him.

It was 17 seconds starting lap three, 20 seconds at Kirk Michael. They refuelled at the end of that third lap and while Hocking was immobile in the pits, hands frantically tightening his faring, Hailwood came in with positively indecent haste. It was a moment of high drama and more followed because those frantic hands were still struggling with Hocking's fairing while the fuel went into Hailwood's tank. As Hailwood pushed off Hocking was in motion—just—and was on the bike—just—with Hailwood running hard before he jumped astride.

At Braddan, Hocking led by 11 seconds. At Ramsey, Hailwood was closing. At Keppel Gate, Hocking suddenly looked down at his rear wheel, his helmet dipping to one side. It was the plugs and at the end of lap four he was in the pits again. It cost him almost a minute. Nothing could stop Hailwood now except another mechanical failure, and the run for home became a triumphal procession with ripples of raised hands saluting him as he went past. He won by 2 minutes from McIntyre and averaged 100.60 miles an hour, the first time it had been done on a British bike. He was suitably astonished at his achievement. The result changed his whole life.

As Ted Macauley was to write: 'Far from revelling in the adoration he was acutely embarrassed by it, and eventually it reached the stage where he was unwilling to leave the shelter of his hotel.' On a more modest level, Taveri still didn't have a contract 'but they promised me bikes for the rest of the season'.

The thunder-clap echoed on at Assen where 200,000 people saw Phillis win the 125 from Redman and Hailwood win the 250 from McIntyre and Redman; echoed on at Spa where Taveri won the 125 from Phillis and

Jim Redman as many remember him, winning and smiling.

Redman, Redman won the 250 from Phillis, Hailwood, and Shimazaki. It brought them to the Sachsenring, a difficult, counter-clockwise circuit in East Germany. 'It was a country,' Taveri says, 'where you had a bad feeling when you went in and a good feeling when you came out. The town of Karl-Marx-Stadt (which was near the track) looked old and dark, everything seemed dark. We stayed in the Hotel Moscow. You got start money and prize money, of course, but you had to spend it because you were not allowed to take it out of the country. We always had problems because there was so little to buy. In the end I had a system. When I was leaving East Germany and I reached the frontier I deposited the money, signed the right papers and the money stayed there. When I came back the following year I was able to pick it up. Year by year I had more money and then even more money! It got so much that I told my wife she could spend as much as she liked but in the evening she had found nothing to buy and we still had the money. I was getting angry. I threatened to throw the money out of the car window . . . but [chuckle] I didn't.'

In the race Taveri had a very bad start and was last. He moved quickly, was ninth at the end of the first lap and third at the end of the fourth. Takahashi, meanwhile, broke the lap record while overtaking Taveri but skidded when he tried to overtake Phillis. Degner, the East German, was clearly ahead but on the last lap Taveri overtook Phillis: 'in the last corner my handlebar broke on the right side. I was lucky. I was doing 200 kph—full speed—but straight ahead from the corner was the road to the paddock. I went down it and was able to turn around, rejoin the circuit and cover the hundred metres to the line. As I passed the pit I made a bad sign to the Honda people there about the bike. I was disqualified for leaving the track.

'In the evening I asked for a bike for the next race, the Ulster, and they said: "Sorry, we have not enough bikes." I thought this was because I'd made the bad sign. Now at this time MZ liked me and I said to the Honda people: "Sorry, but I like to race, I'll go with MZ." One hour later Honda said: OK for Ulster . . . '

The 250 at the Sachsenring went to Hailwood, then Redman and Takahashi. Takahashi took the 125 at Ulster, McIntyre the 250. Only Degner could challenge them in the 125 and won Monza; Redman took the 250 from Hailwood and Phillis; Taveri took the 125 in Sweden and was second behind Hailwood in the 250; Phillis the 125 in Argentina, and the 250. Phillis was 125 champion, Degner second, Taveri third; Hailwood the 250 champion—54 points (44 counting), Phillis 45 (38), Redman 51 (36), Takahashi 30 (29), McIntyre 14 and Hailwood wondered how Honda might view that—the privateer beating the factory. Perhaps that might be buried under the sheer weight of the statistics, although it was unlikely: Honda had filled the first five places in the 250 championship and of the eleven 125 races won all but three. Phillis was World Champion by a distance. Overall Honda had contested twenty-two races in 1961 and only lost four.

And Hailwood, who'd only got bikes from Honda with the help of Stan's muscle? It is perhaps instructive that in his book Redman does not mention this, contenting himself with ruminating that Honda were now the 'sorcerers' and the rest the 'apprentices'. This seems just about the perfect way to put it.

FIVE

A Private Affair

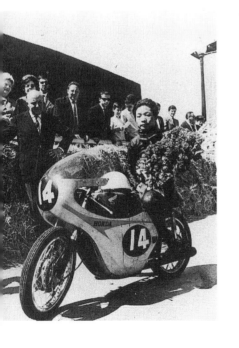

Triumph at Barcelona. Takahashi wins the 125 cc race.

'IN 1962,' recalls Tommy Robb, 'the weather was sunny and we all worked outside in the courtyard of the Nursery Hotel.' Robb had become a rider by taking the traditional route:

My father was always associated with motor cycling on the organization side and I went to meetings with him at a very tender age. At 14 or 15 I started 'stealing' the occasional ride at an odd grass track meeting like everybody else did. I'd go and help with the straw bales, help with the layout of the circuit. I rode in trials, converted a bike for a road in 1955 and won. A businessman had bought an old 175 MV and he asked me if I'd like to ride this little road-going machine. I did and I had wins on it. I was noticed by talent scouts, which they had in those day just like they have at football matches today. I was riding NSUs and my progress was fairly rapid. The scouts worked for all the big oil companies and they had a reasonable amount to spend, I'm talking £100, £200 but it was a lot of money in Ulster then. I was approached by Mobil to ride for the Geoff Monty team and I did ride a lot of bikes for them in 1959 (which was how he'd been in the first 125 race on the Isle of Man that Honda contested).

I was approached by Honda in late 1961 through the then Honda importer for Northern Ireland, Artie Bell [the great ex-Norton works rider]. Would I be interested in joining them? I had already been approached by Bultaco and naturally I had said yes to them so now I needed to be released from that. I approached Bultaco and they said: 'You must go to Honda because they are a bigger company and you have a better chance of winning the World Championship with them.' [This is a kindness Robb still remembers.] I signed a contract with Honda for the 50 and 125 ccs but they also decided to supply me with a 250.

The first meeting of that season was Barcelona in May. Robb soon got a 'close-up of what it was like to be a Honda rider and of the thoroughness and hang-the-expense persistency with which they conducted their affairs. The object was to win and at the Spanish Grand Prix Luigi [Taveri] and I were mounted on their first single-cylinder 50 cc machine. Up against Suzuki and Kreidler they flopped and we found ourselves in the team manager's hotel room with explanations for our failure politely —but, we still knew, firmly—required.'

The manager wanted to know, in fact, why they hadn't even finished

third. Robb said they needed more gears than the six they had. He was asked equally politely how many gears they needed. Eight, he replied. Within a few minutes, Robb would remember, 'the manager was speaking to the factory. I was fascinated. A telephone call from Spain to Tokyo must have cost £3 per minute but our team manager had asked for the call with the same air of detachment that he would use to ask for more water in his Scotch. I was later to learn that phone calls between Europe and Honda in Tokyo lasted sometimes over three hours . . .'

At Barcelona Redman won the 250 from McIntyre with Phillis third, and thereby hangs a tale. (As a matter of record Hans Anscheidt on a Kreidler took the 50 and Takahashi the 125.) The next race was Clermont Ferrand a week later. When Robb reached the paddock he saw, to his complete amazement, two new bikes with eight-speed gearboxes. He decided—and he is a pragmatic man—that Honda must have had 'a magic lamp'. Not that they beat Keidler, and this time Jan Huberts, a Dutchman, won. 'More gears,' Robb said, and Honda reached for the telephone. Takahashi again took the 125, Redman again took the 250, McIntyre second, Phillis third. It meant of course the Redman not only led the championship but was clearly going to win it.

A couple of weeks later they were on the Island. 'Honda chartered a plane and loaded us up for the Island,' Robb says. 'When we arrived we hired a car and arrived at Quarter Bridge in time to see the first riders going round in practice. It looked as though we were off on the wrong foot, but our out-of-breath party were soon in a happy frame of mind. Halfway through practice week two more newly-designed 50 cc machines arrived, this time with ten-speed gearboxes . . . ' The bikes incidentally were revving up to 17,000.

Amongst the riders gathered on the Island was Derek Minter, who stayed in his usual hotel. He was an unfussy sort who had 'always been a man of motor cycles. My father had one and I wanted one and I went very quickly on the thing.' He still speaks with a discreet Kentish accent. He was born near Canterbury and still lives there. 'I first went to the Island in 1953 with a rider called Ray Hallett. I was his mechanic and I cleaned

*Derek Minter on the 250 cc
Honda. He convulsed the Isle
of Man.*

the cycles for him and when I saw the racing over there I thought:
"Blimey, I can do that." Then I bought a Gold Star bike, which was the
nearest thing you could get to racing in the early 1950s, and I decided to
have a little go! I entered a meeting at Brands Hatch but I chickened out!
I panicked because I was frightened. But with memories of the Island still
fresh I made a second decision: I was definitely going to have a go and it
would have to be Brands because that was the nearest track to where I
lived. I raced and I didn't finish last, which was a great incentive. The year
after I went a bit quicker on the Gold Star because I'd got used to it and I
was invited by Rob Harris, the MV distributor, to have a ride on an MV.'
Minter went on to become almost unbeatable on short circuits on Norton
singles.

Now he was poised, although he couldn't know it, to convulse the
Island—and Honda. He was involved with Castrol and so were Honda.
Castrol recommended Minter for a bike and he got one, a 250, but as a
privateer. It was the cosy kind of marriage of convenience which has happened in the sport all down the years.

'The first time I rode it [Minter recalls] was just before Easter, and
from that time to the TT it never ran on all the cylinders properly. It
always felt as if there was fluff in the exhaust, as though a valve had
burnt out. My two British mechanics—Castrol were paying their
retainers—knew nothing about it and I knew nothing about it. We simply
used it because we had no competition as quick in England (in minor
meetings, of course) and I was quite happy. We drove to the Isle of Man,
practised, and I was quite happy with it there, too. The mechanics said:
"Shall we get the Honda team to have a look at it?" I said no because I
wanted to keep us private, and in any case we would be in direct competition with the factory team. My people just about knew how to change
the plugs but, for example, they had no jets for it. So all they did was
change the plugs and check the tyre pressures six or seven times.'
Minter estimated the works bikes would be a good twenty miles an hour

quicker than him and judged that both natural and inevitable. He was drawn number one for the race but that didn't matter particularly. It was, of course, a time trial.

In the morning he did a lap in the van observing, remembering the circuit. He didn't bother much about lunch but he knew, as the race came ever nearer, that his biggest trouble 'was that friends expected me to win because I won so much at Brands Hatch; and of course you could have an off-day and in the race you had Redman and Tom Phillis, who was the same calibre as Geoff Duke, although I hadn't really met him until then. It never entered my mind that I would win the TT. I never dared to think that I would win it.'

It was hot, a heat-haze over the hills. Now he waited by the white line bisecting the road and as he waited Reg Armstrong, a Dubliner in his forties who sold Hondas and was a member of the racing team, walked briskly across and said discreetly: 'Don't forget Jim is leading the World Championship.' Minter, bemused, muttered 'OK.' There can be only one interpretation. Minter was being asked in a direct way not to win.

'It didn't really mean a thing because I didn't, as I have said, anticipate winning anyway and it struck me as stupid. Why did Armstrong leave it until under a minute before the race started?' (The words still haunt Minter and during the interview he says them again, as if he had no need to trawl them from memory because they still smoulder there. 'Don't forget Jim is leading the World Championship . . . ')

'I can't remember who the rider next to me was when the race did start. I was concentrating on how quick I could go on this bike which ought to have been serviced but hadn't been. I pushed off and after Ballacraine McIntyre, who knew the Island like the back of his hand, came sliding by and he was going a good twenty miles an hour quicker.' McIntyre had already made up the 30-second gap. Minter couldn't stay with him. 'I saw nobody else.'

The 125 cc race on the Island in 1962. Degner (Suzuki) shakes hands with Robb (8) and Taveri.

At the Mountain Box, McIntyre had pulled cleanly away from Minter—and let's not forget that Minter had started thirty seconds ahead of him. At Kepple Gate McIntyre's time was 20 minutes 30 seconds and the commentator was calling out over the tannoy: 'He looks all set for a ton lap.' It had been anticipated. In practice McIntyre had done a lap of 97.68 and a contemporary account described that as 'an incredible performance taking into account that he cut the engine at Governor's Bridge and slowed to a stop in the pits'.

Now, coming through Governor's again, he was going for it, Minter trying to cling on somewhere back there. A gasp as he crossed the line: 99.06! The leaderboard (although not, naturally, the order on the road) read McIntyre 22 minutes 51.2, Redman 23 minutes 25.8, Minter 23 minutes 35.0. At Barregarrow McIntyre's engine broke. He slowed, pushed the bike under a rope barrier, held up his hands as if to say 'There's nothing I can do; and chugged off down a side road, the engine puttering. As Minter passed he thought in his own phlegmatic way: 'Well, that's one less to worry about.'

At the end of the second lap it was Redman 46 minutes 42.2, Minter 46 minutes 51.2, Hailwood (Benelli) 49 minutes 43.6. Minter didn't know that Tom Phillis, another strong contender, had developed a misfire on the second lap and because Minter had no pit signals he didn't know whether Redman was poised to slide past him as McIntyre had done. At any instant he expected Redman to do so. Minter pitted at the end of the third—so fast he overshot—and 'because I'd had no signals, when the two mechanics told me I was in the lead I didn't believe them.' Minter had just ridden a magnificent lap and overall had gone a great deal quicker than Redman—1 hour 9 minutes 57.4 against Redman's 1 hour 10 minutes 12.2. As Minter had stopped at the pits the growl of Redman's bike could be distinctly heard, coming, coming, coming. 'While I was in the pits Redman went charging by and I thought good, at least I have someone to chase. To catch someone on the Isle of Man was a hell of a job

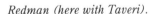

Redman (here with Taveri).

unless you were up with them and it's almost the same when you're in the lead. You have no one to pace you, you don't know how fast you are going in comparison to the people behind. So out I went [the stop had been 52 seconds, giving Redman a lead of 45 seconds] and I'm sure I was the fastest man on the circuit because I was so determined to try and catch him. I did draw nearer to him and suddenly I could see him going round Sulby. I actually caught him going down Sulby and that astonished me—Redman on a works bike and me on the privateer which hadn't had a spanner on it at all since Easter.

'When we got to Sulby Bridge I was right with him, certainly within ten to fifteen yards, we went round Ginger Hall and I was up his backside. After Ginger Hall you had to bear over to the left to go into a right-hander and you were going very slowly. I passed him on the right-hand side. I didn't know until then that there was a bump in the road. I was airborne! I'd never been on the right before. It was determination that made me do it there. It wasn't the height which was the thing—I was only airborne two or three feet—it was the way the whole bike wriggled. I remember glimpsing some cottages and we went round a left-hander and I didn't see him again.' In fact at Ramsey they had the same times on the clock but by Keppel Gate Minter was 10 seconds up and at the end of that fourth lap Redman came in for fuel. Redman was still in the lead overall, 1 hour 33 minutes 38.8 against 1 hour 34 minutes 9.8.

But—and Minter had no way of knowing this—Redman was in deep trouble. His petrol filler cap kept working loose and each time he banked the Honda on the corners fuel spilt. A lap later Redman was in for more fuel and lost another 17 seconds. At the end of lap five: Minter 1 hour 57 minutes 9.0, Redman 1 hour 57 minutes 57.6. It gave Minter a very solid lead and one witness saw him 'pull out all the stops' as he moved in to the sixth and final lap.

On that last lap I was still expecting Redman to catch me again although I didn't look back. You don't have time, do you? I never looked back. Each time I'd passed the Honda pit I looked towards the Japanese mechanics but they didn't put a board or message out to me at all. I'd have thought that if they didn't want me to win they'd have done that. I would still have been entitled to ignore any message as a privateer, but in another sense I would have been a naughty boy for not obeying orders, wouldn't I?

Going up the Mountain the last time I lost a thousand revs and I didn't know why. It was confusing to me. But the bike was getting slower and it was only when I began to come down that it was doing 14,000 again. It held 14,000 at Creg-ny-Baa and from Creg to Brandish it was still holding 14,000 so I thought that whatever had happened before must have been me. I reasoned that maybe I must have been taken a corner back there too slowly, maybe five or ten miles an hour too slowly to get the revs. I must say that the engine didn't sound any different. I crossed the line, shut the engine off, took three or four hundred yards to stop and went through the gateway onto the path which led back to the assembly area.

Derek Minter was calm and resigned. It had been a good race and while he knew that McIntyre hadn't won, he wondered who had—Redman or Phillis? 'A few minutes later my two British mechanics came to me and said: "You beat them." I said: "I didn't." They said: "Yes, you did." I still fail to understand why neither Phillis nor Redman beat me, it was a mystery to me. It must have been that they didn't know their way round the Isle of Man like I did.

'I'd been in the assembly area about ten minutes and by then everybody knew I'd won—[it was of course prudent to wait until all the front runners had come in, unlike a head-to-head race] and people came over to congratulate me, but Honda didn't. I was literally in disgrace and Redman didn't do anything because he was so cheesed off.'

The Honda mechanics did, however, have a look at the bike. Minter left it with them and 'we went back to the hotel and just had a bit of a celebration, nothing drastic because I didn't drink at that time and I don't now.' Minter had won £250 plus bonuses, which 'brought it up to the region of £500. Today you're talking in thousands . . . '

As Minter and his friends sat in the hotel a Japanese mechanic entered and spoke to him. What he said staggered Minter. 'They'd taken the bike to scrutineering and had decided to lift the bottom end out. They found the crankshaft was broken but jagged so it held together enough to get me to the line. I asked how many miles it had done like that and they said about half a lap. I said: "This must have been how I lost 1,000 revs." '

Minter wondered how far the Honda mechanics estimated one of their race engines would go before it needed an overhaul. They thought about 300 miles. His, he knew, had done at least 600 . . . and if the bike had broken up as Minter was coming down the Mountain at 140 miles an hour? 'You don't get frightened about that, you never think of those sort of things. Anything could have happened but you always have a clutch to pull in and that should free the back wheel.' He pauses. 'The Honda mechanics did overhaul the bike for me on the Island and when we got it back it was a damn sight quicker than it had been.'

But the other, brutal face of the Island was to show itself. Honda had now produced a 350 bike—it was an enlarged version of the 250—which during the season would be replaced by new bikes. In the 350 race Hocking led Hailwood with Phillis on the Honda clinging to him. Redman went to watch at the bottom of Bray Hill and described the sight as 'awe-inspiring', but he noticed that the Honda, which didn't handle well, was 'bucking and bouncing'. Hailwood would say: 'Phillis was killed trying to keep up with Hocking and me. What he lost in speed he tried to make up with sheer riding skill and daring.'

The second lap began and people noticed that the Phillis's name wasn't being included in the tannoy commentary any more. Redman, listening intently, was immediately concerned. He knew full well that if a rider stopped the commentator would habitually say that he'd had mechanical problems or, if he'd crashed, that he was unhurt. It's a reflex action by any commentator: to bestow reassurance. Silence was satanic. To make it worse Phillis's wife Betty was in the grandstand. Redman, waiting 'in agony' for a word, any word, to echo from the loudspeakers, sensed somewhere deep inside himself that Phillis had been killed. When he saw Reg Armstrong's face he had all the confirmation he needed. There was no need to speak. Phillis, straining so hard to stay on the pace, had hit the wall at Laurel Bank, and the words of Stuart Graham come tragically to mind: 'Laurel Bank and its approach from Dorans Bend was very, very, very bumpy; it was nasty, it was dangerous—a fast left and then a right-hander with a stone wall on the outside . . . '

Redman controlled himself hard, the thought-processes moving as precisely as those of a rider, isolating the priorities. His wife Marlene was nearby and he sent her to collect the two Phillis children, Debbie and

Jimmy, who were at a nursery. Then he went to the grandstand.

Hocking was so distraught that he retired and returned to Rhodesia to be a farmer. He forced himself to do just one further race on a motor bike—the 500 this same week—and was gone, never looking back. He was 24 and would talk about 'the false sense of security' you get when you're actually racing, but the compulsion didn't go away. He carried it with him back to Bulawayo and within months was driving racing cars. Perhaps he felt they were safer. In December 1962 he was practising for a race called the Natal Grand Prix at Durban in a Lotus Climax, although rumour has it that Stirling Moss ought to have been in it. (He wasn't. He was still recovering from an horrific accident at Goodwood at Easter). So Garry Hocking took it out and he was good; some people who knew said he was very good.

He was killed.

You can approach it from many directions. You can assemble the witnesses and examine their testimony, rake over the wreckage, make reports. You can listen to people fumbling among their emotions, reaching for something. You will hear justifications that the man knew it was dangerous, nobody made him, he wanted to. You can justify it to yourself by this parable: an anonymous old person in some transient hospital ward doesn't choose the manner of their death, they just die. Why should you grieve any more—or any less—for one who had a choice? That does not alter the sense of waste, the sense that when it happens it just couldn't have been necessary, the sense that nobody of 24 should die for any reason. And of course in motor sport it happens all at once so that the familiar reassuring world you know so well—Phillis approaching Laurel Bank as he had done so many times before, Hocking easing a car out of the pits—is brutally broken in a handful of wild seconds, and no sane witness can have the mechanisms to absorb it until a long time afterwards. There is a very great emptiness when brave men who have the choice accept it, balance it, ride it through, and don't come back.

No man is an island.

There are postscripts, necessary to our story, about the Isle of Man, June 1962. Taveri: 'In the beginning, Jim Redman was not happy that I came in to the team. I was in competition with him because he liked to win and I liked to win. He was the big man at Honda, then Taveri comes in and he

The 125 cc at Assen, Taveri leading Hailwood.

was not happy. He never told me, but I could feel it. Then Tom was killed at the TT and I think that changed Jim's mind. We became good friends. Jim was always fair and I learnt many things from him. I was just a rider, he understood about the money and so on.'

On the Island, Robb and Taveri had their ten-speed gearboxes for the 50 cc race and, as Robb says, 'these gave us a better spread of power because the bikes were revving up to 17,000. We still didn't win, but the fact that Luigi finished second with me third to Degner on the Suzuki gave us hope for the future.' Minter, incidentally, had a 125 production Honda as well as the 250 which had already passed into legend. 'Whether it was me or not I don't know, but it was quicker than the works bikes going round the Island. It was a bike which the ordinary person could buy. I think I embarrassed Honda because they decided to give me a genuine racer. I rode it, came back, and told them it wasn't so quick. I said there was something wrong with the rev counter; it wouldn't go up and back as it ought to have done. They said: "No, no, it's alright." Anyway . . . I finished about fourth on it.'

Minter remains gently bemused by what machines can and cannot do. He has tried to rationalize this and it leads him back to the man, not the machine, and the man is himself: 'I reckoned the production machine was a good five miles an hour quicker. Of course it may have been the way one rider comes out of the corners a bit quicker than other riders; skill could have played a part. I'm not saying that I know the Isle of Man like the back of my hand now.' Pause. 'But I did then.'

This is Taveri's own montage of the West German Grand Prix.

Robb took the place of Phillis at Assen later that month in the 250: 'Unusually for me, I got a good start and I was dicing with Redman and Degner. Jim was leading as we rushed into one of the corners on the back of the circuit when all hell was let loose. Being used to a 50 cc machine with its ten gears I forgot that the 250 had only six! I got mixed up in my gear change, found myself in bottom, much too slow for the corner. The

Weltmeisterschaftslauf

1962
SOLITUDE

machine jack-knifed and I was pitched off on to the grass and straw bales. I picked myself up. My bike had come to a stop in the middle of the track and Degner, hitting it, took off like a moto cross rider, stayed on board, and continued the race. Provini, however, was furious . . . he slewed his bike into a broadside at the corner, hit my bike, threw his own down, glared at me, shook his fist and only just failed to beat Redman by half a wheel.' Ah, the tricks of memory. In fact it finished:

Redman	58 minutes 52.2
McIntyre	58 minutes 54.4
Provini	58 minutes 54.8

Robb had torn his knee-cap but, pinning up the gap in his overalls, he competed in the 125 and while he was locked into combat with Taveri, Degner, and Hailwood the pins worked loose and began to stab the open wound. Robb finished third . . .

Spa was only a week away but Robb was sent back to Belfast to recover. Competing at Spa was out of the question. 'While I was moodily staring out of my window at the panoramic view of the city I had from my hill-top home, my thoughts were still of the boys on the Continent and I resolved to lift myself by the bootlaces to get reasonably fit. I had a Bultaco in the garage so I hobbled out and straddled the bike in a crouching, racing position. What happened? I ripped out the stitches in my knee.'

McIntyre took over the 125 ride but retired. Taveri was third. They improved on that at Solitude in the 250—Redman, McIntyre, Tanaka, and a West German called Beer gave them the first four places. Honda power, you know and only three years since they'd first ventured to the Island.

McIntyre was a great rider. He'd never 'given motor cycle sport a thought while I was at school. In fact I was nineteen before I saw my first race—a scramble—and I was twenty before I competed in my first race.' He was the son of a riveter, a useful footballer, and at 15 had got a job in a garage 'to learn a useful trade, not because of any passion for motors'. He brought his first bike at 16 (a 1931 Norton for £12). His mother 'took one look and raised all the objections about oil and noise and danger'. McIntyre persuaded her, became a dispatch rider in North Africa during his National Service, and as now in 1962, I repeat, a great rider.

And they all went to the British Championships at Oulton Park between Solitude and the Ulster Grand Prix. Minter was still using the private Honda 250 on the short circuits; 'that was the next time I met Redman after the Isle of Man. I was astounded how good the bike was after the Honda mechanics had overhauled it. I don't know whether I was fastest in practice. I always took the first lap steady so I could weigh the circuit up, see where the others were, and on the first lap Redman toyed with going round the outside of me at one corner and the next lap at the same corner I was doing a good ten to fifteen miles an hour quicker because I knew it was all right and he tried the same thing. He kept straight ahead on to the grass because he was going too quickly for the corner.'

Accounts of what happened immediately after that vary, Redman claiming that Minter braked violently. 'At the end of that meeting they took the bike from me and said: "You aren't going to ride it any more." After that they told me I could go to Japan to ride in the Japanese Grand

Prix but I would have to pay my own fare, although they'd give me a bike to ride. I said: no chance.'

McIntyre was to compete in a handicap race at Oulton. 'The weather,' Robb says 'was terrible. I went over and spoke to Bob, who was changing his sprockets on his bike. We didn't have time to talk. "I'll see you later," he told me.' 'I was leading the race,' Minter says, 'and everybody says Bob was catching me but he wasn't because I had good pit signals and every lap I was getting an increased sign. On that corner [Druids] there was a puddle of water and I kept aquaplaning through it and I kept getting further and further over to the left to miss it.' McIntyre, handicapped to start from the back, was making a characteristic charge. 'The next thing I know I come whistling up there and the yellow flags were flying. I saw somebody had come off but it wasn't until two laps later, when I had a sign from the pits to tell me I had a big lead, that I thought it must be McIntyre.

'When I finished I asked and they said "Yes". I know it's a cruel thing to say but I thought there couldn't be much hope for him because he really ploughed in there. His bike must have just aquaplaned and he just sort of carried straight on. I think he hit a tree because there were a load of trees there. I mean, you hadn't got to go far before you came to them.'

Ken Sprayson had spoken to McIntyre earlier on in the meeting: 'This sort of motor cycling was a bit of a free-for-all. You set up shop in the middle of the paddock because there were no pantechnicons and no motor homes or anything like that. Riders had vans or cars and trailers and they mucked in with everybody else in the paddock. Everybody would be together. It's just unbelievable when it happens, I mean you just don't believe it.'

The world moves on. They went to Ulster and Minter was 'actually leading the 125 race' when he found himself jousting with Redman again coming into a place called Quarries Bend. 'I fell off and damaged the third finger on my left hand, but what happened I haven't a clue, haven't *A close-up of Taveri in action.* a clue; all I know is I finished up in Belfast Hospital.' Robb took

McIntyre's 350 and was second to Redman when the oil cooler split—'I must have looked like a jet plane taking off with streams of smoking oil soaring into the air.' Redman won, Robb third.

Redman, of course, was the man Honda had designated to win the 250 title and Robb, and Ulsterman in Ulster, knew he had been cast in the role of support. He gazed at the crowds who were all willing him to win, but the winning belonged to Redman. Emotions were heightened further because he and Redman had what he tactfully calls a 'clash of personalities'.

Factory riders do as they are told or they do not remain with the factory long, so Robb duly obeyed, following Redman at a discreet distance; the rest were nowhere. Robb did not 'dare' to overtake, but with three laps left Redman's bike began to fire on only two cylinders and was 'going so slowly I couldn't have sat behind him. It would have looked ridiculous.' It became one of Robb's' very greatest days.

Redman now made his position in the 250 championship impregnable by winning at the Sachsenring and Monza and it demands to be said that in the nine races so far (only Argentina remained) he had finished first or second in every one. At the Sachsenring, Taveri took the 125 world title. 'It is difficult to explain my feeling,' he recalls. 'I was happy, of course, to win my first championship but I was happier to give to Honda what they had expected of me. I felt they were very happy, too, but I couldn't tell by their faces because they don't show their emotions in the way we do. There was a bar in the Hotel Moscow and everybody was drinking and joking. It was a big festival—not for my championship but because everybody had to spend the money!'

No special celebrations?

Taveri's wife Tilde: 'Well, nine months later we had a boy!'

At Monza, Robb had a bizarre incident, although many people feel rightly that Monza is bizarre in all its aspects. 'Rimo Venturi on a Bianchi was second, I was third. Some of the lads came up to me after the race and said: "You've got to put in a protest." They told me I'd finished sec-

Robb and Redman. 'Jim took off like a scalded bloody cat...'

ond. Venturi had evidently pulled into the pits to change plugs, started the bike, set off, noticed that the bike was still misfiring so he came round the back of the pits and in again but he was credited with doing a complete lap. Honda made me protest and the result was rearranged so that I was second, but they still let him keep the prize money. Anyway I had the second place and the points for that, which was important to me.'

Finland—Tampere—was after Monza and although there was no 250 there were all the other classes. 'Tampere was the most dangerous, most exhilarating circuit,' Robb says.

In those days I loved trees and telegraph poles, I enjoyed racing between them, but this particular circuit was tarmacadam with shiny patches and wet patches. The trees were within twelve inches of the side of the track and by trees I mean trees. You couldn't see a gap between them. Mike Hailwood fell off and hit a park bench on his 350 and that cannoned him into the trees. Luckily he got away with it, although the bike was written off. In the 350 practice I discovered the bike had so much power that I couldn't get on with it in the slippy conditions, so I asked if I could ride the 285 because if I finished first or second I was going to finish second to Redman in the World Championship. Honda agreed. This bike was a dream, a real dream. Before we went out I said to Jim: 'You don't need the points. If you find that you can, would you let me finish well up.' At the start Jim took off like a scalded bloody cat, he really did, but it was one of those days when I found my moto cross and grass track experience came into play. I was sliding and slithering and those trees were looming—and concrete posts—and I was enjoying myself. I caught Jim and went past him and eventually got quite a good lead. I won. I don't think he was too pleased but it did give me second place in the championship.

A question: were you frightened? 'Everybody feels frightened. Don't get me wrong, I'm not trying to make out we're brave people—we're not. We're all frightened, but it's fear that gets the adrenalin flowing, isn't it? It's fear that keeps your nerve ends tingling, isn't it?

'I mean, this place Tampere, right on the Russian border, had a slippery corner at the bottom of a hill and the bike was sideways—not the way they do it today by drifting sideways, the bike was going sideways. I mean, I crashed in the 125 race. I braked beside the pit area and the next thing I knew I was in the trees . . . but it was great, terrific, I loved that sort of race. It was a test to stay on board and keep it going straight without wheelspin.' Taveri won the 50, Redman the 125.

A turbulent, saddened season was over.

Ralph Bryans in 1963—here on a 350 Norton.

SIX

Robbed

'I got into motor bike racing by accident,' Ralph Bryans says. 'I had a bike purely as a means of transport to get to technical college in Belfast. I had a friend who was very interested in racing but we were both seventeen and his mother would not sign the medical certificate to enable him to get a competition licence. I forged my mother's name on a certificate, went to a handicap race on a rainy day, and won it. I'd got the bug. That was 1959 and I remember it was miserably wet. By 1961 I was being sponsored by an insurance agent on a Norton 350. By 1963 I won the Irish championships at 350 and 500.' Bryans was a name being noted as he moved in the background of this season of 1963.

It was to be a time of a slight tactical withdrawal by Honda. Taveri: 'There were no Japanese mechanics. I had one of my own men to help me but he wasn't a mechanic so I had to work on the bike myself. Jim Redman was in a similar situation.' Moreover, Suzuki were direct challengers and took the world 125 championship. Honda won the first race in Spain but no more until Monza in September. Redman was again on the 250 although by now Yamaha were direct challengers and by the fifth race (Spa) had started to win. No matter. Redman was unstoppable on the Island in June. It was so hot that the tarmacadam was melting and Redman noted this even as he drove from his hotel to the paddock. It's going to be dangerous, he thought, very dangerous.

He decided, prudently, to have a good, long look as the race unfolded and if necessary let others make the running. It was the right decision. Twenty-six riders didn't finish and Redman could see 'scars' in the tarmac where riders had fallen and their footrests gouged the melting surface. The engine heated so much that it began to burn his legs, but he kept on and finished 27.2 seconds in front of Ito on a Yamaha. It was his first TT win.

That night he stood the trophy on the hat stand in the hall at the hotel and everybody chattered about the race. That was Monday 10 June. The 350 race was on the Wednesday and by then the weather had broken. It nearly broke Redman. It nearly broke Robb, too. It was cold, it was raining, mist had wreathed itself about the Mountain. In the morning Hugh Anderson won the 125 race—Redman was sixth—but at least Redman had been out there, had been able to gauge the conditions for the 350 in the afternoon. He took the lead, anticipating the Hailwood (MV) would overtake him at any instant; but, like Minter in 1962, he didn't look back. He just rode. So did Robb, whose bike had developed an oil leak immediately before the race began that had somehow cured itself. He was ordered to be circumspect in case the leak returned.

Redman was astonished at Ramsey to get a signal that he held a 10-second lead; Robb was delighted at Ramsey to look down at the wheel and notice that there was no oil on it. He had let a lot of other riders go by and now he decided to accelerate. Redman and Robb—separated by a long gap, of course—headed into the mist of the Mountain. At Creg-ny-Baa Redman emerged from the mist and there was Hailwood alongside him. They braked for Creg, Hailwood went through, waved, Redman twisted the accelerator and re-took him; they braked again and Hailwood retook him. Redman twisted the accelerator again and retook Hailwood . . .

Robb reached the Graham Memorial but a patch of road had a sheen on it where the tar had melted in the hot weather and had now reset perfectly smooth. The bike slithered, tipped onto its side dragging Robb along the surface of the road; and the surface was rough here. The chippings in it clawed at his leathers, tearing them away. When he stopped he was bleeding but, astonishingly, only his right finger was broken. He was laid down in the Memorial and just then the mist started to crawl back over the hillsides. As he lay he heard the distinctive sounds of another bike approaching—and crashing. A few moments later a Swedish rider was being ferried into the Memorial on a stretcher, his chin badly hurt. The Swede, concussed and no doubt seeing the pure white softness of the mist, said he thought he'd gone to Heaven.

On lap three Redman had a 23-second lead and then came the pit stops. Redman was subsequently told that, as Hailwood moved away again, he had stuck his tongue out at the Honda mechanics! It was unwise, as these gestures usually are. A few moments later his engine expired and Redman was left alone to beat the Mountain. The mist was so thick now that he removed his goggles to see better; the cold stung his eyes, the rain was so heavy that it ran in rivulets across the road, and once, at Glen Helen, he aquaplaned wildly. He held that and when he crossed the line to win he was so exhausted he could barely get off the bike. He felt the elation of survival, not victory.

And that was 1963—almost.

The second last race was in Argentina. No one who went there is likely to forget it, and nobody went back until 1981. 'Before the practice started Mike Hailwood, Jim Redman and I went to our pit,' Taveri recalls. 'The time arrived but there was no practice. Why? All the bikes were ready but no ambulance. One hour later an ambulance came and about two or three hours later we had the practice. When we came back from that, everything in the pit was a mess and I said: "Somebody has taken our things." Mike said: "My money's gone." He went running to the organizers and shouted this to them. They said: "Oh yes, we will come and have a look eventually . . . "'

'We had a car to take us from the circuit to the hotel. Some people stopped the car and wanted to get in themselves. We got out and a fight

Taveri got himself hit over the head with a starting handle in Argentina. The irony: he was an utterly peaceful man ...

started, Mike and Jim and me fighting with these people. I was the last to get back into the car and that was stupid because one of these people got hold of a starting handle and hit me over the head with it. The next day for practice I could hardly get my head inside my helmet ...'

Redman remembers Argentina vividly, too. 'Luigi, who had retired from the race, was having a near stand-up fight in the pits as he tried to signal me my position. Officials insisted he should not be on the road in front of the pits, despite the fact that there were Coca-Cola and coffee vendors there and they were not told to move. This is how ludicrous the situation had become ...'

Taveri again, talking urgently under the impetus of vivid memory: 'After the race there was more confusion. The car was standing there and although the car was for us, spectators were trying to get in again. I thought that this time I had better keep my mouth shut so I was standing there with my hand baggage but I didn't say anything ... then we had problems getting our prize money ...'

Truth to tell, 'the bikes were tired. We understood we couldn't push too hard and Jim asked me what we were going to do. I knew he was always faster than me in the 250 so I said: "OK, it's your race, but the 125 is mine" and he accepted that. Some laps before the end of the 125 I felt my engine wasn't good. It was making funny noises and one lap before the end the engine breaks. Jim wins. I said: "Ah, Jim, I give you a present, now you give me a present in the 250." "Yes," he said. We go to the start and when I push the bike the engine goes whump! My race is already finished.'

The last race was at Suzuka and, Taveri says, 'When we came to Japan

Honda had all new bikes, four cylinder 125s and a new 50 cc, very, very, very nice bikes. We would be competitive again in 1964.' Taveri won the 50, Redman the 250. The 50 cc bike was a twin cylinder machine which evidently reached 19,700 revs and certainly did over a hundred miles an hour.

'I'd raced for an English team on a 125 Honda,' Ralph Bryans says. 'The connection had been made through a friend who was very friendly with Tom Phillis and Jim Redman. When they came to the Ulster Grand Prix they used to stay with this friend. At the end of 1963 I went off to Spain to do some meetings there and I signed a works contract with Bultaco to contest the 125 and 250 World Championships in 1964. In December 1963 I received a telegram from Redman asking if I would be available to ride for Honda. When I looked at the two opportunities, Honda was definitely the one to have but I was in a bind having signed for Bultaco. I explained the position to them and they kindly released me. Off I went to Japan. I met the Japanese personnel, had two or three days testing at Suzuka, and came home with the contract in my pocket. I'd never been as far from home as that before and everything was very different, the people, the lifestyles, the way they do business, but I got on very well with everybody. I had no problems at all in that direction.

'It was the time when the Bullet trains had just been introduced so we went down to Nagoya on one—fantastic—and then took a taxi to a hotel called the Station Hotel which was about 25 miles from Suzuka. We always stayed there in the future. When it came to testing, Honda were hard task-masters. The day started well before dawn. A taxi would arrive while it was still dark and we ate breakfast in it on the way, a flask of coffee and some sandwiches. I was used to this sort of thing because I'd done testing in Northern Ireland and daylight is not in plentiful supply there in the middle of winter. At first light you would start testing and you'd test until darkness fell again. When you arrived at Suzuka the

Two last looks at Tommy Robb. In a corner (right) and doing the other thing he did well: communicating.

mechanics were already there, the machines would already be there.

'The first machine I rode at Suzuka was a Honda racer called the 93. That was to get familiar with the circuit. The next step was to get onto the full-blown works bikes. I fell in love immediately with the 125 four-cylinder. It was a beautiful machine to ride, tractable, fast, light, everything. I absolutely detested the 50 cc, I didn't know what to make of it initially and the riding technique on very, very small machines is totally different anyway. For example, the 50 peaked at about 19,000 revs and you wouldn't get any power until maybe 18,000 revs. The difference between that and the Manx Norton 500 I'd been riding was that the power came on at 7,000 revs.

'I also tested a 250-four. It was on the last day, I was starting to put up respectable times, and if memory serves me correctly I had broken the 125 lap record. Jim Redman was testing the 250 and having difficulty with the handling. This was due to the fact that Honda had used Avon tyres in 1963, Avon had withdrawn and Honda were now using a Dunlop triangular tyre—a small section front, a large section rear—and whenever you canted the bike in a corner you were getting imbalance on the side walls of the tyres.' Bryans went out on the 250. 'On the first corner after the start, a fast right which tightens up into a tight-right, I was going too fast . . . as it transpired. You never know how fast you are going when you're on a racing bike: you look at the rev counter and use your discretion. I was canting the bike over, it slid and spat me straight off the front. I landed on my head. I was closing the power off, that's for sure, but . . . I knocked myself out for about fifteen, twenty minutes. I woke up in the back of an ambulance. I had slight concussion. Jim and another rider testing at that time, a Southern Rhodesian called Bruce Beale, were standing there. I was a bit worried because I had concluded that there was only one place available on the team and it must lie between Bruce and myself.

'I didn't have to go on to hospital or anything silly and the day after we went back to Tokyo where I did some shopping. The day after that we went to the Research and Development centre and we had a proper sit-down business meeting there. I wasn't sure how the crash had gone down. I had, of course, apologized for partially destroying one of their machines, but nobody seemed to be really bothered. Mr Sekiguchi, who was head of Research and Development, said to me that the difference between a very, very fast rider and a crash is very, very small. They understood. They produced a contract. I signed it and flew home.

'As it's not a good thing for a Grand Prix rider to go into the first race cold without experience of the bikes, it was arranged that I should have some semi-works machines to use at selected international races before the season began, so Honda loaned me some old works 125-twins. They flew them over and I picked them up at the airport. I did some races in Italy, some in England, and the North West 200 in Ireland. The first Grand Prix was the Spanish [at Montjuich, Barcelona in May] and Honda earmarked me for the 50 because of my physical build. I weighed in at 9 st 2 lb and was 5 ft 7 in tall. Luigi Taveri had signed a works contract with Kriedler, the West German company, for the 50 but for Honda in the 125.'

The day before practice a thin, angular man with dark curly hair arrived. His face was already familiar. He had come from Northern Rhodesia where he had been working in the ventilation section at a copper mine at a place called Kitue. 'It was great money but a real dead hole

Thirsty work, this bike riding, as Takahashi discovers.

in the bush,' he would say. His name was Nobby Clark. He would get closer to Honda than any other non-Japanese. In fact he would get inside Honda.

'I was born in Bulawayo, Southern Rhodesia [Zimbabwe]. I went to technical school there and then served a five-year apprenticeship on the Rhodesian railways as a turner and fitter. One of the other apprentices was Gary Hocking. I was always keen on bikes and I can remember being taken out on a Douglas during the Second World War by a young RAF pilot—there was a training field near where we lived. I was also a big fan of Ray Amm and I'd followed his career when he was racing in Europe in the 1950s. [Amm, a fellow Rhodesian, won the 500 TT in 1953 and 1954 on a Norton.] I had my first ride—by that I mean the first time I had control of the throttle—in 1947 when we lived in Bechuanaland [now Botswana]. The roads were just sand tracks, no tarmac anywhere, very few cars, no police. Heaven! I went to Europe in 1960, travelled around with Hocking, and helped him until he retired in 1962.

'In 1963 Jim Redman asked me if I would like to work for him and prepare his bikes for international and Grand Prix races. I would travel with a Japanese rider, Kunimitsu Takahashi. We got along really well. Tak-san, as he used to be called, was a real great guy and a friend.' But now Clark found himself at the copper mine in the bush: 'I had planned to go to Japan in 1964 to see the Olympic Games. I was going to hitch-hike up Africa and then get the Trans-Siberian Express to Tokyo. I had kept in touch with Tak-san in the meantime. One month before Easter in 1964 a letter arrived from Jim Redman, who had just been in Japan. Honda said if I could get to Barcelona for the first Grand Prix in Europe and work with the team they would pay for my trip to Japan at the end of the season. They would also get me tickets for the Games. It took me about two minutes to make up my mind plus write a letter tending my resignation at the mine.'

The mass start in 1964: Suzuki versus Honda.

Traditionally, the Olympic Games are held in mid-summer; this year of 1964 they were between 10 and 24 October; but all in good time, all in good time. We are still at Barcelona in May and Nobby Clark has just arrived. 'There were two others in the 50, Takahashi and Robb, and the first race was an unmitigated disaster,' Bryans recalls. 'The engines broke. We were left with just one engine for the next meeting at Clermont Ferrand a couple of weeks later.' Anscheidt won the 50, Taveri the 125, Redman second to Provini in the 250.

'Ralph came in my van,' Robb says, 'and from Barcelona we went to the Austrian Grand Prix [non-championship] which was held on the auto-bahn just outside Salzburg. The 125 developed an oil leak and so we went to a friend's in Switzerland because he had a workshop. We spent a night stripping the engine to cure the leak. We finished about two in the morn-ing and I started it up. Suddenly there was a pool of oil on the floor where one of the drillings at the factory had gone right through the head, so we had a job to do on that. We got to Clermont Ferrand, booked into a hotel, and we both woke in the middle of the night with fleas crawling through the hairs on our chests.'

Robb practised that first day and while he was weighing the 125 in on the second day 'Redman told me that my contract had been terminated. I said: "But I've a contract to go right through until after the TT [the follow-ing month]" He stared at me and told me there was nothing more to be said . . . I packed and drove home. Why it happened I don't really know. I've tried to piece things together since then, but I'm saying no more.' Robb left in the van. 'To be perfectly frank, I just don't know why it hap-pened. It was quite a shock but that was it, it was all over,' Bryans says.

Anderson won the 50, Taveri the 125, Phil Read (Yamaha) the 250.

Two days later Robb's phone rang. It was Yamaha.

Now it was June, they were all back on the Island, and whatever the politics of what had happened Redman was to do something exceptional.

Robb rode a Yamaha on the Island—a 250—and however hard his fate had been at Clermont Ferrand, motor racing was about to show him its innocent face again. The Yamahas had trouble with their plugs and in practice Robb's bike stopped on the Mountain. He noticed an abandoned tractor in a field, got a 'rusty' plug from it, put it in and continued. In the race he limped home and had to push the bike from Governor's Bridge.

That 250 race was on the Monday and Redman reasoned that Phil Read and the Yamaha were favourites. Redman took the lead, Read chasing him hard, and they were together on the second lap when Read was forced into the pits—plugs, of course. Read lost around 60 seconds but, touched by rarest inspiration, went so fast that he took the lead on lap four. Then . . . plugs! Read clambered off the Yamaha at Quarter Bridge, took the plugs out, and flung them away in disgust.

It left Alan Shepherd (MZ) in second place and not far behind. On the last lap at the Ramsey hairpin Redman felt the bike 'slew' and in an instant it was virtually out of control. He 'hauled' it back and, as if by magic, it righted itself. He didn't know that an oil seal had split and was smearing the rear tyre on the left-hand side. This oil now flowed onto his leg, seep-ing down to his foot, which started to slip off the pedal. He crossed the line to win in 2 hours 19 minutes 23.6 seconds, an average speed of 97.450 miles an hour—a record. Shepherd was a mere 41 seconds behind.

In the 350, Redman and the Honda were completely untouchable and

Left *The 350cc race at Suzuka in 1964.*

after he'd reached an average speed of 100.75 miles an hour on lap three he eased off and won by a distance. His overall speed was 98.50 miles an hour and would have been a hundred if he'd wanted. He did that in 1965 . . .

The 125 was the harsh one. Redman set off with only three cylinders firing—the fourth didn't join in until after a couple of miles—and actually led, altogether Honda's overall strategy was for Taveri to become World Champion. Redman understood that but knew, too, that there were no team orders on the Island. Taveri was a lighter man and Redman estimated that that alone was worth five miles an hour going up the Mountain. Taveri overtook him on the last lap and won by 3 seconds, with Bryans third.

'The first race I finished on the 50,' Bryans says, 'was at the Isle of Man, where I was second. We went to Assen and I won'—Redman took the 125, 250, and 350. 'We went to Spa and I won there, too. The Belgians got mixed up afterwards. I'm an Ulsterman, of course, and that's part of the United Kingdom and we have the British National Anthem but the Belgians didn't know whether to play the Southern Irish anthem. As a compromise they played the Japanese anthem! The Japanese team were not given to an awful lot of emotion and it was both nice and strange standing up there on the podium receiving the winner's wreath and watching the mechanics cry when the anthem was played. They were very emotional about that.'

Bryans was beginning to assert himself and Honda in the 50—a twin which pulled 19,700 revs and did a ton—although as Clark attests 'he was called Baby-san by the mechanics for his youthful looks, and he was a rider who could do anything and get away with it'. Redman was shifting the whole balance of interest in the 250, an event traditionally in the shadow of the 500. Yamaha and Suzuki, sensing the many advantages of beating Honda, mounted a real challenge and it reached such an intensity that the 250 was sometimes moved to the end of a meeting as the climax. Recapping briefly, here is what had happened so far:

Left *Redman leads from Yamashita.*

Montjuich:	Provini (Benelli), Redman (Honda), Read (Yamaha)
Clermont-Ferrand:	Read (Yamaha), Taveri (Honda), Schneider (Suzuki)
Isle of Man:	Redman (Honda), Shepherd (MZ), Pagani (Paton)
Assen:	Redman (Honda), Read (Yamaha), Robb (Yamaha)
Spa:	Mike Duff (Yamaha), Redman (Honda), Shepherd (MZ)

They went to Solitude, where Bryans took the 50 and Read the 250 from Redman by 3.1 seconds. It was all 'hair raising' and 'torture', as Redman would remember. At the Sachsenring there was no 50 race; Read beat Redman in the 250 by 1 second. At the Ulster there was no 50, but again Read beat Redman by 1 second in the 250. The 50 cc people went to Finland and, says Bryans, 'I was leading the championship by a long way. I changed down a gear too much and broke the engine. Had I won there

Far left *Redman on the podium after winning.*

I would have taken the championship.'

'When Yamaha won the 250 Belgian Grand Prix in July,' Clark says, 'Honda knew that there was no more they could do with their ageing 240-four cylinder. They started work from scratch and by the time the Italian Grand Prix came round they had a brand new 250-six cylinder. No one knew about it. In Japan it was tested at a track near the Research and Development and after testing the two outside exhaust pipes were removed so that if anyone saw the bike at close range it looked like just another four cylinder. Even when we picked it up at the airport in Milan it only had four exhaust pipes on it.

'When we got it to Monza we had it inside our garage within seconds and the doors were closed. We prepared it for a test run. When we did wheel it out and fired it up, people were speechless. The noise it made! The fact that it was a 250-six seemed impossible and yet here it was. It revved at 18,000—something else which hadn't been heard of before. In the race it stayed with the Yamahas but slowed when it began to over-heat. The problem was solved for 1965 . . . '

Read won on the Yamaha and won the World Championship; Duff was second on another Yamaha, Redman third.

At Monza there had been no 50, although Bryans did ride a 125. 'To give you an idea of the testing,' Bryans says, 'I received a telegram at Monza directly after the Grand Prix and it said: "Report to Japan on the first available flight", which I did. I arrived in Japan on 15 September and my daughter was born on that day [Monza had been 13 September]. When the Honda personnel came to the hotel to pick me up for testing they informed me that I was a father. A telegram had come overnight.' What did Bryans do? 'Testing, testing, testing! The next—and last race—was the Japanese Grand Prix and Honda were very keen to win it on their own circuit.' At Suzuka, Bryans took the 50 but Hugh Anderson (Suzuki) the title. Honda were pleased with Bryans and he signed a contract for 1965.

In many ways 1965 would be his season. 'Honda wanted to win the 50 World Championship very, very badly because at that time the bread and butter of their production was 50 cc bikes. It went right through to the last round in Suzuka.' Bryans's main rival was again Anderson on the Suzuki, although it was Degner who took the first race—Daytona—for Suzuki. Bryans won at the Nürburgring, Anderson at Mountjuich, Bryans at Rouen, Taveri on the Honda at the Island, Bryans in Holland, Degner in Belgium. Bryans needed to beat Anderson to take the title in Japan, but Anderson crashed on the last lap and Bryans finished second behind Taveri. It was enough. Honda, he remembers, were 'quite pleased—maybe that was the lack of emotion, maybe that was because they expected to win titles. After the race we went back to the Station Hotel, had some dinner, a few beers and played cards.'

'We'd had a good season in 1964,' Clark says. 'I duly saw a lot of the Olympics and then Honda wanted to know what I wanted to do. I could go back home or I could stay. I chose to stay. I worked in the Research and Development department. During the season I had learnt a little bit of Japanese customs and language. They were worried about how I would take to the food. They said I could have steaks every day if I wanted. I told them I'd like to live like a local and eat whatever was on the menu. At the

Research and Development they had a canteen where you could eat breakfast, lunch and dinner. One thing they could not get used to was that I could eat rice three times a day. I stayed at a bachelor's hotel, had to share a room and slept on the floor—like a local.

'At the R and D we were issued with white overalls and boots. The overalls were cleaned every week. We used to wash the floor with brushes and soap twice a month, normally on a Saturday after official working hours!

'There were always more bikes than mechanics so you had to be able to work on any engine. We also built the racing bike engines from scratch, prototype road bike engines, and the Formula Two car racing engines which Jack Brabham was to use. We had a time limit to work to. You were not expected to work to it when you were new, but after a couple of engine overhauls you were—the idea being that you could always work slowly but if you had not been taught to work fast you would never work fast. If a mistake was made you paid a fine. A certain amount was deducted from your wages per month and the duration could vary from one month to eighteen.

'Mr Honda would visit every section of Research and Development every day, and sometimes twice day. He remembered what was being done in the different sections and on the different projects. He helped us, if necessary, with constructive ideas, he was never frightened of getting his hands dirty or oily. If he did not like some new idea on design he would tell the designer to change it and made sure it was changed.

'Everything was secret, just as it is now. Most of the riders did not speak Japanese and did not know how much English the mechanics understood, so when they talked among themselves they used ex-

Redman, the man who was 'intensely loyal'.

Redman again.

pressions which nobody else understood—for example, when a con-rod broke the term was "the motor hung a leg out of bed" and when a bike seized it "yanked". The mechanics would frown on anyone who mentioned what trouble they had had in practice or the race when they were talking to the Press or to riders from other teams.

'All the data sheets which were with the engines always had the maximum horsepower blanked out. At Research and Development there were notices up the message was: Don't talk about what you are doing or what you see or what you hear. All the motor cycle, car and aircraft magazines from all around the world were brought, read and any interesting or important articles were translated. The aircraft magazines were a source of what new materials were being used and what new types of construction there were in the aircraft industry . . . '

Bryans would have another reason to remember 1965 and, now we've looked at the background, no wonder. 'The 50 was extremely unforgiving and on a pure road circuit you had to treat it with the respect it deserved. Today's riders would laugh at it. I came off once. It was in practice at the Isle of Man and it locked up on the way to Bedstead Corner, dumped me on the road. It was in the right hand kink. I stood up and turned the throttle and it dropped a valve in. That locked the back wheel. I went skittering down the road on my backside. I must have travelled fifty, fifty-five yards before I stopped. I was totally unhurt. What goes through your mind at such moments? Making sure you don't hit anything. It's not the crashing that kills you, it's the sudden stop. You kick the machine as far away as you can and if you stay on your back you can actually steer yourself. You dig your elbows in and you can manoeuvre your body so that if you are going to hit something you will hit it feet first. It's like the Cresta Run without a toboggan underneath you! You can steer yourself and turn round and do all sorts of things. One of the fastest crashes I had was on an Ulster road race. I was looking at the rev counter and the next instant I was flat on my back in the middle of the road—and that was a long slide, over a hundred yards. I destroyed my boots, helmet, leathers, goggles, the lot, because of friction with the road surface as I was steering myself down the middle of the road. And I got up too fast! I didn't realize I was still doing about thirty miles an hour when I decided to stand on my feet. It was comical. The impetus took me on and I was taking great big strides and now the soles of my boots were being worn away . . . '

Redman was under pressure in 1965, and so were Honda. In the 125 class Suzuki produced a water-cooled disc-valve twin that took the first three places at Daytona (Anderson won), and the first two in West Germany (Anderson), the first two in Spain (Anderson), and the first three in France (Anderson). Honda's second place on the Isle of Man was their first in the top three. 'They withdrew after that because they were being so easily beaten and went home to have a rethink. What they did was build a 125 five cylinder,' Bryans says.

It was essentially two and a half 50 cc engines joined end to end and it appeared at the Japanese Grand Prix in October. Although Taveri led on it, the bike broke down. Honda finished second, third, and fifth.

Redman was third in the 250 Championship behind Read and Duff. After four races he had no points and the pressure was coming down on him. (There was a rumour that Franta Stasny, a Czech, might join the team.) Redman fended it all off at the Island by winning the 250 from Duff by a whopping 3 minutes 40.6 seconds, and did the first ever hundred mile an hour lap on a 250 (100.09). Redman won two other races—Spa and the Sachsenring. He took the 350 title for the fourth year, but something profound was happening.

The year before, Redman wanted Hailwood to join Honda but the team refused without giving any reasons: 'it shocked and upset me more than I showed at the time.' Hailwood has recounted how, just before the Japanese Grand Prix in 1965, he noticed a letter with a Japanese stamp among the mail that dropped through his box. When he opened it he found an invitation to ride a 250 Honda in the Japanese Grand Prix. MV said they would release him, changed their mind, and then changed it back again. So Hailwood went to Japan and was shocked by how badly the Honda handled.

'That was Mike's first ride on the 250-six, when he made his famous statement,' Bryans says. 'He was asked what he thought of it: "Bloody awful," he replied. He couldn't understand how Jim Redman had ridden the thing.' Only five riders finished: The first M. Hailwood (GB), Honda, 1 hour 1 minute 49.1 seconds . . .

He was taken to a hotel, had an amiable chat with H. Sekiguchi, head of Research and Development, about the shortcomings of the bike, and signed a contract for 1966.

This brings us back to Jim Redman and a necessary tribute to him by Murray Walker:

To our consternation and dismay and alarm and apprehension [Walker is speaking as a patriotic Briton] we heard that Honda were coming in to the 500 cc class. That was where Redman was to display his character. He had been multiple World Champion in the 250 and 350 and, to be fair to him and everybody else, he'd been riding bikes which had the usual Honda attributes: a jewel of an engine, a camel of a frame. You'd watch him wrestling the bikes round the circuits, seek him out after the races and ask: how did it go?

'Marvellous. The bike was an absolute dream.'

'Engine?'

'You know the engine. Perfect.'

'Handling?'

'Perfect. Spot on.'

Jim was intensely loyal, he was a marvellous company man, and he would never be disloyal. Against that background, when Honda came into the 500 cc and Mike was his team-mate, Jim insisted on being given preference.

It was certain that the season of 1966 would be interesting, but before we get to that it is time to travel with Nobby Clark inside Honda and the racing world they inhabited.

'In Europe we had an interpreter in the early 1960s, but later we did without because I had learnt enough to do the translations at the borders and hotels. We would arrive in Europe in the spring and there was always a lot of work to do; parts had to be divided up because we never carried everything with us. We had four vans and a station wagon. There was always work to be done on the vans, mainly fitting them out to suit our needs. In those days there were no motorways in Europe, except in Germany, and travelling, especially in convoy, was hell. It took, for example, seven days to get to Barcelona from our base in Amsterdam. The borders were another pain. If we had, say, fifteen bikes plus five spare engines and parts it meant we had twenty-five carnets [official documents]. When the customs saw this pile they went crazy. Sometimes they would make us count all the spare parts, nuts, bolts, washers, and so on. I am sure they did it so that the next time we'd choose another border post to cross at.

'Once when we were on our way to Italy we were just about to leave the German customs when suddenly they decided to check the front of the vans. They found about forty-five cartons of cigarettes. These they took to a room and put on a table. They brought us all in to the room and asked whose cigarettes they were. We all took a carton. After a few minutes we were told that as non-European residents we were entitled to two cartons. We all took another carton. There were still twenty-five left on the table. After a while we were told we could take the lot and everyone thanked the customs officers in their best German . . .

'When we went to the East German and Czechoslovakian races, which meant we were away for three weeks, we took our own supply of Coca Cola. This was 800 cans. We sometimes worked over 100 hours a week. We were forbidden to drink any alcohol, even beer, while we were working. We could, but only when it was over. We had an Australian mechanic in 1964 and he told the Japanese that when he had a headache a beer would fix it, but he never managed to get that sort of medication! After a race we'd give it a thrash but you always had to remember that next day you'd be on the road again.

'There were times when we didn't get to bed for a couple of days, although Honda were not the only team to go without sleep. When we were told that we would have to work all night, you switched off the sleep button. Every couple of hours you could have a cup of coffee or soup and a cigarette. The big thing was to say no when you were asked if you were tired or sleepy. The Japanese really respected you if you were prepared to stay at it and only go to bed when the work was finished.

'If we had any parts that failed during practice or a race the parts were redesigned and made before the next race, even if there was only a week between the two. After every race the bikes were stripped down complete and rebuilt, the engines were opened, and everything checked. A record was kept on all the bikes and engines, and when a part reached a certain mileage it was changed. All our pistons had to be hand-finished before we could use them.

'I really think Honda were in the vanguard of the Japanese invasion. They did not copy things, they improved the original item far beyond its original design. When a race was won by any of the other Japanese factories it was bad for us, but once the Japanese flag was raised one could sense that all the teams were proud. Then you got on with preparation for the next race.'

SEVEN

Rainy Day People

'To know about Mike Hailwood,' Murray Walker says, contemplating the received information of all those years ago, 'you really have to know about his father, Stan Hailwood. Stan was a brilliantly gifted entrepreneur/businessman who had a club foot and he started his career walking round drapers' shops in Manchester with an attaché case full of ties. If you can imagine a harder way of making money than that, I can't. But Stan was an inspired salesman who could have sold ice boxes to Eskimos. He could be utterly charming and, on the other hand, the most ruthlessly unmitigated bastard you ever met in your life.

'Stan managed to build up the most successful chain of motor cycle dealers in the country and became a multi-millionaire. Stan begat Mike, who was always a quiet, inoffensive, cheerful bloke and with a father like Stan you either had to be like that or you had a cataclysmic row and left home very rapidly. Stan put Mike into Dartmouth Academy to join the Royal Navy and Stan had a row with the Admiral in charge and Stan took Mike away. Then Mike started to fiddle about as a sort of apprentice mechanic and Stan put him on a bike.

'A family friend, Bill Webster, who was a motorcycle dealer and racer from Crewe, loaned Mike a 125MV to ride in a race at Oulton Park—at which I was present—in 1957 and Mike rapidly revealed that he was a bloody good rider. I always had a theory that Stan was living out through Mike something he'd wanted to do himself. Stan had raced a bit—Morgan cars, sidecars—and bearing in mind his club foot he wasn't particularly good, although he wasn't bad either. But he certainly wasn't brilliant. When it became clear that there was something a bit special about Mike, Stan absolutely poured money into him. He even sent him to South Africa in the winter of 1958 to race there.' Hailwood won their championship on a 250 NSU.

Hailwood's reputation grew quickly and when Tommy Robb met him back in England Hailwood said: 'You're Tommy Robb aren't you?' and Robb replied: 'Yes, and you're THE Mike Hailwood. I've been reading a lot about you in South Africa.'

Let us explain the background further, and begin with a question. How ruthless was Stan Hailwood? 'Mike had a very rich dad who gave him the best of everything,' Derek Minter says. 'A lot of people don't know this, but I was offered by dad—it was at Castle Coombe—£50 to keep my bicycles in the van so Mike could go out and win. Dad offered me fifty quid, that was a lot of money in the fifties, but something came over me. I was determined that wasn't going to happen and when I went out I screwed the bike harder than I had done before and I won the race and broke the lap record. That is all the God's honest truth.'

'Stan bought Mike a 250 NSU which was unobtainable to ordinary people, but because he was Stan Hailwood and he had the dealership, and could give business to people, he could get anything,' Walker says. 'He bought any bike likely to give Mike an advantage. There was a gifted tuner called Bill Lacey, and Stan, who lived in a giant ancestral home in Oxfordshire, bought Bill Lacey! Stan made him an offer he couldn't refuse to work for Mike full time. Bill Lacey was told to spend what he needed. Workshops were built in the stables and they had AJSs and Nortons and Matchlesses and NSUs and Ducatis and everything you can imagine. They had spare tanks and exhaust pipes hanging from the ceiling, cases of sprockets, engines . . .

'Mike was the first bloke to have a transporter in the current sense of that word, an enormous great thing with a workshop inside it as well as racks for the bikes. One of Stan's gigantic strengths was a flair for publicity; he was an enormous extrovert and he had "Here Comes Mike's Bikes" painted all over the sides. And of course there was an enormous amount of bitterness and jealousy about this young puppy who was blowing everybody off and people said "We all know the only reason he wins is because he's got dad behind him."

'Wrong.

'It takes two to make a bargain and in car and bike racing the two are the machine and the man. Mike could have put his leg across a garden gate and won. He was that good. He was absolutely brilliant, the best rider who ever lived.' He was also, let us say immediately, handsome, macho, well heeled, and perhaps much misunderstood. Walker again: 'From the age of seventeen he was the Golden Boy. He received both adulation and media concentration of an intensity which was certainly as great as anything that exists now. Women threw themselves at him partly

The man who was as handsome and determined as Hailwood: Giacomo Agostini (here with a very young Johnny Cecotto).

Hailwood destroys all opposition at Barcelona in 1966 on the 250.

because of his success, partly because of his money, and partly because he was good looking.'

It was a devastating combination.

This is not the place to recite exhaustively what Mike Hailwood had done up to 1966 on bikes; but to cover the ground quickly and give you some measure of it all here is a vignette or, more properly, a summary. He was World 250 champion in 1961, World 500 champion in 1962, 1963, 1964, and 1965, and he captured something of the spirit (take a deep breath, here comes that awful phrase) of the Swinging Sixties when youth, talent, and good looks were all and the world, perhaps for the very first time, seemed to belong to the under 25s, not the over 50s.

'He was unbelievably versatile. I've seen him at Brands Hatch get off a 500 cc four-cylinder MV with right-foot gear change having won the race, walk across the grid and get onto a 125 single cylinder two-stroke with left-foot gear change and win that, walk across the grid and get onto a 350 cc single cylinder AJS—totally different power and handling characteristics—and win on that.' Walker remains slightly in awe of this even as he describes it two decades later. 'Stan had been known to turn him out of the house. Sometimes he threw him out in the middle of the night after they'd had a row and Mike would go to Bill Lacey's home until it was sorted out. Stan's house was fairly close to Silverstone and it was a tradition when there was a big meeting there that if my father and I were doing the commentary Stan would invite us to stay. The cynic in me suggests that Stan was asking us not only because my father was editor of *Motor Cycling* and therefore not at all a bad bloke to be on the right side of, but because Graham and Murray Walker could give an extra amount of publicity to his gifted son. It was good thinking. It worked because I'm damn sure we did without realizing it.

'I arrived there one evening and Stan had a vast armchair and he sat there with one leg up along the arm of it. I asked how everything was. "Not too good, Murray. We had a bit of a problem today. We were testing the Norton at Silverstone and Mike came off and he's hurt his leg quite badly. But he's insisting on riding tomorrow. You know Mike likes you, go up and have a word with him."

'Mike was also a gifted musician and I went upstairs and he was sitting half-on half-off the bed with his leg all bandaged up playing the clarinet. I said "How's the leg?" "Not too good." "What's all this about riding tomorrow?" "Well, the old man says I've got to so I suppose I have." I knew who was telling the truth. Mike started from the back, he had a pusher to get the bike moving, and he won . . . '

This is the rider who, in 1966 and 1967, was to attempt—virtually on his own—the ultimate examination of what a human being's mind and body can tolerate, the 250, the 350, and the 500 championships, and to compound that he would be pitched directly against a master, Giacomo Agostini. They had much in common, Hailwood and Agostini: wealthy parents, the looks, and yes, let's use the word, charisma. Between 1965 and 1976 Agostini would become statistically the most successful rider ever to haul himself on to a motor bike. He won fifty-four 350 races and sixty-eight 500 races. The nearest to that total of 122 would be Spaniard Angel Nieto, with ninety. Hailwood himself finished with seventy-six.

Agostini joined MV in 1965 and although he hadn't ridden a 350 before he astonished the bike world by winning in West Germany, Finland, and Italy. At Suzuka in October he was in the lead and moving towards the championship when he was halted by a broken spring. Hailwood won the race on a Honda, Redman took the championship. Charisma? Agostini had plenty of that. Girls went weak when he signed autographs for them and there was a rumour, a delicious rumour, that Agostini planned to get married in secret. He had actually reached the altar when angry MV officials arrived and forbade him to say "I do." Is the rumour true? I don't know, and it's certainly too nice a story to check just in case it isn't. But as a rider Agostini had what Hailwood had, an all-embracing smoothness so that he, the bike, and the circuit blended, and going round fast corners fast seemed to be the most natural movement in the world.

Hailwood signed for Honda in October 1965, the same month the Agostini got so close to the 350 championship. In the first race of 1966—the 250 at Barcelona in may—Hailwood destroyed all opposition, although Redman had powered away in the lead, lost it in a right-hander, and as he struggled uncertainly to his feet watched the Honda burst into flames. This left Hailwood, as a contemporary account records, 'in solitary splendour' and he won by a lap; won the next, West Germany, from Redman; won the next, Clermont Ferrand, from Redman; won the next, Assen, from Phil Read, with Redman third. In the 350s he struggled against Agostini; but the real problem was the 500.

'It wasn't,' Hailwood would write, 'just the usual matter of trying to win, it was trying to stay on the thing. It really was the most frightening experience.' He found several phrases to capture that: 'trouble into the corners and out of them' . . . 'it whipped like mad and bent in the middle' . . . 'it wobbled all over the road.' It seemed the frame couldn't cope and Hailwood reportedly sent a Norton frame to Tokyo so that Honda could have a look at it. Eventually Hailwood would decide on a drastic step. He went to Milan with an engine and asked a specialist frame-builder there to make one. He tested it at Modena, Ferrari's own track, and felt it had a future; but news of this private enterprise emerged and 'Honda were furious. They sent me a strong letter emphasizing that they like to keep everything secret'. Nothing fundamental changed. Soon enough Hailwood realized that he'd have to ride the bike Honda had given him, and he did. Hailwood had no complaints about the engine but reportedly wasn't at all happy with 'sticking it into the old 350 frame'. The engine had four cylinders, and, as Brian Woolley has pointed out in his *Directory of Classic Racing Motorcycles*, they weren't really needed because there was such a 'spread' of torque available. The frame was 'a full twin-loop with the bottom tubed detachable to facilitate work on the engine'. The bike also had 'heavy-duty telescopic forks of a new design'.

Luigi Taveri became more than an eyewitness to this. He gives two examples. 'We were in Japan for a Grand Prix and in the hotel one evening we were having a big discussion. A rider called John Cooper said: "When I have a Honda four cylinder I will show people how fast I can go." I said: "When you have the four cylinder it will make you look bad." Then he says "No" and tells me that at Monza in the Curva Grande he goes at full speed on the Norton. He didn't believe what I had told him and he was getting angry so I told him I hoped that one day he would ride the bike. A couple of years later he did in England and he did nothing on it, nothing. This bike was so difficult that only Mike could ride it.

'Another time we tested in Holland—at Zandvoort—and Redman and Mike made a joke with me. "You ride the 500 and you'll see what happens." I did about five laps, the bike had about a hundred horsepower, and I tell you, you had to have a big heart to make it go at full speed on the straight, *ja, ja, ja*. The Honda was enormous, it jumped from side to side.'

Nobby Clark of course also saw it all. 'The infamous bikes were the 500s. I don't think that anybody thought that a bike could be built which was so fast, had such a small power-band, and a frame which was like a rubber garden gate. The theory was: forget the frame because if you could go down the straight faster than anything around you would not have to worry about the corners or curves. You could make it up on the straights. When Mike tested the first 500 at Suzuka in the wet he said he could not ride the thing. There were bits and pieces welded to the frame to try and stop it bending. In the end it looked like a canary cage but it still did not handle. I think that if the Honda racing engineers and designers had listened to Mike they would have had a bike which nobody would have beaten. They knew he would always give his best and his natural talent was worth at least twenty horsepower. In fact, I think that in 1966 and 1967 it was not Honda winning, it was Mike.'

There was another problem. Hailwood assumed that he had been hired as the man to win the 500 Championship for Honda. It was, after all, the one class they hadn't won, whilst he had won it on MVs in 1962, 1963, 1964, and 1965, as we have seen. Rumours suggested that Honda were making only one 500 bike and Redman wasn't happy about that, thank you, especially after all he'd done for Honda. (They had told him once: 'You rode our bikes when they were slow, now you can ride them when they're fast.') Honda made two 500s and Redman got the best one. Hailwood found himself cast in the role of supporting actor and it was not a role that came naturally to him.

Author Peter Carrick has written that 'this first Honda 500 was phenomenally fast and in the West German Grand Prix at Hockenheim Redman reckoned he was travelling in excess at 165 miles an hour on parts of the circuit. Before 130,000 spectators the Rhodesian dominated the race . . . the all-conquering MV which had taken John Surtees, Gary Hocking and Mike Hailwood to nine World Championship wins in nine years and now ridden by Agostini was totally outpaced.' Redman's time: 1

hour 4 minutes 00.8 seconds; Agostini 26.1 seconds behind him. In the 500 at Assen, Hailwood broke the lap record, although MV had produced a new bike with its three cylinders enlarged. Hailwood wound the Honda up after a slow start, cut 4 seconds a lap off Agostini, and on lap four the record went. He was just ahead of Agostini—around 30 yards—on a banked left-hander when the gearbox broke. Hailwood parked the bike and said: 'If I'd finished the lap the time keepers would have had hysterics.'

Redman remembered that vividly. 'Mike went down and nearly had me off! While I was steadying myself Agostini built up a lead of 5 or 6 seconds. That quickly went up to 12 seconds, then 15. I went after him, I was going too fast, I was braking too late and I thought to myself: Steady it down, steady it down. With nineteen laps to go it was still 15 seconds and I thought: I need to pull back 1 second a lap. And I did. With nine laps to go it was 7 seconds but then it stayed at 7 . . . 7 . . . 7. The lap after that I really went for it and the gap was down to a couple of seconds. I got him on the start-finish line, slipstreaming and overtaking him. Those last two laps were a nightmare because half the track was under water and the other half was in brilliant sunshine. I think it was one of the best rides of my career.' Redman had beaten Agostini by a mere 2.2 seconds.

A young man whose name was almost completely unknown except via his father, as it were, came in fifth. He'd been fourth at Hockenheim the month before. His name was Stuart Graham. 'My father, Les Graham, was 1949 500 cc World Champion. He was killed in 1953 in the Isle of Man. It didn't put me off. I was eleven at the time and our whole life was racing. I served an apprenticeship at Rolls Royce and started riding a bike on the roads. I decided I'd like to do a race and I bought a 125 Honda Sport off Bill Smith. It was a help to be the son of Les Graham, it enabled me to gain more support. I progressed up the privateers' ladder and decided to explore further afield. You could take two week's holiday, do the Dutch followed by the Belgian, and then bring the van home. The idea was to be sensible, move around in midfield because if you broke anything you didn't pick up any money and therefore you didn't eat. There were two or three works teams then, followed by the privateers, and what you'd got to do was be fastest of the privateers. With the fourth place in Germany and the fifth in Holland I arrived at the Belgian Grand Prix lying third in the World Championship behind Redman and Agostini, but in fairness all I'd done was knock up the points.'

And now they all came to Spa, that rolling, intimidating course in the Ardennes: it was a place prey to rain and to compound that a place of high speed. Graham: 'The race started in a thunderstorm on the old, proper circuit, trees, houses, no armco, nothing. The wet never bothered me unduly. My father was well known for being good in it and I rode naturally in it—rode as I felt.'

Just before the start, lightning burst across the sky and the road was awash at Stavelot. 'On the line an official held up a sign *"Il pleut à Stavelot"* (it is raining at Stavelot)'—a vast understatement. Redman remembers that vividly, too: 'We were on dry tyres so I managed to get the start held up for a couple of minutes while we had the tyres deflated a little bit. If they'd been pumped up hard you'd have had no chance, no chance at all. Anyway, I was thinking: I've won the first two races; in conditions like this the thing is just to finish. Third would do fine.'

They set off into the storm and on the first lap one rider—Derek Woodman (Metisse)—scudded off and broke his thigh; another, a New Zealander called John Wells, did the same and broke his ribs when his Norton came to rest in a river. At the end of that first lap the storm had moved across and now battered the pits. Redman was third, 'just inches between Ago and Mike and myself and I couldn't see in all that spray. We reached what the riders used to call the Cocoa Straight [it was actually called Burneville but the British dubbed it Cocoa because the name was so similar to the manufacturers of that, Bourneville.] I pulled out so that I could see and I must have been doing 150 miles an hour. I didn't know there was a lake at the other side of the track. I felt as if the bike had been completely plucked away from me and as I went down I put my left arm out and—crack. I thought: It's broken. I was going along the road skittering over the wet tarmac at a hell of a speed facing backwards. Using my legs I tried to turn myself round. I saw the bike coming at me and I lashed at it with both feet and—crack. I thought: Leg broken. The bike headed towards a small concrete milestone and demolished it, and thank God it did because I passed over where the milestone had just been and the next thing I was in a ditch full of water. I looked back and I saw a gap in some wooden fencing and I thought: Thank God the bike got there first and made the hole I've just come through. Then I saw another hole and I realized the bike had made that one, I'd made this one . . . '

By the fourth lap Agostini was lapping at over 90 miles an hour and had squeezed a lead of 6½ seconds over Hailwood. Some distance behind Graham was struggling in combat with Guyla Marsovsky (a Swiss on a Matchless) and Peter Williams (AJS).

'The conditions were quite ridiculous, diabolical,' Graham says. 'Guys were falling off all over the place, and don't forget that when you were going slowly on the old course at Spa you were doing a hundred. I could hardly see the road. The rain lashed down, the mist was so thick that there were times down the straight where you assumed that the lightest patch was the road and the darker bits were the sides. It was crackers! But when you're 24 you're young and hungry, you're out to do it all, and you take the most horrendous risks. I was thinking "Stuart, this is absolutely crazy, you're an absolute nutter" but I kept on. I didn't see Jim Redman's crash . . . '

Williams came into the pits leaving Graham and Marsovsky wheel to wheel, while on lap five Hailwood dug deep into the Honda—it had no top gear, that had gone in practice, but it scarcely mattered in this race—and overtook Agostini despite 'having to go down to second gear through floods at Masta'. By lap six Hailwood had a 17-second lead.

'I was dicing with Marsovsky and we kept swopping places and then I got a pit board—my wife Margaret holding it—telling me I was fourth. I was cold, it was still horrible but I thought I'd keep on.' So did a rider called Jack Findlay (Matchless—Walker describes him as a 'tough Aussie'). A pheasant flew into his face breaking his goggles and when he reached the pits he had to be lifted off the bike. He went to hospital to have shards of glass removed.

'Hailwood must have stopped because next lap there was Margaret holding out the board: Third. I thought this is all right. Marsovsky was in front of me and I made my mind I was going to get past him again.'

With four laps to go, Hailwood had gone—gearbox. He drifted into the pits 'shivering, violently, soaked to the marrow'.

Now Graham 'took a chance and I did get past Marsovsky and I got a board: Second. I remember wondering who was first. I had no way of knowing. Keep going, I told myself, keep going. I was getting signals through the spray and now they were 20 seconds, 18; next thing it was 17 and I thought that I must be catching somebody.' We'll never know who, but it was probably a back marker. It certainly wasn't Agostini, who won it by 48.4 seconds. The ordeal had lasted—for Agostini—1 hour 19 minutes 43.1 seconds and he had maintained an amazing average speed of 98.915 miles an hour. Graham finished second, 1 hour 20:31.5.

'When I reflected, at least it was Agostini who had beaten me and that is where he should have been, anyway. But second was bloody marvellous and it put me in second place in the championship. I was travelling around with Ralph Bryans, we were great buddies, and when we left the track we went to see Jim in hospital. It was near Spa on the road to Liège. Jim said—I assumed half-joking—to Ralph: "We're buggered now, you'd better get young Stuart to give you a hand, it was bloody good finishing second."' As the van moved away from the hospital, Stuart Graham insists that he thought no more about it. He and Bryans headed east to a town called Karl-Marx-Stadt and the Sachsenring.

'There were three rules for riders in those days,' Redman says. 'Survive coming off the bike, survive the impact, and survive the first aid services when they came. In some countries you definitely didn't want to fall off. I was rushed to hospital and when I woke up—and I'd had breaks before—I felt my left wrist wasn't as it should have been. It was also in plaster. I said to my wife: "Right, let's get out of here, let's get back to England" and on the cross-Channel ferry the pain was so bad I asked if there was a doctor on board. One came. He said: "You must get that plaster off as soon as you can or you'll have gangrene." When we arrived back in London I went to a man who specialized in those things—a lot of the riders used him—and he had the plaster off within two minutes.' The wrist was badly broken. Jim Redman would never ride in a race again.

But what of Hailwood? In the 500 championship he had no points at all, Agostini had 20. Six races remained. With Redman gone, Honda's 500 thrust would be centred around Hailwood—and, as we shall see, Graham. It meant Hailwood going for the 250, 350, and 500 and even now strong men become misty-eyed when they contemplate the scope of the attempt. Worse, the MV was ferociously fast, the Honda had that notoriously bad handling.

Of course Mike Hailwood would make the attempt, and in doing so would pass further into folklore. He himself would evaluate it in his matter-of-fact way: 'I would say that riding ability counted throughout those two seasons [1966 and 1967] more than for a long time. I had to ride as I'd never done before to give the big Honda any chance at all against the MV. I chanced more than I dared hope to get away with. Remember, I knew exactly what the MV and Agostini could do; and I would say the advantage was theirs. I'm not knocking Ago and I'm not praising the MV more than it deserves, nor am I overstating the bad handling of the Honda.'

The Sachsenring was a race with a unique atmosphere. Graham would call it 'a daunting place' just as East Germany itself was daunting. This was the Soviet Zone of occupation—as it would remain until November

Hailwood at Governor's Bridge.

1989—with its own currency (not accepted in the West) so that winnings were spent in a wild spree before leaving, as Taveri had had to do. It was a grey, squeezed, drained country with bomb damage still visible everywhere and even the name Karl-Marx-Stadt was a proclamation of who was in charge now. (The town had formerly been called Chemnitz.)

'When we got there Ralph said: "There is a chance of you riding for Honda, Honda want to talk to you. Would you be interested?" So there I was, a privateer in my first international season and I thought: This is pretty hairy stuff. I met them and they wanted me to ride a 250 six cylinder—Redman's bike. They said they wanted me to run through the rest of the season with a view to a contract in 1967. The idea was for me to ride a 125, too, leaving Mike to take care of the 500. So I rode this enormous six cylinder thing. It was fantastically fast. Compared to my 500 it was much quicker. It had six or seven gears and went up to 16,000 revs. After the old plodding single-cylinder Matchless it was a horrendous thing to handle and it had been set up for Jim Redman. It was terribly bumpy. I was jumping all round the place scaring myself silly.'

In the 250 Hailwood won, Read (Yamaha) second, Graham fourth. 'In fact,' Graham says, 'it killed a lot of my confidence. I was super-confident on my 500, I felt I could do anything with it, but this Honda was a totally different machine. And this was the Honda works team and you know what the Press is like—third World Champion signs for Honda, all that stuff, suddenly I had gone from a reasonable privateer to something like star status. Christ, I was green! Mike was very good and looked after me very well, Ralph did too, and Luigi Taveri was very helpful but really I was a raw young recruit.'

In the 500 in East Germany Hailwood didn't finish and neither did Agostini, Hailwood breaking down after five laps, Agostini shattering Hailwood's lap record and then crashing 10 kilometres from the line. They moved south to Brno in Czechoslovakia. 'I was trying to keep myself out of trouble, trying not to make mistakes,' Graham says. 'I was doing quite well in practice when Mike's machine broke—I think two of his bikes broke—and in the end he had to use mine.' But Graham was not to be spared Brno, 'which in its old form was a hell of a place, two villages, through the town, through the forest and the road surface made the Isle of Man seem smooth. The place was primitive and on top of that I was trying to learn the circuits and cope with this factory Honda. Meanwhile I continued to ride my 500 Matchless as I needed the start money and of

Above right *Honda's modern dynasty, typified by Freddie Spencer, double World Champion in Sweden, 1985.*

Above *Tradition demanded that he went in the pool, and he did.*

Right *Wayne Gardner was next in line. Here he is in the wet at Spa.*

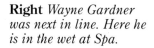

Right *Which brings us to Eddie Lawson, World Champion in 1989.*

Right *A rare montage from the collection of Luigi Taveri which, if you glance back at the previous picture of Lawson's bike, shows graphically how far the sport has developed. Here is Taveri at Hockenheim in 1966 . . .*

Right *. . . and hill-climbing in the early 1960s.*

Below *People remember the lovely, throaty noise. Look at all those who covered their ears.*

Below right *Giacomo Agostini, direct challenger to Mike Hailwood.*

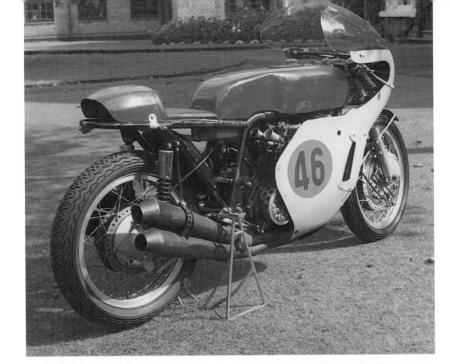

And this is the bike Ken Sprayson built for Hailwood. We'll never know if he'd have beaten Agostini on it.

1985 was Spencer's year, but Randy Mamola won the 500 at Assen.

Ron Haslam in the wet in 1985.

Above *Spencer gets a lift from fiancée Sarie at Silverstone.*

Above right *A sip of champagne after Spencer won the 500.*

Right *Spencer on his way to the World 500 Championship in Sweden.*

Right *Wayne Gardner moving towards second place at Misano, 1985.*

Above *The loneliest place in the world. One man, one machine, one circuit: Suzuka, 1985.*

Above right *Wayne master. Gardner rides the storm to win Silverstone, 1986.*

Right *He'd won in Holland, too.*

Right *Symbolically, Gardner was second in the last race, Misano, and second in the championship.*

*Gardner's year, 1987.
Here he wins Rijeka.*

*'Hey, you've made it,
you're champion.'
Gardner on the podium in
Brazil. Girlfriend Donna
shares the moment with a
beautiful smile.*

*Gardner drinking water
during testing in Brazil,
1989.*

Newcomer Michael Doohan looked impressive during those tests . . .

. . . and during the Australian Grand Prix, too.

Gardner thought he'd win the championship until he broke his leg.

Above *Eddie Lawson, the epitome of maturity and pragmatism.*

Above right *The timeless machine. Luigi Taveri with Agostini at Salzburg in the 1960s, smiling.*

Right *Luigi Taveri in Japan in the late 1980s still smiling.*

course I was fine on that. I qualified on the front row of the grid alongside Agostini and Mike and Frank Stastny [on the Czech Jawa] and all the rest behind, so that was reasonable.'

The race was the start of Hailwood's assault. He finished 1 minute 16 seconds in front of Agostini, who had not completely recovered from his crash in East Germany. Graham, unplaced, decided to concentrate on Honda and the 250, which was, after all, the future and, as it seemed then, quite something of a future. So—Finland at Imatra. 'Mike and I put on a demonstration in the 250 and, on another daunting circuit he won, I was second.' Stastny's Jawa finished a lap behind.

This time in the 500 Agostini won, Hailwood 40 seconds behind him. The championship: Agostini 34, Hailwood 14. Three races left. What really mattered was that only your five best results counted—a cruel and unfair way of deciding anything and designed to keep a championship alive across a whole season. Agostini already had five finishes, the lowest of them second place worth 6 points. Any result now in the remaining three races was worthless if he didn't win. Second place would have to be discarded. Hailwood, starting his charge so late, could count whatever he got because he had only finished in the points twice; or to put it more starkly, every time Hailwood won a race he got 8 points and Agostini got none. The 500 Championship was still possible.

The Ulster Grand Prix at Dundrod was all Hailwood. Redman made an attempt to compete but his arm stiffened and he prudently withdrew.

'Dundrod was a fairly hairy sort of place and I was on the spare 250-six, which handled like a drain,' Graham says. 'Jim Redman came over and asked: "How are you, Stuart? Are they looking after you all right" Then he said: "What's that thing you're riding?" He got very, very cross with the Honda team manager and said to him: "Where is there a decent bike for the lad to ride?" But the team manager replied that they hadn't a spare, so I rode the old machine'—and didn't finish in the top six.

In the 500 Hailwood beat Agostini by a cavernous 1 minute 29.4 seconds, and that was Agostini 34 points, Hailwood 22. And so they came back to the Island. 'By this time,' Graham says, 'they had a new bike for

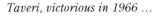

Taveri, victorious in 1966 ...

me which was a lot better than the old one, a much better frame, a much better engine. The problem was that I was in the awkward position of being directly compared to Mike all the time. Mike was riding one bike. I was riding the other, and he was miles quicker. He was lapping at 104 miles an hour and I was lapping at 99 and it didn't matter that everybody else was doing 99, too. In general I was cracking along quite well and Honda were saying: "Look, we don't want you to take any chances, it is a learning year, we realize we have dropped you in at the deep end, we'll sort everything out for next year."

'I finished second to Mike in the TT and I went well. My only regret was that the pit signals weren't accurate enough and I missed a hundred mile an hour lap by about three hundredths of a second. I always settled down to what I called a sensible pace at the Isle of Man. The only man who *raced* round it was Mike. He could do that.' That was the 250, of course.

In the 500 Hailwood established a new absolute lap record of 107.07 miles an hour, beating Agostini by an even more cavernous 2 minutes 37.8 seconds. Agostini 34, Hailwood 30.

Before we leave the Island, an anecdote from Clark: 'We were ready and waiting for practice in front of the grandstand. An ACU official came up to me and told me to tell the mechanics to stop warming the bikes up. When I told him the bikes were not ours he really got bent out of shape—it turned out they were Benellis! A little while later the same official came up and asked me how many 250-six cylinder bikes we had. When I said we had five of them up at the start for practice he said he wanted the engines measured. He thought we were running 297 cc—six cylinders and said that if one was found to be bigger than 250 cc the ACU would officially disqualify Honda and we would not be able to start in any race. Officials duly arrived at the garage after practice and measured the engines, which were found to be all correct and under 250. This really annoyed us because it meant so much more work for nothing . . . '

Only the Nations Grand Prix at Monza remained and you see the scenario clearly: Agostini an Italian, MV an Italian company, Monza the ultimate Italian crowd in temperament, in chauvinism, in naked bias. Hailwood had already won the 250 title so that in the 250 race he and Graham put on another exhibition. But it wasn't quite as straightforward as that . . .

'We didn't have a lot of opposition and we were racing round together. I was gaining in confidence. I then found I could pull a gear higher than Mike and my bike was effectively faster than his. On the quick straight and the swoopers round the back I could actually pass Mike . . . because physically he was a lot bigger and heavier than me. There was a time during the race where I had got it theoretically worked out that I could win it. I could pull out of his slipstream and go past and he'd have to scratch as hard as he could on the corners, where his skill came in. So I was thinking: Now what do I do? Dare I beat the great Mike Hailwood? And he wasn't really bothered because he'd already won the championship. I have a feeling even now that he would have let me win the race. Next thing the bike started vibrating, the crankshaft broke and that was that. It happened on the start-finish line about four laps from the end. I was very disappointed.'

The 500 was a bitterly cruel race. Agostini had only been 0.8 seconds slower in practice but he made a mess of the start and was swallowed by the mid-field, Hailwood leading. At the end of the first lap Agostini was 1.4 seconds behind, by the end of the next lap was actually in Hailwood's slipstream and a great roar went up from the grandstands. According to one contemporary report this roar was so vast that it drowned the howl of the engines. On lap three Hailwood permitted Agostini to take the lead—tactically it was the right thing to do—and as they crossed the line a mere 0.6 seconds was between them. Across lap four and five Hailwood stayed there, knowing he could pick his moment. On the final lap another great roar went up. The Honda's exhaust valves had broken. It was over. 'Wild scenes' followed, but not for Hailwood, who was very angry indeed and said so. Agostini, incidentally, finished two laps ahead of Williams (Matchless).

There were some strange postscripts to 1966. Ralph Bryans gives one. 'Taveri and I were on the 50 and 125s that first year when Honda produced the 500. He won the 125 and I was second in the 50. (Anscheidt-Suzuki won that.) I won on the Island but by then you had to go flat out just about everywhere to get round fast. I lapped at 87 miles an hour on the 50!'

Honda did not contest the final round of the 50, which was moved from Suzuka to Fuji. They claimed the banking was dangerous. It meant Anscheidt, unopposed as it were, needed first or second—and finished second. The entries were low, only 2,000 spectators came and the racing was 'processional'.

Privateer Bill Smith went there for the final 250 of the season. 'When we arrived at the pits there were illuminated signs saying which team had which pit. We reached ours and it said: Bill Smith Raving Team!' These many years later Smith is still laughing out loud about that. Smith, incidentally, estimates that Honda were paying Hailwood 'about £25,000 a season, which was a lot of money then'. Yes, and more than most Britons earn now.

'In 1966 they contested everything in bikes plus they were supplying engines to the Brabham car team in Formula Two and running their own Formula One team,' Bryans says. 'Their budget for just that one season must have been frightening.'

'In November Honda suddenly contacted me to say that unfortunately they didn't need my services for 1967 because they had decided to with-

draw from the 50 and 125 and were going to concentrate on the 500,' Graham says. It was done politely, of course, but it seemed to be like an undercurrent coming to the surface. Honda were stretched and if you trade in excellence that's not a good thing to be.

Paradoxically, perhaps, Honda kept Taveri under contract for 1967, although there was nothing for him to ride, and a career that had embraced the 125 championship in 1962, 1964, and 1966—and twenty Grand Prix victories on Hondas—was over. 'Normally,' he will say, 'it's the races you win that you think are your best, but there were races I didn't win which made me happier. One year at the TT my 125 was not competitive but I stayed one lap with Phil Read [Yamaha] and he had a better bike. So I felt I was riding better than he was. I even forget where I finished, but I was happy.

'I always thought that I didn't have so much talent, then in races when I had the same equipment as the good riders I did well so I started to think I must have some talent. I never thought I was the best. I always respected the opposition.'

These are lovely words that capture, accurately, Luigi Taveri the man. They are reinforced by man who knew him well, Nobby Clark: 'Like Hailwood, Luigi was highly respected. He was a very good test rider, he could give a lot of feedback on the modifications to engines and frames. He never pushed his way around. He was a real gentleman.'

But it is still the end of the 1966 and everything leads inevitably back to Stanley Michael Bailey Hailwood and what he'd do in 1967.

EIGHT
Let's Twist Again

'PERSONALLY, I believe Honda made a big mistake. Mike Hailwood was riding the 250, 350, and 500 practically single-handed. They were asking a lot of him. I did help Mike as much as I could by beating Bill Ivy [Yamaha] and Phil Read [also Yamaha] on occasions in the 250, and I won two races, but you could see the strain piling up on him. Oh yes, you could see that,' Ralph Bryans still remembers that strain, still remembers it piling up. 'And that 500 bike was an absolute camel to ride, it did everything but go where you pointed it . . .'

The year of 1967 for Hailwood would be thirteen rounds of the 250, eight rounds of the 350 and ten rounds of the 500 where Agostini was waiting again. Laconically, Hailwood would say: 'Honda seemed quite content to leave it all to me. They seemed to assume that, as I was winning a few races, there was no absolute necessity to engage anybody else. It was a good economic proposition for them—they were getting three men's work for one man's pay.' Hailwood saw that Bryans, a natural 50 and 125 man, wasn't happy with the 250, however hard Bryans was trying, and looked around for promising recruits for Honda to hire to spread and share the burden. All he saw was 'average riders'.

'Early in 1967 the bombshell came,' Bryans says. 'Taveri had retired and I was the only works rider left to contest the 50 and 125, only to be informed by Honda that they were temporarily withdrawing from these classes. Jim Redman had of course retired and I would be offered what they called "practice" rides in the 250 to keep my hand in until they had developed machines capable of winning the 50 and 125, but there was only one 250 machine for me and if I did it any mischief there wasn't another one. It is not the most conducive way to give a man confidence.'

The 350 championship proved to be no trouble—Hailwood finished eight points clear of Agostini—but the 250 was a desperate, breathless lunge all the way to the line from April to October. It ended in a dead heat, Hailwood 54 but only 50 counting, Read 56 but only 50 counting. It was decided on the number of wins and Hailwood got that 5-4. But the 500 and that big, unwieldy bike—the 500 was something else.

Mike Hailwood (with Frank Cope) and his Honda 6.

It began at Hockenheim, a flat circuit in the middle of West Germany: a strange accommodation of a place with dense, sombre woodland running up to the edge of the track, high speeds, and a vast, curving, concrete grandstand built for political rallies in the 1930s. At Hockenheim it went wrong. Hailwood took the lead but the gearbox broke and he had to watch helplessly as Agostini won.

'Immediately after the race Mike was completely and totally unapproachable,' Bryans remembers. 'He would not speak to anyone. A lot of people didn't think he was very serious about his racing, but believe me he was—very, very serious. At this moment everyone was told: leave him be, clear off, leave him alone. He stayed in his caravan. I'd seen him like that before from time to time. By the time prize-giving came around he was his usual cheery, bouncy self.'

In France—Clermont Ferrand—there was only a 250. Bill Ivy won, Read second, Hailwood third, Bryans fourth. The Isle of Man in June was always going to be shaped into classical proportions, Hailwood versus Ago. Hailwood took the 250, his tenth TT victory equalling the record of Stanley Woods, an Irishman, who'd done it between 1923 and 1939. Hailwood then won the 350 to beat the record. Murray Walker interviewed him straight after the race: Hailwood, a strong man with short dark hair almost curling at the front, leathers open all the way down his chest, and a gold charm hanging on a chain.

'Mike, you have just created history by winning eleven TTs. What does this mean to you?'

(Polite chuckle.) 'Well, I'm very proud to have done it, naturally, but it doesn't worry me all that much.'

'And what is left, Mike? I mean you have won—what is it?—three hundred races. Where do you go from here?'

(Another polite chuckle.) 'Down.'

'What are your plans?'

'I believe Honda are coming back next year in full force (draws hand wearily across face) so I presume I'll be riding again next year, anyway.'

'Well now, what about Agostini? What sort of opposition would you expect from him in the 500 compared to today?'

'Much more, I think. I believe the MV is easier to ride and I know he'll be trying harder than he did today. I think he was saving himself or something. I don't know.' Grin.

'And I presume it is a masterpiece of understatement to say that you are anxious to win?'

'You could say that.' (Whole face grinning.)

It is a well-bred Englishman speaking, of course, and a well-bred Englishman dealing in the ease of an interview; being polite, being dismissive of his new record, never quite revealing the true hunger he had for Ago and the 500 or anything else.

The day before the race the big Honda was pushed up a wooden ramp by a Honda mechanic for the weigh-in, and the mechanic had an arm draped over it to keep it upright; but it was as if the bike was as large as a pony and just as awkward to control. And the mechanic was only pushing it.

The day of the race there was that distinctive pre-race atmosphere, submerged tension, the normality of spectators and officials wandering about, and yet it was building in spite of itself. Agostini, leathers folded down to the waist, a yellow pullover underneath, sun glasses, joked with

Between the Belgian and German Grands Prix, Hailwood took part in what looks like a hill climb at Mount Generoso on the Swiss-Italian border. This is just before he crashed.

Hailwood pleasantly, affably, almost intimately. These were real men they were behaving as real men would, civilized off the track, hard as hell on it, civilized again afterwards.

Agostini had been much quicker than Hailwood in practice, and anyway this was his twenty-fifth birthday. As he moved towards the grid a pretty girl scampered up and asked for his autograph. She gushed. Some girls squealed even if Ago thrust his hand through his dark hair to smooth it. She didn't, just gushed and smiled nervously to be in his presence while he signed.

Hailwood, number four, went in the second batch and the Honda engine growled before it burst into a jungle roar as he ran it forward, got on side-saddle, slipped fully on. John Dee, watching, could almost touch the electricity in the air. Thirty seconds later Agostini went. The MV engine was more shrill, seemed to gurgle before it growled, and Agostini was away past the front of the grandstand.

At Quarter Bridge, Hailwood angled the bike down, so that his knee-cap was virtually caressing the road. When Agostini did precisely the same hands were stabbing stop-watches. The gap was still the 30 seconds they had carried from the staggered start, but at Ballaugh Bridge it was 23 and Agostini was coming fast; at Signpost Corner it was 19 seconds. When Hailwood flowed over the line to complete lap one he had averaged 107.4 miles an hour and broken his own record from a standing start. Twelve seconds later here was Agostini and he'd done 108.4. Hailwood's record had lasted merely those 12 seconds.

'I was watching from the grandstand,' Dee says. 'When I saw Hailwood and Agostini going down Bray Hill it was . . . death-defying. When they reached the bottom I just don't know how they got round it. I mean, Hailwood took a line between a manhole cover and the kerb and the gap was two feet, three feet at most. The vast majority of spectators desperately wanted Hailwood to win and that meant the whole atmosphere was supercharged.'

Now they were into lap two.

Ken Sprayson, expert frame designer, was also a spectator. 'The most impressive thing I've ever seen was Hailwood on the top of Barregarrow against Agostini. They were doing 180 miles an hour flat. They came over the crossroads, a slight right-hander, and turned down a hill. Hailwood came through the top of the crossroads and dived down the hill. That was really something and I'm not an impressionable sort of man. Ago did the same but the fact that the Honda was a bit wild gave the moment that little bit extra . . .'

The gap after lap two was 8.6 seconds. This time Hailwood had gone round at 108.8 miles an hour and had taken the record back. The pit stops came at the end of the third lap. Hailwood arrived first. 'You could hear him shouting "hammer! hammer!" ' Walker could hear this above the noise of the engines and the noise from the grandstand. Hailwood sat erect on the bike and suddenly he seemed a tall man, tall enough to be master of the big bike not its servant. Then he stooped and the hammer someone had thrust into his hand was banging at the end of the twist grip on the handlebar. The crowd could see that the hammering was costing time. But Hailwood had no choice. The twist-grip had come loose. As he hammered Agostini decelerated past him, the gurgle of the MV dying away as he moved in for his pit stop. Agostini stopped ten feet ahead of where Hailwood was. Hailwood tossed the hammer away, felt the twist-grip and shoved the bike forward. He had been stationary for 47.8 seconds.

'I can't imagine anything worse than that twist-grip,' Walker says. 'Not only do you hang on to the handlebars with it but it controls your engine speed . . . and if it had come off . . . well, Mike was averaging 108 miles an hour . . .'

Agostini was stationary for 37 seconds. He now had a 12-second lead. Hailwood attacked it and on lap five at Kirk Michael it was down to 3 seconds; at Sulby they were level. At Ramsey, Hailwood was in the lead for the first time, by a single second. At the Graham Memorial, Agostini had

Mike the Bike and the Honda 500.

counter-attacked and they were level again. At Signpost Corner, Hailwood came through like a train and the crowd waited for Agostini . . . and waited. Thirty seconds. Where was he? Forty seconds . . . fifty . . .

His chain had broken and he'd steered the bike off at Governor's Bridge. The classic was over except that on the last lap Hailwood felt the twist-grip working loose again. 'The bloody throttle kept sliding,' he would say and added: 'Thank God I got a signal at Ballacraine that Agostini had retired. I slowed right down.' Journalists crowded him. 'How do you feel?' one asked. 'I feel OK—knackered.' (Smile.) By then Agostini had coasted back to the puts to deep applause. He got off the bike and turned away from it, his face sombre.

The piling on of the pressure had only just begun. Hailwood won at Assen, Agostini second; Agostini won at Spa, Hailwood second. Agostini won at the Sachsenring, Hailwood at Brno, Agostini won at Imatra although Hailwood had built up a 22-second lead. His goggles misted, the bike aquaplaned and went off, and Hailwood only missed a tree by inches. Hailwood won the Ulster after Agostini's clutch burnt on the start-line. Agostini lost four laps while it was rebuilt and kept doggedly on to finish twentieth. The 80,000 crowd appreciated that as much as they appreciated Hailwood winning.

Then—Monza. Agostini had 44 points, Hailwood 38 but the mathematics were more subtle. Agostini had already used up his quota of six finishes, Hailwood had only five. Canada would follow but Hailwood sensed that he had to win Monza and we come back to the same equation as 1966; Agostini, an Italian, MV, an Italian company, and this chauvinistic, rather frightening crowd. That September day they did what they were always going to do: they fashioned Monza in their own image, fashioned it into a cauldron. Hailwood took the lead and as they crossed the line to complete lap one he was about 250 metres ahead of Agostini; and now he began to increase that by a second a lap. He smashed the lap record by 3 miles an hour but with four laps to go the vast crowd could see him waving his right foot as he passed the pits. There could only be one meaning: the gearbox was in trouble, maybe he couldn't change down. Agostini closed and closed, but with two laps left Hailwood still held a 17-second lead. The Honda was trapped in top gear and Hailwood was impotent to stop Agostini flowing past him while the crowd abandoned itself to something approaching hysteria. Hailwood limped on. Agostini won it by 13.2 seconds. At the end of the pit lane straight Hailwood stopped and propped the bike against a wall, abandoned it. 'I was 3 minutes from winning that race, 3 minutes, that's all and a stupid thing like that had to go wrong. I could have cried. The disappointment was too much for me.' Hailwood took it, as Bryans says, 'hard'. He took it so hard that initially he refused to go on the rostrum and had to be persuaded to do so.

He won Canada (Agostini second) and he'd been right about needing to win Monza. Both he and Agostini had 46 points which counted, both had won five races so it was decided on second places. Agostini had three, Hailwood only two.

If you really want a last insight into Mike Hailwood, please listen. Bill Smith says: 'The greatest thing I remember about him is that we arrived at the Japanese Grand Prix one year and Mike had a very cavalier attitude at that time. Honda were paying real mega-bucks money and Mike didn't give a damn. They showed him a bike and he said: "No. It's the biggest load of rubbish I've ever seen." I mean, there he was in Japan going to ride a Japanese factory bike and he knocked it. Then he went out and annihilated the opposition, he made the other riders look stupid. That was Mike.'

'One day at Suzuka,' Clark says, 'Mike had gone really fast on the 250 but asked for harder rear suspension units to be fitted. He was told the ones on the bikes were good enough. He took them off and threw them into the lake at the back of the pits. Only then was something done about it. The mechanics would work all day and night for Mike. He was highly respected as a rider and as a person. He would give his trophies to the mechanics after a race. It was a great pity he did not win three World titles in one year. I think he was the most respected rider of all time.'

No sporting competitor could ask for a better epitaph.

In February 1968 Ralph Bryans received a telegram telling him to report to Japan 'as soon as possible'. He wasn't in the least surprised. He'd had a lot of telegrams like that, more than he could remember, and perhaps this one was to discuss the coming season. More probably he reasoned it would be to do some testing. He'd done that, too, more times than he could remember. 'I was met at the airport and taken to an hotel in Tokyo. The next morning the head of Research and Development came and had breakfast with me. He said that unfortunately Honda had decided to withdraw from Grand Prix racing.' It was, as Bryans remembers so vividly, a modern hotel and they took breakfast in the coffee shop, which was full of the sort of people who inhabit hotel coffee shops. They might have been a couple of businessmen quietly discussing a deal. But it was the ending of a whole era.

'The reason given was that Research and Development was far, far too busy working on cars. Honda said they would loan me an ex-works 125 and 250 which I could race anywhere in the world at my discretion provided they were not World Championship races. So in effect I was paid for the 1968 season not to ride in Grands Prix.' The logic of course was that he would be a privateer and the prestige of Honda would not be at stake. It was entirely understandable if the factory were not putting its muscle behind it. 'We had a bit of a party with all the mechanics in a club, we had a few laughs and that was it. It's sad, but that was it.' Ralph Bryans caught the plane home.

A couple of days later Hailwood received the same summons (he was in South Africa). He, too, thought it was to test. He was taken to dinner by Mr Sekiguchi and the news came as a 'terrible shock'. He was offered the same deal as Bryans but with 250, 350, and 500s of 1967 vintage. He would be paid and decided the 'money was too good to turn down'. But the Grands Prix? No. He too caught the plane home. He had won nine World Championships, seventy-six Grand Prix races. He would never win another.

Actually, Sekiguchi said that Honda planned to concentrate more on their Formula One team as a way of preparing themselves for the car market. They'd hired a former bike rider, John Surtees, to drive the Formula One car and in his single-minded way Surtees was urging and cajoling Honda and no doubt stretching them himself.

The individual 500 apart, Honda could gaze back—if they wished, although it's not something they do wish and Mr Honda is reported to be

19th October, 1967   KHS/LPD

S.M.B. Hailwood Esq.,
7 Wheatlands East,
Heston,
Middlesex.

Dear Mike,

    I have now completed a proposal drawing for your new frame. Before making this, I would like verification on points like ground clearance, footrest position etc.,

    Could you let me know where I can contact you within, say a week of replying to this letter, so that I can forward a drawing for discussion and approval by yourself and Roy.

    Best wishes,

              Yours sincerely,

              K.H. Sprayson

Above *Ken Sprayson, never one to waste words, tells Mike Hailwood how the frame for 1968 is coming along—but needs questions answering.*

Right *And this is what Hailwood replied.*

HOTEL NEW OTANI
4. KIOI-CHO, CHIYODA-KU, TOKYO TEL. 265-1111
CABLE ADDRESS : HOTELNEWOTANI TOKYO

Box 39, Bryanston
Johannesburg,

17th Dec 67.

Dear Ken,

    Thanks very much for your letter and the proposal plan for the Honda. It really looks very nice, and 20 lbs sounds very light. Also the height sounds very low, how does it compare with, say, a Norton? As for the angle of lean achieved when racing, I really couldnt tell you, but if you get on to derek Carpenter at dunlops, I am sure they will be able to tell you. But I'm sure it wouldnt exceed the 50 degrees laid down by the FIM.

    The footrest position looks about right, although I'm not very fussy where they are, as I seem to be able to ride with them almost anywhere within reason.

    I think the best thing to do about the forks is to take the head races out of the Lyster frame, as I think they are the same as the later type. They only strengthened the forks themselves and not the head. As to the tank and saddle, if you are unable to make them yourself get someone else to make them and I will pay for them. I should like the saddle to resemble the familiar honda pattern as far as possible, and the tank should be five gallons and it could come down between the back top frame tubes, as on the lyster job and the later Honda model , to lower the centre of gravity a bit more.

    Unfortunately, my usual mechanic, Roy Robinson, is down here in south Africa for the winter, and I havent a clue when he will be back in europe, and off hand I cant think of anyone I know who would be suitable to build up the machine when it is ready, who arent fully employed allready, I was wondering if you could make a few suggestions? Ask Bill Boddice, he seems very keen, but I should think he has enough work on his plate without worrying about something like this.

    Must apologise for not writing sooner, but we have been charging all round the southern hemisphere racing and things.

    How long will it take you to make the frame, now the drawings are complete?

    I will be back in England on or about the 15th january, and I will give you a ring when I get back. I certainly hope that this will be the answer to our problems. I dont know if you read the MCN, where it said that the spanish organisers are having a 500cc class there in '68, so we really will need something that handles brilliantly for that. So as you suggest, we must have a lot of testing to get it as near perfect as possible before the beginning of the season.

    Looking forward to hearing from you soon.
Hope you have a happy Christmas, dont get too pissed.

          All the best

          Mike Hailwood.

P.S. Thanks very much for your cooperation this matter.

so unsentimental that he had one of his winning bikes flown out to sea in a crate and dropped in a) to consign it to the past and presumably b) so no other competitor could examine it—on this vista: they had won the World Manufacturer's title in the 50 cc twice, the 125 four times, the 250 five times, the 350 six times, and the 500 once. Historian Peter Carrick would write: 'Motor cycle racing had been an impoverished, second-class sport until Honda came on the scene. They changed all that. With big-money contracts they wooed the most successful riders and put glamour and glory into the continental circus. Honda injected racing with a new vitality, a vibrant atmosphere and a smart image.'

Walker provides a slightly different analysis. 'For years and years and years Honda made a fundamental error in assuming that power was all. They assumed that if you produced more power you were going to win the race. But what you must have is a balanced package and it applies even more to racing bikes than racing cars. If you put an enormously powerful engine on a bike and it won't handle—as Hailwood's didn't and the early 250s didn't—you've got a major problem. However, the early 250s were so superior in every other respect that when you put people like Bob McIntyre, Jim Redman, and Derek Minter on them they would win the race. There came a time when Honda, who were naturally four-stroke people, found they weren't winning against the two strokes and Honda got into some incredibly advanced four-stroke technology with oval pistons and a fantastic number of valves per piston (eight, something like that) and even that wasn't enough.'

Ah, the handling . . . the handling that had frightened Hailwood and those who watched him. He decided to do something about it, and as a first step dispatched a Norton to Honda's Research and Development for scrutiny. Hailwood knew that the big Honda needed an entirely new frame. At a meeting at Oulton Park in early spring 1967 Ken Sprayson was in the paddock doing what he habitually did: welding. It was why the British company, Reynolds, employed him. Reynolds made tubing. Hailwood came over and asked casually: 'Could you do a frame for the Honda? What about making one for the 500?'

Sprayson said he 'would be willing to have a go' but, being both phlegmatic and pragmatic, stressed that it would probably take three or four months and would have to be done through Reynolds. 'I think that put Hailwood off because I didn't hear any more about it for a long time.'

Hailwood was put off because he needed a new frame immediately and turned instead to a man called Colin Lyster, a frame expert. They decided to travel to Milan and see what an Italian welder could do. The welder built a new frame—as Hailwood would claim—in sixteen days, the engine was fitted, and Hailwood tested it at Modena. The handling was not perfect but it was better. He entered a race at Rimini and won. What Hailwood hadn't done was tell Honda what he was doing and when they found out they were 'furious'. The new frame needed a lot more work on it and Hailwood simply dare not risk it in the coming Grand Prix season; 'so it stayed in my van'.

In September 1967 Sprayson was at the Motor Show at London's Earls Court when Hailwood approached him again. How did he fancy making a frame? (At this point of course Honda had not announced their withdrawal from racing in 1968.) Sprayson would now have time, (the whole winter) and, provided it was done through Reynolds, he said he'd make the frame.

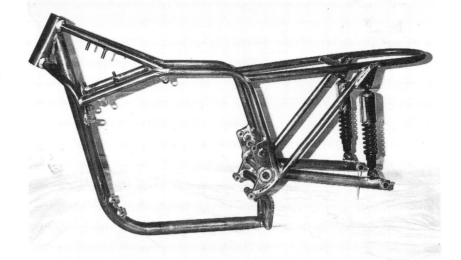

The frame that Ken Sprayson built.

The engine fitted snugly.

Ken Sprayson had joined Reynolds as a fitter in 1948. 'During the war the company made aircraft engine mountings and I was on the assembly line, but the wartime contracts were dying out and they were looking for work to replace them using the skills they had built up. Basically, they were a tube-making firm and would do anything with tubes. If you wanted them made into armchairs they would make them into armchairs.' One of their first jobs after the war was making parts for cash registers. Before the war they'd supplied the British motor cycle industry with tubes and now 'Norton came along and asked if we could help out with the welding of their frames. I was in the right place at the right time and although I was only a kid at the time I got to do all the specialist stuff. Norton brought a frame, we made a sample, we made jigs for that sample, and then we made all the frames (it was the Norton Featherbed). I was put in charge of a development and experimental department. We did a lot of other motor cycle jobs. During the 1950s we probably did every frame you can think of for all the little companies that had sprung up after the

The bike—rear view and side on.

War. Anyway, in 1953 or 1954, Norton approached us and said: "We have these frames on the Isle of Man but we don't have anyone with the welding skills to repair them if they get damaged. Could Reynolds send someone over to look after them?" We had a bloke who did all this kind of thing and he went over and set up a welding service. Initially it was for Norton but very quickly it became for everybody—and was free. He ran that up to 1958 and was over for the TT when he had a thrombosis and died.' It was the eve of the TT week.

'The boss called me in and told me to go and take over [he adopted the traditional route: a motor cycle and the ferry]. I've been going there ever since . . .'

Sprayson would soon find himself busily employed, so busy that he hardly had time to note whose bike he was welding. 'I started off behind the Falcon Cliff Hotel and moved about in the years to come—a lock-up garage would do. The Auto Cycle Union would put notices up telling people where to find me, and Reynolds used to put little advertisements in the newspapers.

'I remember the first time Hailwood came into the garage. It was the late 1950s and he was with his father. Stan said "Can you do this for Mike?" and I said "Get to the back of the queue, we'll see what we can do."' Sprayson was not particularly close to any of the riders—except, perhaps Geoff Duke—because 'you only get close to them when there is some mutual involvement'.

But now it was autumn 1967 and the involvement was about to begin. 'The problem with the Honda was that the engine was a pretty square box and if it was placed low on the frame it was virtually impossible to get the tubes underneath. You could get them down the front but there was nowhere to bring them up the back.' One solution, naturally, was to raise the engine—Lyster had tried that—but 'you almost needed a pair of step ladders to get onto the bike'. What Sprayson wanted was the engine low and on a self-contained frame because 'you have to be able to take the engine out to work on it'. Sprayson 'fiddled about' and found there was a triangular gap just wide enough to get ⅞-inch tubing through between the chain and the back of the swinging arm. 'Whether I was lucky or not I don't know, but I'd found the way. The fine point was still giving Hailwood, [who leaned over at an angle of 57° through corners] clearance. Putting tubing outside the engine effectively made the unit wider and as Hailwood leaned that would have given him less clearance. When the frame is all connected up it looks simple, but it was hard work and I'd had to start with a blank piece of paper. The actual construction took about two weeks and we were delighted that the engine could be put in and out with comparative ease and yet the machine had no excessive height or width.'

By then, of course, Honda had withdrawn from racing, although they were prepared to allow Hailwood to ride the bike under his agreement not to take part in Grands Prix. What Sprayson had done had been a fearsome undertaking. 'In those days the Japanese went mad on horsepower. We knew from experience that the Norton had 52 bhp, this Honda was 98, and they produced one which did 106. Norton went up to 56 but the horsepower came in at a sudden peak so as soon as you opened the throttle you got the lot. It wasn't controllable but when Norton detuned to 52 it made a wider curve so you could feed in the power.'

Anyway, 'Hailwood, myself, and the only non-Japanese mechanic to work with Honda, Nobby Clark, worked all night to get the thing together. Hailwood left about two o'clock in the morning and we finished it at four.' It was sent down to Brands Hatch for testing but Brands was being resurfaced so it—and Hailwood—went straight to Italy for a race at Rimini. At this stage he hadn't ridden the bike. The race was over twenty-eight laps and Agostini was in it, too. Hailwood took the lead and stayed there for ten laps before he tweaked the accelerator a little too hard and slid off onto grass. It cost him half a minute and although he had a shattered windscreen he broke the lap record. He finished second and blamed himself, not the frame, for his mistake. Shortly after he went to Imola but had trouble in practice with the 1967 engine and Clark spent a whole night changing to a 1966. This time Hailwood won but he couldn't persuade Honda to change their minds and go for the TT with it.

'The bike was never really developed,' Sprayson says. 'In effect those were the only races he did. Understandably, big companies are a little bit reluctant to go outside to get things done which they ought to be able to do themselves. While they are racing they like to keep everything in-house. Was I disappointed? I'd got used to it because we'd had the same thing with Geoff Duke, the same thing with John Surtees—they only came to us when their contracts were finished. They were still on peak performance, still basically as keen as they'd ever been, but they had not got the factory incentive behind them. We did the AJS for Surtees and as soon as we'd made it he went car racing [with Ferrari then Honda].

'One thing Hailwood did say to me, the year after he'd done a lap of 108 miles an hour on the Honda in the 500 against Agostini on the Isle of Man, was that if he'd had the bike we made it would have been 110.' Sprayson is reflecting on the era now: 'As I say, Redman kept himself very much to himself. They are all very nice people in motor cycling, but there are some quiet ones. Surtees kept himself to himself too. Hailwood mixed with everyone. Geoff Duke was very friendly, but wasn't a party goer, he was a quiet sort of chap. But it was all casual, all friends together. Tom Phillis: I was probably one of the last people to speak to Tom . . . you don't actually hear that Tom Phillis has retired, you don't hear anything publicly, but the word goes round quickly. You're very sad but the thing is, at the back of your mind, you expect such things to happen however much you say they won't happen . . . so really I suppose when they do, it is not the shock it would be if your next door neighbour walked out and dropped dead in the street . . . I suppose you have to accept these things. Phillis was a very nice chap; again, he was one of the crowd, friendly with everyone. Bob Brown was another . . . '

Some last words to mark the era from Nobby Clark:

Jim Redman was a very good rider, a very cagey rider, he never raced faster than he had to and he was the first man to win three races in one day at a Grand Prix, the Dutch in 1964. He did an awful lot for Honda in putting their name on the map. There were four types of bikes which were really great to work on and ran like clocks if they were properly put together: the 125-four of 1964, the 250-four of 1964, the 350-four of 1963 and 1964, and the 350-six of 1967. That 125 was a great bike, gave very little trouble . . . in fact the only time it gave us a problem was at Monza when a valve dropped and Luigi Taveri felt it immediately and stopped the engine. There was no damage to the head or cylinder. We only had to replace the piston and valve. I think the 350-six was only beaten once in a Grand Prix and that was when Ralph Bryans rode it in the Ulster. I don't think the bike was ever pushed to its limits and certainly there was no development done on the engine. One just felt that when it was wheeled on to the grid it was a winner.

In 1968 Giacomo Agostini won all ten 500 cc Grands Prix. We'll never know what Hailwood thought about that. The bike that Ken Sprayson built, and which might have altered all that, is in a museum now and Sprayson still wonders about what might have been. 'The fact that Honda allowed us to make it coincided with their withdrawal and that's probably the reason we got permission. The thing is, if we had been allowed to race it in a Grand Prix we would have had more money, we would probably have ended up making them for Honda.' There is another bike in another museum. Soichiro Honda ignored the habit of a lifetime and kept the 125 with which Hailwood had won the 1961 TT at his home on a special stand. When Mr Honda retired in 1975 it was presented to the Murray Motor Cycle Museum at Snaefell.

Both bikes are silent now.

NINE

Don't Bank On It

'I was approached,' Bill Smith says in his own firm, calm way, 'in 1969 by Honda because they had a four-cylinder 750 cc road bike and they wanted to know what was the best form of publicity for it. I said: "Race one." They agreed, so we decided to contest the Bol d'Or in France. Tommy Robb and I went and it was a 24-hour race on a banked circuit, at Montlhéry just outside Paris. We'd do two hours on, two hours off. So we turned up with the bike and it was really out of this world, but the French authorities said that because we were works riders we weren't going to be allowed to compete. We went berserk trying to get a licence and it almost created an international incident, but we didn't get a licence. After a lot of arguing we had to get Frenchmen to ride in our place and we picked two students literally out of the paddock and they won. They'd been recommended to us. It started a huge explosion of superbike sales on the Continent because nobody had hear of a four-cylinder road bike before.'

There was a logical, perhaps inevitable, sequel. If the bike could win the Bol d'Or so easily with students on it, why not go the richest and most famous race in the world, the Daytona 200? Honda contacted Smith again.

'I was asked by the Honda factory to get a team of riders together to go for the big one. I picked Robb, Ralph Bryans, Steve Murray, and myself. Honda flew the bikes over to me in January 1970 to test them because Daytona was on 14 March. They were beautiful, all made of titanium, and super quick. We went to Oulton Park to test and there was snow on the ground. Ralph was a bit anxious about racing again on a quicker bike than he'd ever been on before. He was worried and I could see that.'

'I was flattered to be asked to join the team, but to be perfectly frank the machines were underdeveloped,' Bryans says. 'They were brand new and I don't think they'd been tested before, which was very untypical of Honda.' Murray didn't get a ride at Daytona because Honda understandably wanted an American to maximize their impact and picked Dick Mann.

'We had no idea how good he was,' Robb says, 'so, full of confidence, we had a meeting to decide how best to split up the money between the three British riders. About £9000 was up for grabs and it was agreed that no matter where the three of us finished we would share an equal amount of the cash.'

They had a flight wracked by turbulence from New York to Florida—Robb likened it to a ride on a moto-cross bike and he was frightened—but they settled into a luxurious hotel and soothed the memories of the journey away quickly (as people do) in the swimming pool.

Mann arrived and Robb was delighted to see that he was 'a veteran, like myself, and had no high-flown illusion about his ability, though he was truly a professional and a clever performer'. In fact, he was a pro amongst pros. The chemistry was always going to work. The culture shock came in the pits. Mechanics had to wear freshly-laundered white overalls and no girls in 'sexy' dresses were allowed near in case they proved to be a distraction.

Smith sets out the background. 'Honda said "Here are the four bikes but there are different specifications on the camshafts." One had 96 horsepower, two had 92, and one had 89. So you can imagine which bike I gave Dick Mann [throaty chuckle implying the 89]. Being greedy I picked the fastest one for more myself [second throaty chuckle implying the 96].' Bryans expands on the background. 'There were no Honda works mechanics there. It was left to a team of American mechanics and some lads who had come across from England to sort the bikes out.' Now Smith examined Daytona itself. 'It was a hell of a bottle [slang for courage] circuit because of the banking. You'd fly up to the top like a wall of death and you needed guts to keep this Honda flat out. They'd got them so highly tuned that they were breaking cam chains, and you could imagine being stuck up there at 160 miles an hour. It was very, very, dangerous.'

'We had very severe handling problems,' says Bryans. According to Robb: 'The circuit consisted of a speed bowl banked at each end with an infield where the only real riding came in. The rest was just a straight blast and on occasions our Hondas were doing almost 180 miles an hour. I remember passing Gene Romero on the Triumph 3 at 174 miles an hour, but I had to ease up at the bend because I didn't fancy soaring above him on the steep bank.'

Practice was an end in itself—sometimes almost literally the end. 'I hit the wall at the top of the banking,' remembers Bryans. 'I had got too close to the wall, turned the throttle, the back wheel stepped out and hit the wall. The bike jack-knifed and shot me over the top. We both cascaded down to the infield. The fuel tank was ruptured and the bike caught fire. There happened to be a fire truck within a hundred yards, two intrepid firemen hopped in, approached where the bike lay but lo and behold they'd parked the truck too far away and the hose wouldn't reach. When they'd got out of the truck one of them dropped the keys and they couldn't find them . . .

'That was the day I began to think of my future in racing motor cycles. As a professional it was a very grave error I had made in hitting that wall, because there was absolutely no need to do it. We were bedding in tyres, chains, brakes, and I was over-exuberant. I applied too much power in the wrong place. It could have been fatal.' Bryans would start the race from

A glimpse of the future: Wayne Gardner and Freddie Spencer.

the back of the grid. Smith had struggled too because 'my bike kept busting the cam chains as it came off the banking'. Robb wasn't in the fastest fifteen qualifiers. Mann meanwhile was fourth fastest.

Smith was out before the start (cam chain again). Mann briefly led and then settled to ride a steady race. Bryans was out after four laps ('the timing chain broke and that was the end of that'), and Robb went soon after with the same problem. Several riders, including Hailwood on a BSA, led but broke down and guess who won? Dick Mann by 10 seconds.

There were sequels to Daytona. Bryans continued to wonder about continuing to race. 'I borrowed a 250 from Luigi in Switzerland of 1961 vintage and competed in the North West 200 in Ireland, won the race, and announced my retirement immediately afterwards. There was a time when I used to think I'd be lucky to survive to thirty years old. So to hedge my bets I retired when I was 29. I had accepted that I might not see 30, oh yes, you see a lot of good men go, and motor cycling road racing didn't take many prisoners in those days.'

The last races on the Island to count as Grands Prix were in 1976. Thereafter the British Grand Prix moved to Silverstone, then Donington. 'The reason the TT died,' Murray Walker says, 'is that the two-stroke motor cycle became the thing to have, but they were brittle and prone to breaking down—so you'd get these riders coming over to the Island where they had to spend two weeks and they wore the machines out quickly. And the Continental riders always complained that you needed about three years experience before you even knew your way around the course.' Even those who did, remember, habitually toured it slowly, patiently each year to remind themselves; and Minter would say many years later that 37.75 miles is almost too much to remember. 'It gave,' Walker says, 'an unfair advantage to the home riders, so the Continentals were never all that keen on coming over in the first place. Then when the two-strokes arrived the Continentals found themselves spending a lot of money and doing badly in an event they didn't like anyway. Another factor was that it lasted two weeks, the first for practice, the second for the racing. The reasoning was: If we go on the Continent we can race in two meetings for the price of one and so the Isle of Man (in its traditional centre-of-the-world sense) just got phased out.' That said, racing continued there and still does.

As another historical footnote, the sight of Hondas did not completely cease at the end of 1967. Privateers continued to race them—an Australian, T. Dennehy, in 1969; Dennehy and Lewis Young in 1970; J. Campiche, a Swiss, 1971. I record all this is a quiet concluding paragraph because, while no doubt these were good men and true, it was an aeon away from Redman and Hailwood, Bryans and Robb, and little Luigi Taveri and Stuart Graham.

TEN

Four Into Two Doesn't Go

THE telephone rang in Bill Smith's Chester office. It was Yoshio Nakamura. 'He asked me if I would go to the West End of London to meet the young team that was to design Honda's new 500 cc racing bike. That was the autumn of 1975. I went and we had a meal in a Japanese restaurant. I didn't know before the meeting that they were coming back in. They asked me what type of bike I would make and, knowing Honda, I thought they'd want it to be a four-stroke. I said it needed to be a mono-coque.

'I was really appalled when I met the designers because—typical Honda—they never pick people with a track record; they pick engineers straight out of university, give them a clean piece of paper, and say: "This is what you do." We'd never do that in the West. They paid the penalty for that because the first bike was a monocoque but was so badly designed that to take the carburettors off to change the main jets, which you have to do at race meetings, you had to take the engine out of the chassis. They got the 500 four-stroke going quite well, but it was never competitive enough to match the Suzuki and Yamaha two-strokes because in terms of brake horse power per litre you just can't compete against the modern day two-strokes with a four-stroke, even though Honda have wonderful technology.

'Such was the naïvety of the Honda engineers that they hadn't con-sulted the FIM regulations, which stated that the maximum number of cylinders was four and the maximum number of gears six. If Honda had had their way, they would have had an eight- or twelve-cylinder 500 with a ten-speed box and it would have annihilated everything else. The 500 four-stroke was brilliant, but it was never going to be competitive.

'After the shambles they had with the frame they called in a chap called Ron Williams of Maxton Engineering, who was a well-known frame en-gineer. He designed virtually a new frame layout that was taken over to Japan and perfected. They worked on the four-stroke for the next three or four years before they finally gave up because a straightforward three-cylinder two-stroke could win very easily.'

At that meal in the Japanese restaurant, Bill Smith was being paid two compliments: that he was being implicitly trusted to keep secret the fact that Honda were coming back into Grand Prix bike racing and that he could impart invaluable advice. In fact the public announcement was not made until December 1977 by the company's President, Kiyoshi Kawashima. He said Honda would race again in 1979 with a four-stroke engine. This provoked something approaching disbelief. No four-stroke had raced for three years. The inherent efficiency of the two-stroke had simply blown them away.

It was not hard to understand why. Two-strokes have twice as many 'power strokes' as fours, an inviolate physical law. There was a way to compensate for this by having more cylinders, but, as Smith pointed out, the regulations stipulated four cylinders only. What Honda now attempted was to create the effect of eight cylinders by making oval cylinders with eight valves within each. Taken together, it was an extremely risky move and soon demonstrated how stubborn Honda could be. They would be forced back to the drawing-board at least three times and meanwhile the riders suffered. That was obvious from the very first day of practice at Donington. The two chosen riders, Takazumi Katayama and Mick Grant, were slow and, as *Motocourse* would point out, 5 seconds outside Wil Hartog's lap record on the RG5000 Suzuki'.

Grant, a Yorkshireman, had already tested the bike in Japan. 'I'd been with Kawasaki for four years and I left them on good terms. The offer to join the new Honda Grand Prix team came right out of the blue. The temptation was that they would be resuming where they had left off in 1967 and when details of the bike began to filter through it started to get really exciting because it seemed so innovative. I tested it at Suzuka in early 1979 and I can't remember if we were able to string three laps together in three days. It was bloody awful. Everything went wrong and there was very little power, although the bike was very well balanced. They didn't seem aware of what the rest of the world was doing. For example, they'd spend hours in the dyno house but they'd use a three-year-old 500 Suzuki for comparison. What they should have done is start where they had left off in 1967. We did a lot of testing and after a session you'd go in to a room with twelve engineers for the debrief—one engineer for the gearbox, two for the tyres, and so on—and they'd all be firing questions and every time I would say: "None of it is any good!" Excellence is something well balanced. I'm not being derogatory, I'm being honest.

'I'll give you another example. They chose 16-inch wheels (instead of the customary 18 inches) and if we'd been running the 18s we'd have known the problems weren't the tyres. There were loads of things like that. It was frustrating because the engineers did not have race experience. I once asked one of them what he'd been doing before and he said he'd spent three years putting front fenders on to Honda Accords! They worked extremely hard, though. In 1979 the engine would only tick over at 7,000 revs but by 1980 they had that down to 1,000—2,000 like a normal road bike. When you consider that it had no flywheel, that was a fantastic achievement.'

The Grand Prix debut at Silverstone was a disaster. 'By that time I knew what to expect,' Grant says. 'They had open practice and on the straight a 250 Yamaha was pulling away from me—not a lot, but pulling

Spencer, all smiles.

away and that was enough to show me the scale of the problem. I had never ridden harder.'

Grant and Katayama qualified on the last row of the grid. 'I bump-started it. You had to be on the 7,000 revs and I missed that two or three times. Katayama caught his—it was all a matter of luck—but because he wanted us to go round together he sat there looking back waiting for me. It was very embarrassing. It must have lasted a full couple of seconds. At last I started off and went up through first, second, and third gears, but I was doing a "wheelie" because I had my weight at the back going towards the first corner.' Unfortunately, the angle of the bike meant that oil was being pumped out of the flat-sided piston and when Grant reached that first corner he had a well-lubricated rear wheel: 'I went down. When I was back in the pits the Honda people said: "No more wheelies!"'

The next race was the French, at Le Mans. It became a bizarre 'joke', Grant says. 'We must have been quite an embarrassment to the organizers. We just failed to qualify by a couple of places, but that didn't stop us taking part in the warm-up lap, did it? We were hoping a couple guys would drop out during the warm-up and when it was over we took the bikes on to the grid still hoping the French would let us in. Unfortunately, nobody had dropped out and the grid was full, but all the crowd wanted to see the Hondas. Pandemonium! The noise the crowd made! There's a tall fence at Le Mans separating the crowd from the track but they came down to it and seemed on the verge of tearing it down so they could reach the grid. It was one of the times in my life where people really wanted me! However . . . the team manager signalled for us to take the bikes away and that was it, really.'

In 1980 Ron Williams began to redesign the frame and it was used at Donington in June, where Grant tested it. In July, Katayama took it to Imatra for the Finnish Grand Prix, qualified slowest, and didn't race. He had two bikes and had damaged both. By now the press were beginning to hammer Honda who, according to one witness, 'closed ranks and got on with the job'. At the next race, Silverstone, the machine did go the distance, giving Katayama fifteenth place; and at least he was on the same lap as the winner, Randy Mamola (Suzuki). At the race after that, the Nürburging, Katayama was twelfth. Suzuki finished with 108 points, Yamaha 102, Kawasaki 13.

'At the end of 1980, Gerald Davidson [the team manager]—a man of definite ideas—suddenly decided I was getting on a bit, so I was out in the cold,' Grant says. 'I carried on until 1985 and I did some good things after that. Every time I overtook a Honda I thought . . . well! But looking back on Honda it was a rich experience and one that I wouldn't change.'

That wasn't the whole story of 1980. At Easter, before the Grand Prix season had even begun, an intriguing series of races had been held at Brands Hatch, Mallory Park, and Oulton Park. They were called the Trans-Atlantic Challenge. Unfortunately, disputes with the organizers led some British riders to withdraw, while Grant took part with a broken ankle—he'd broken it in Japan, a mere three days before, testing a Honda. The American team looked useful, particularly since it was headed by Kenny Roberts (World Champion in 1978 and 1979) and Mamola. The first race, at Brands, was thirteen laps of the 2.61 mile circuit and more than 50,000 spectators came to savour it. Brands, which dips and rises, is difficult to master, whether you're talking bikes or rac-

Erv Kanemoto, his eyes missing no detail at Spa.

ing cars. On lap three a silver Yamaha—number five—with a rider wearing a matching silver helmet moved past Graeme Crosby and in to a lead he would maintain to the end. He had the face of a choir boy, he had quiet manners, he was eighteen, and he had never been out of the United States of America before. He was called Freddie Spencer and few among the 50,000 had ever heard of him. In the second race he led from flag to flag, as they say, beating Roberts, with Mamola third. It was a fascinating glimpse of the future, and, as it happened, Honda's future.

In the Superbike championship in the United States, Spencer rode a Honda in all ten rounds, won three times, and finished third overall. He was intuitively fast, always had been. This same year Yamaha lured him to compete in the Belgian Grand Prix at Zolder; but he felt homesick, didn't enjoy being closeted in his hotel at night, and he'd only been on the bike once before, at Laguna Seca a few days previously. He disliked Zolder (many people do) because it rained the whole time and the track was bouncy-bouncy. In the race he was involved in a shunt on the start line—'I got baulked and my knees hit the gas tank and broke the fuel cock and I had to pull in after the first lap because gas was all over my tyres.'

That was 1980.

It is time to take a closer look at Frederick Burdette Spencer. He was a private man whose instincts were always towards the reclusive rather than the gregarious. He preferred the sanctuary of the motorhome to the hustle of the paddock. He was born on 20 December 1961 at Shreveport, Louisiana, a town in the north of the State in what they call the Bible Belt. The Spencers were staunch Baptists and Freddie attended the Crawood Christian School. The family ran a grocery store, but speed was in their blood. Freddie Senior had in his time gone racing with whatever was to hand, not only motorbikes but cars and karts as well. He was still racing. A daughter, Linda, would be drawn towards karts; a brother Danny drawn towards the motorbikes; and so was Freddie.

Legend insists that he began dirt track riding when he was six. Legend also claims that when he was twelve a challenge was made by a road race club to the dirt trackers to see what they could do on roads: Spencer, on a 100 cc Yamaha against riders on 250s, finished last. Legend further has it that he was riding in more than a hundred events a year and that the family arranged their holidays to allow him to race. His father decreed that if Freddie was serious about racing, then it should be treated seriously. And there was another dimension. Riding so much he was learning profound lessons across a wide variety of subjects. 'Dirt-tracking,' he would say, 'teaches you how to keep the throttle open when the wheel slides away. You learn how to control the bike by shifting your body weight.' And this: 'If you win your first heat, you often don't race again until 52 heats later. By then the track has probably changed completely . . . '

He turned professional at 16—in 1978—and as fate would have it was spotted by a fourth-generation American called Erv Kanemoto, who could tune engines with intuitive skill. Kanemoto saw instantly that Spencer was 'something really special'. His father asked me to do some engines for him and from then on I really wanted to be involved.' A partnership was born that would deepen and mature until it reached global dimensions.

In 1979 Spencer was becoming widely noticed domestically and when Honda needed a replacement for an injured rider in the Superbike series they went to him. He won twice. Soon, however, Honda were not alone. Yamaha wanted him. Kawasaki wanted him. The question was: what did Freddie Spencer want? Well, as he says himself, he wanted to be well paid. Even at school curious fellow-pupils had wondered how he could expect to make a living of out of merely riding bikes. Honda made their offer for 1980 and allowed him to ride a Yamaha at Daytona—for which Honda did not then have a bike themselves. Spencer accepted the offer and in December 1979 became a works Honda rider. He was 17. At Daytona he had a clear lead on the Yamaha when a bearing broke; on the Honda Superbike he was either fiercely fast or the machinery failed him. As a matter of record, shortly after Daytona he was on the Honda at Charlotte, North Carolina, when an oil filter went and the oil on the back wheel put him down heavily at more than a hundred miles an hour. He was badly shaken. I mention this only in case a picture is forming of a young man who was so consummately skilled that he didn't know what it was like to experience his own mortality and go down dangerously and ignominiously.

Spencer knew. It happened on banking and what he did was masterly. He jumped off before anything else could happen. In the Trans-Atlantic Challenge in England he was the second-highest points scorer (76) behind Roberts (92), despite a crash at Oulton Park. He would say subsequently that this might be the one race of his life which he'd like to re-ride. He was in the lead but didn't back off, as he could have done, and was criticized as being too young to be manipulating monster bikes. It hurt him.

Spencer at Misano, May 1982

At the end of 1980 Spencer wanted to take on Europe *in* Europe, which meant the Grand Prix championship. His contract with Honda had only been for one year and was therefore up for renewal (or renegotiation). Spencer knew what everybody else knew: the 500 two-stroke was off the pace and might well always be so. Honda hinted that by 1982 all this would be changed. Spencer resigned and 'during a break in the American season I went to Suzuka and rode the NR 500 for a couple of laps and we decided to take it to Laguna Seca to race it. At first I was about 6 seconds outside the lap record, because I was trying to ride it like a normal motorcycle where you accelerate on the edge at around 13,000 revs. The four-stroke would rev to nearly 22,000 and so eventually I narrowed up the power band and brought the gears so close together that I was changing between 13,000 and 21,000 revs. I was shifting gears all the time, but you had to keep it in the power band if you were going to race it hard. Its great shortcomings were its weight and lack of torque.'

In spite of all this, Freddie Spencer was what he had always been—impressive. In a heat at Laguna Seca he actually beat Roberts. A decision was taken to race the bike at the British Grand Prix at Silverstone on 2 August.

The problems came tumbling at him, the first being the all-important push-start: 'If you didn't hit it just right it would skid the rear wheel and I had a sore chest that weekend from banging the gas tank to get that thing started.' He practised push-starts alone out there on the track hour after hour, but 'in the middle of one of my practice sessions Carlo, quite an old Italian mechanic who went on to work for Marco Lucchinelli, came across after watching my efforts and said: "I will show you." So this old guy took three or four steps and the bike started first time. I watched him and from that point on I didn't have a lot of trouble starting it.'

Spencer also made a decision of his own. He would abandon prudence, would dismiss any notions of chugging round to finish, would instead push the bike to its limits and see what happened. He qualified tenth fastest with a time of 1 minute 32.53 seconds. (Direct comparison: Crosby, Suzuki, on pole with 1 minute 30.40 seconds). On the fast, level Silverstone circuit Spencer, hemmed in the middle of the pack, went for it. On the third lap two of the leaders had crashed and that left a quartet isolated at the front: Roberts, Mamola, Kork Ballington, and Jack Middelburg. Behind them, charging furiously was Spencer. There were moments when it did seem that Spencer was catching the quartet. Then he felt a piston hit a valve and his race was over.

Kanemoto, who had been gaining experience in Europe by working with Barry Sheene, was summoned to Honda American in Los Angeles. Spencer was also summoned from Shreveport. It was all done with the Honda secrecy we know so well. In a room a box was unpacked and there before their very eyes was the new three-cylinder two-stroke engine. It looks, Kanemoto ruminated, like a moto-cross engine. The engineer in charge of the project was called Shinichi Miyakoshi, and he had been actively involved in Honda moto-cross engines. ('This was regarded as sensational,' Murray Walker says, 'that Honda, the great masters of four-stroke had thrown in the towel, accepted defeat, and gone two-stroke. If they couldn't beat Yamaha and Suzuki they would join them!')

Spencer tested the new bike at Suzuka in December, then at Laguna Seca, then in Brazil before the real assault began at the Argentinian

Bike racing had now become extremely glamorous...

... and the Rothmans girls were not far away.

Grand Prix at Buenos Aires on 28 March 1982. Spencer would be partnered by Luchinelli, for whom, it was reported, Honda had paid a fortune. The affable Italian had beaten Mamola to the 500 World Championship in 1981, 105 points against 94. Both were on Suzukis. Lucchinelli had started in 1974—a hill climb—and had been with Suzuki since 1976. He'd had to wait until 1980 to win his first Grand Prix, the German, but in 1981 added another five. Clearly, he and Spencer constituted a formidable team, but they faced equally formidable challengers. There would be Franco Uncini on a Suzuki and Mamola, too; there would be Crosby, Roberts, and Sheene on Yamahas. If you let your eye travel down the list of bike manufacturers who had won the 500 title since the last fling of MV Augusta in 1973, you would see that Yamaha had won the two years after that and Suzuki every subsequent year.

Spencer found the new Honda 'nimble' but 'a bit down on power'. The whole bike world waited to see what would happen, and the whole bike world was intrigued because the secrecy had been rigorously maintained. Rumours were the currency everyone traded in. Rumours said that the Honda had broken lap records when prying eyes were not looking; rumours also said that it was already faster than the Yamaha of Roberts. Nor did this speculation end when people actually saw the bike in the pit lane of the Autodromo Municipal de la Cuidad at Buenos Aires. Three cylinders? Reed valves? (Technical note. Miyakoshi would say about the former that only three reduced friction; but the latter was completely revolutionary. Everyone had run discs for as long as anybody could remember, but the reed responded precisely to the rise and fall of compression in the crankcase, opening and shutting.)

Immediately Spencer was fast. In fact only Roberts was faster—1 minute 34.05 against 1 minute 34.10. Lucchinelli was fourth. It was hot for the race, hot as Louisiana itself. Spencer took the lead at the end of the first lap, Sheene hounded him and took the lead for himself, Roberts coming hard took both of them. This was a classic. This was a thinking race. Now Mamola began his charge but was crippled by gear problems. He had fancied himself to win. With only a few laps left, Spencer brushed

against a straw bale but he recovered and was holding third place. Roberts was travelling so fast to hold off Sheene that he actually clipped a back marker in the hairpin, but he recovered. Meanwhile, down the long back straight, Sheene pondered the wisdom of an all-out assault, decided his brakes might not tolerate that in the hairpin, and kept himself safely in second place. Spencer held third. After 32 laps—127.488 kilometres—the result was Roberts 50 minutes 44.82, Sheene 50 minutes 45.49, Spencer 50 minutes 46.19. For good measure Lucchinelli was fifth, Katayama sixth.

Honda were back.

But it's not easy, not easy at all. At the very next race, Austria, Spencer went only as far as lap nineteen before mechanical troubles halted him, and although Lucchinelli was breaking the lap record at will—he set a fastest lap of 191.302 kph—and seemed poised to win after a savage contest with Uncini (their bikes repeatedly touched), but with no more than a lap left Lucchinelli over-cooked it, flicked on to the grass, and went down heavily.

France (Nogaro) was boycotted by the leading riders because they considered the facilities 'well short of civilized standards', the track 'too bumpy and offering serious safety hazards', and 'the overcrowded paddock a fire risk.' The race was run none the less and stands as a sort of curiosity, with a lot of names few people remember getting points.

Spencer took pole in Spain but retired on lap seven when he was in the lead; he was second at Misano and set fastest lap; he set fastest lap at Assen but fell in the rain. And so they came to Spa, where, as we have seen, it also rains—as Jim Redman discovered all those years ago.

Nothing fundamental changed.

Spencer was second fastest in qualifying behind Middelburg and felt that the Honda liked the track. 'The road runs downhill away from the tight corners,' he said at the time, 'which helps my acceleration and I don't feel the lack of horsepower so much.' He bided his time in the race, running seventh after the opening lap, moving up to fifth then third while Roberts, locked in combat with Uncini for the championship, forced the Yamaha towards its limit. On the ninth lap Spencer was second and suddenly Roberts began to wander all over the track. His rear tyre was shredded. Spencer went past and stayed comfortably in front. He beat Sheene by 3.80 seconds and was so intoxicated that as he angled the bike towards the entrance to the paddock he fell off it. He clambered to his feet, a great big grin spreading inside his crash helmet and punched the air, fist clenched. This was his first Grand Prix victory. It was Honda's first 500 victory since Hailwood had crossed the line at Mosport, Canada, on 30 September 1967 precisely 37.7 seconds ahead of Agostini. As many people noted, Freddie Spencer was still only 20.

Three races later—Anderstorp—he took pole but was crippled by a misfire on the warm-up lap. This does not dilute the impact of what was to follow. Takazumi Katayama was about to experience the great moment of his life. He was a Korean citizen (via his parents), although he had been born in Kobe, Japan and did not speak Korean. He had flirted with car racing, settled on bikes, and had joined Honda in 1979. With Mick Grant he had wrestled and struggled with the four-stroke Honda. Now in Sweden he qualified the two-stroke third, took the lead quickly, and simply stayed there. (Katayama, incidentally, was also a very successful

Spencer during the French Grand Prix.

pop singer in Japan.)

Spencer won at Mugello (although Katayama set fastest lap and crashed). At Hockenheim, Spencer was in the lead, but on the last lap slowed too much as he approached the contorting series of corners that feed out on to the start-finish line. In any case, Spencer had trouble with the ignition. He braked and Mamola, up with him, nipped by on the inside; but Uncini, who tried to do the same, never made it. They collided, Spencer's collarbone was broken, and as he walked away he collapsed with concussion. Victory would have given him second place in the championship instead of the third he had finished with; and that was 1982.

It is now time to meet Kenny Roberts from Modesto, California, who, approaching 1983, was a formidable presence. He first rode in 1969 and from 1978, with Yamaha, had won sixteen Grand Prix races. Now it is April 1983, we are in a restaurant in London, and Roberts is outlining his life. As we wait for the food to come he constantly revolves his neck, slowly, deliberately. 'I've big back muscles,' he says. 'Motor cycling com-

Enter Wayne Gardner. A characteristic study ...

… and another.

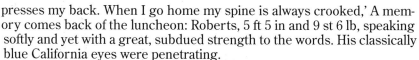

In time his face would become familiar everywhere. He'd also learn other skills, serving drinks as well as consuming them.

presses my back. When I go home my spine is always crooked,' A memory comes back of the luncheon: Roberts, 5 ft 5 in and 9 st 6 lb, speaking softly and yet with a great, subdued strength to the words. His classically blue California eyes were penetrating.

'I'm sure that motor cycling is 100 per cent science. For me, art is something you just do; there it is, you've done it, and there's no need to

know how. If that was the case with motor cycle racing I wouldn't have to spend days before a race testing, practising. I could just fly in, race the bike, and go home. No. It's a science; it's the relationship between power, gyro-effect, engine torque, G-forces—all the things that make the bike go a little bit quicker round the track. You have to be able to use every little piece of momentum. If you could programme a computer to know all the things that you know after years of racing, then it would do the thing for you perfectly.

'If you pick your butt up too fast you pitch the bike sideways. In a corner, if you slide your hand off the handlebar it hits the ground. I get holes in the bottom of my boots. You push so hard with your feet that you need new boots after every two races. I'm piercing through rubber and thick leather. The force is unbelievable. Danger? You're always thinking about it, but you never think about it. It's weird. You have to be so confident to push a bike that far, anyway. To ride in a Grand Prix you have to be at the point of throwing the bike away. At Daytona I'm going 180 miles an hour into the S-bend and all I see is a blurr. At the 150-yard marker I have to get down from 180 to 60 or 70 miles an hour. The blurr goes and a picture comes into focus. I've put every piece of concentration in to the braking.

'For three days at a Grand Prix meeting you just tune yourself for the day. It's a very nervous feeling. Some guys can't do it. You are actually making the motor cycle do what it doesn't want to do. The bike says: "I don't want to do that" and you say: "Yes, you are going to do that." '

He ate precisely, the hands manipulating knife and fork with precision. He was, and is, much more like your idea of an all-American than Spencer; he has been raised to be open, available; he expects to answer questions and is unafraid to answer them as he wishes. As the meal came to an end I wondered about the championship. 'It is' he said, 'a long way to go.'

Spencer won South Africa from Roberts and at Le Mans, the second race, Spencer won again, Lucchinelli second, Ron Haslam (on another Honda) third, Roberts fourth. Spencer won Monza while Roberts, who had been on pole, backed off towards the end with a misfire. He had been holding Spencer, although he freely confessed that he had no advantage anywhere over the Honda: 'Every time I looked over my shoulder, there was Spencer'. In points that April evening, Spencer had 45, Roberts 20, and there were nine races to run.

At Hockenheim, Spencer took the lead but was slowed by engine problems. Roberts went by and it seemed that Spencer, desperately nursing the bike towards the finish, would have to watch impotently while a cavalcade of other riders went by. Then it rained. When the race was stopped after fifteen laps Spencer was fourth. Roberts won it from Katayama and Lucchinelli. In points it had become Spencer 53, Roberts 35, and there were eight races to run.

Jarama was an absolute classic. Spencer moved into the lead on lap three (taking it from Haslam), Roberts was behind him on lap five; Roberts moved into the lead on lap nine, Spencer re-took it on lap twenty, Roberts re-took it soon after, Spencer re-took it on lap thirty-three. Four laps remained, just four laps of 3.132 kilometres each. Roberts clung to Spencer as they flowed through the corners with such evocative names—Nuvolari, Fangio, Varzi, Le Mans, Farina, Ascari, Portago, Bugatti, Monza—and then came to 90-degree right-hander to the pit lane straight. They were approaching the final lap. They were also about to lap Middelburg who was on a Honda. As they crossed the line to begin the last lap they were level with Middelburg and all three were running hard towards Nuvolari—the sharp right-hander at the end of the pit lane straight. Middelburg came back at them and tried to outbrake them going into Nuvolari. Spencer sneaked through, but Roberts found Middelburg four-square in front of him. It cost Roberts perhaps half a second and he now threw himself and the machine at the track, urging, squeezing, pounding, but still he couldn't catch Spencer. The difference at the end was 0.55 of a second. The last lap was the hardest, Roberts would say, anyone had ridden against him, so far in his life anyway . . .

Spencer now led by 68 points to 47 and there were seven races to run. Roberts won in Austria—Spencer had a crankshaft problem on lap twelve—and Spencer won in Yugoslavia, Roberts fourth, making it Spencer 83, Roberts 70. Roberts won Holland, Spencer third; but that wasn't the story of the race at all. On the third row of the grid was a young, eager, and almost completely unknown Australian called Wayne Gardner and this was his World Championship debut.

'I've always been involved with mechanical things,' says Gardner. 'My dad was a truck driver and engines have always amazed me—buses, trucks, cars. I had a go-kart when I was young and then I went on to bikes, from dirt racing to road racing. It was just a natural progression. In fact it was a hobby that turned into a career, a very well-paid career. When I first started and I wanted to go road racing, my dad said: "Well, it's dangerous and I don't want you to do it but I'll help you as much as I can"—I don't come from a wealthy family—"financially and morally". He was saying to himself: If we say no to Wayne then he'll probably go and mix with a bunch of bad people and then go into drugs and then get put into jail. So my mum and dad were really good. They thought: Even if it is a dangerous hobby at least it's a good hobby. Racing is very good for having discipline of the mind, taking responsibility, being physically fit, and you've got to have a certain amount of brains to put the whole thing together.'

Gardner came to Britain in 1981 and competed in domestic races; 'but I'd always wanted to do Grands Prix. I went to watch one—in fact it was Spa, 1981. I drove one of the sponsor's cars over. They needed a chauffeur, so I was hired because I couldn't afford to go any other way. At Spa a guy from Suzuki GB came up and said: "We'd like to talk to you about next year's racing in the United Kingdom with a Suzuki machine." Barry Simmonds, who was Honda Britain's team manager, saw this and as soon as the conversation was over came rushing up and said: "We'd like to speak to you about next year." I was caught for words. I said: "Oh, yeah?" All that was in the pit lane. About ten minutes after, Yamaha UK came up so there were three offers within the space of that ten minutes. I was flabbergasted. I didn't know what to think. It was just Donna [Gardner's girlfriend, now wife] and myself wandering around trying to get my face known.'

He joined Honda Britain. 'Suzuki said I couldn't ride a 500 and Honda Britain didn't have a 500 for me to ride, so basically I knew I just had to ride four-strokes (1000 cc four-strokes in the British F1 Championships, but not Grands Prix). 'I liked the professionalism of Honda. I remember seeing Ron Haslam in the Honda GB colours and I just thought it looked

Honda also made run-arounds to run around accompanying the bikes.

a better outfit. It was a new experience to me joining a factory team because I'd never been in one before. I took it as it came. Ron Haslam was still in the team and I tried to be back-up man. I did pretty well, I won some races, and it was an interesting year. For me it was really good because for the first time in my career I was actually being paid! I kept thinking of all the years in racing when I'd spent money to make a name for myself and finally I was getting something back. All of 1982 I thought not so much of winning but of getting my payments. It wasn't a great deal of money. Every time I'd start a race I'd look in the programme to see how much prize money there was because I didn't know where my career was going to take me. I was trying to get cash to set myself up in the future if everything fell through. In 1983 I had a different approach. I stayed with Honda Britain and I wanted results. Once I was a little bit financially secure I tried to push harder and stop thinking about money all the time.' Honda had offered him a 500 for 1983 (the RS500) to race in Britain again and he started to win. He was at Assen in a supporting race—the F1—and Simmonds said: 'We've got some 500s, we'll let you ride one in the Grand Prix.'

'Fine.'

Gardner qualified sixteenth. 'I got off to a good start and was running fifth in the race when Franco Uncini (Suzuki) crashed at the end of the straight. There was a corner there that has been changed now. Coming out of that he high-sided and fell off [slithered and was pitched over the handle-bars] 'and I came round the corner trying to avoid going into the back of him. But he'd got up and tried to run off the circuit. I was taking avoiding action and was going around the back of him to miss him; but in the same space of time I thought about that he got up, panicked, and tried to get off the track. I probably hit him at . . . second gear . . .60, 70 miles an hour. There was nothing I could do. Even though I was inexperienced there was no way I could have avoided it. He didn't look, he just got up and bolted and we collided. It nearly finished my career.

'On TV it shows his helmet hitting the front of the bike. His helmet came off and it was a nightmare. I can still see it over and over again. He broke my knuckle with his shoulder. I went down into a ditch and they carted us off to hospital. I knew he was serious but I didn't know how serious. His brother was there and I was bawling my eyes out and his brother said: "He's fine, he's getting better, come and see him." They took me up to the intensive care unit and I was expecting him to be sitting up in bed, OK? I was in a wheelchair because I had hurt my ankle. I remember looking in there and he was on the bed with wires all coming off him and his face was all cut because his helmet had come off in the accident. I just couldn't believe it. I just broke down and cried and cried and I said: "I've killed a man" and he was twitching because he was in a coma. I said: "Right, that's it, I've killed a guy, I'm going to quit racing, motor cycling is a crazy business." Fortunately, Roger Marshall was with me and he said "It's OK, it's OK" and I was released from hospital, but Franco had to stay because he was in a coma for two weeks.

'Then he came out of it and he's made a full recovery, but it was real tough. Driving back Roger said, "You can't quit, you're going to be World Champion" and I said I was going to quit and I cried just about all the way to England. I wasn't old enough to be able to rationalize it. It hurt a lot. I can still see it happening over and over again. I rang my dad and he said come home to the family but I went back up to Lincolnshire, where I was living then and sat around for two weeks. A lot of the press were calling me a murderer, saying I shouldn't have been in the race. The press came down on me really hard and they wouldn't leave me alone.

'Anyway, he started to get better, and I was contracted to ride a race and he came out of the coma. I was kept updated and that made me feel better and Roger said: "We've got to get back racing. You've got to get back on that bike." So I went to Donington and I thought I'd just have a steady ride and I ended up winning the race. Then Franco came out of hospital, I was feeling a bit more confident in myself, the press laid off me. Even though it was a bad accident, it was kind of a good accident in another way—if you can phrase an accident like this—because it left a maturing scar on my mind that always tells me about the danger, always tells me not to overstep the mark, because people do get killed, can get seriously hurt. It's like a little bit of a reminder which has stayed in the back of my mind. Don't forget what happened.'

The world moved on, of course, while all this unfolded, moved on to Spa a week after Assen where Roberts won, Spencer second, and that was 105 points to 100. Then came to Silverstone.

'Everything,' Roberts says, 'went badly for me that year.' Silverstone was an utterly tragic event, riven by chaos, confusion, and accusations, and although this is no place to examine all the aspects of that, the consequences must be faced because they are central to our story. Roberts took pole with 1 minute 28.00, Spencer immediately behind him with 1 minute 29.38. Spencer took the lead, Roberts stalking him from fourth place until he grasped the lead as they (and Mamola) turned into Stowe Corner at the far end of the extremely fast Hangar Straight. That was the third lap.

A couple of laps later two riders, Norman Brown and Peter Huber, crashed. Both were killed. The race was not stopped immediately and when it was the acrimony began. Who had hoisted which flags and when and where? Some riders were very angry indeed. Some officials became very angry indeed. Eventually the race was restarted, the second running to be counted as part two and the result to be combined with where the riders had been been before the crash.

Roberts says: 'They did have a second half and they called it all a race. I don't think they should have done. It should have been a completely new race. I mean, you don't really get going until after five laps—when (essentially) the race had been stopped. It meant Spencer was second, not fourth. That still stands out in my mind.' Spencer had been second before the crash, and although he came fourth in part two he held second place on the combined placings. However you want to define it, Kenny Roberts won the race and that tightened it up to 117–115. There were two races to run.

Approaching Anderstorp, Roberts judged that the Yamaha might have an edge. It's tight but there is a long straight and he'd be feeding a lot of power into the Yamaha along that. He was 'surprised the Honda went so well'—Spencer was on pole a full 1^1/$_2$ seconds quicker than Roberts. In the race Spencer was away fast, Roberts stalking him again until lap seven when he took the lead. Spencer clung on and with nine laps left was right there but couldn't get through. At moments he would thrust the Honda virtually alongside the Yamaha but no further. The last lap would be decisive. Ahead lay the right-loop of the Sodra Kurvan then the straight, 800 metres long (it was also an airport runway) then the right-angled right-hander Norra Kurvan, then a breathless sprint to another right-angled right-hander called Laktar Kurvan, then the breathless sprint to the line a couple of hundred metres away.

As they came out of the Sodra, Roberts had screwed so much power down that the Yamaha's front wheel began to lift. He knew the Yamaha had more power than the Honda, he needed it all, and for an instant kept the power on. Still the front wheel rose. He eased the throttle back and the fractional deceleration brought the wheel down, but Spencer had within the instant caught him. Spencer tucked in behind and slipstreamed all the way down the straight and the Norra Kurvan was rushing at them at 160 miles an hour.

At the approach to the corner Spencer snaked out to the right and drew level. He had the inside line. 'It was the slowest part of the course and I suppose we were doing around 40 miles an hour,' Roberts says. 'No, I wasn't expecting him to try it there . . . He was "underneath" me—on the inside—and I didn't see him until I was leaning in to the corner. Desperate? Yeah. Was I surprised? Yeah. I was suddenly in a no-win situation. If I had taken the racing line—and there was only one line through that corner—we'd have met in the apex and we'd both have fallen. My first thought was to save the bike because I had to try and save the race.' Now Roberts caressed the brakes—just another instant, but easing them off, easing them off, and his front wheel was fractionally in front. It was too late. Spencer was still there on the inside, Roberts—far to the left of the racing line—still trying to dive back onto the inside in front of Spencer. The track wasn't wide enough and they both went off. Neither fell. Spencer got control faster than Roberts and set off, winning by 0.16 of a second.

'I was very angry after,' said Roberts. 'I can take losing, but I wasn't about to risk my life so he could win a World Championship. Afterwards what I said to him is not printable. I told him it wasn't worth dying for. I told him if he ever did it again I'd throw him off the victory car.'

Afterwards, too, Roberts stood on the podium alone—it was a temporary wooden structure placed on a piece of grass—waiting for Spencer. He stood erect. His hands were locked behind his back, his face sombre. He knew it now: Spencer 132 points against his 127, and there was only one race to run—Imola. Second place would be enough for Spencer to become the youngest ever 500 World Champion. Imola turned on another American whom we have not yet met, another Californian—from Upland, a small place midway between Los Angeles and the town of San Bernadino—who had been competing in Grand Prix racing for two years and, during this season of 1983, had partnered Roberts at Yamaha. He had 68 points but that was no longer relevant. What he could do was win the championship for Roberts by coming second and holding Spencer down in third place. He was called Eddie Lawson.

Hysteria gripped Imola because Italians like shoot-outs. Roberts, who had been in California for the month since Anderstorp relaxing, took pole, Spencer second. Roberts had stated his intention to retire after the race. That, all else aside, was a powerful stimulant. Lucchinelli, in his last race for Honda, might—so the whisper went—try and beat Spencer himself. Lucchinelli was Italian, of course . . . and here we are at Imola with 100,000 spectators rooting for the local boy. Lucchinelli lived at Imola while the others were from Shreveport, Louisiana; Modesto, California; Upland, California.

Spencer burst away from the line with Lucchinelli behind him, Roberts third, Lawson lost somewhere back around tenth. Lawson was out of the equation. If Spencer won, it didn't matter anyway. What would Lucchinelli do? If he overtook Spencer, and if Roberts overtook Spencer, Roberts was champion. A great finale for a great career. A fitting end. But Lucchinelli wasn't flirting with anything like that; Lucchinelli was holding Roberts in third place. Again Roberts stalked, waited, composed himself, and on lap three went through. He battered the lap record by 2 seconds, he covered the 5.040 kilometres in 1 minute 53.36, an average speed of 160.056 kph and each moment brought him closer and closer to Spencer. He caught and passed him on lap eight. He'd been harrassing him for several laps, drawing level, staying there, trying to force an error, and now, as they moved away from the start-finish line, he went through.

He couldn't intimidate Spencer in any way because Spencer was slotted into that championship-winning second place. What he could do was slow the pace to allow Lawson—now up to fourth and back in the equation—to get past Lucchinelli and get to Spencer; but Spencer saw it all, responded, and took the lead. Desperation drove Roberts on, he retook the lead, and then, 'slowing it down was all I could do, maybe as much as a couple of seconds a lap, but that wasn't enough'.

On lap seventeen Lawson hauled himself past Lucchinelli, but there were only eight laps left. Lawson went for Spencer, and on lap twenty the gap was down to 5 seconds and Lawson could see Spencer. Just in front, Roberts was riding like an old master, using every corner to slow the pace further. But if Roberts was going slowly Spencer could go past him and increase the pace, shedding Lawson whenever he liked. He did it with four laps to go and all at once Roberts had only one tactic left: to win the race and hope. Lawson, valiant to the end, would run third, several seconds off the pace. Roberts moved back into the lead and Spencer positioned himself 50 metres behind and remained there. There was simply no point in risking anything else.

The last lap was a long one. All machines break down and until Frederick Burdette Spencer came through the chicane behind Roberts he was still at the mercy of mishap; but now he could virtually see the line, only now did he say to himself: I've done it.

Roberts took the race and made a last great gesture, a vast wheelie. Exactly 1.23 seconds later Spencer did the same thing. The hysteria engulfed them; the paddock became a madhouse and Spencer needed a police escort to reach the press conference.

As Roberts says: 'Slowing it down was all I could do . . .'

Spencer was 21. Honda had first contested a 500 cc Grand Prix race at Hockenheim on 22 May 1966. It was the year Redman, who rode it, crashed at Spa; the year Hailwood finished second to Agostini in the championship, just as he would the year after. Now, these many years later, Honda had done it; they had their 500 champion. As the crowds ebbed away into the stately, fading splendour of the town of Imola, as the transporters prepared for the long journey home, there were ghosts in the paddock. Mike Hailwood had been dead for eighteen months, killed in a car crash in England. Many in that paddock had him in their thoughts.

ELEVEN

Spencer Into Two Does Go

The Bavarian with a face that looked like it had been hewn out of Alpine stone wasn't expecting the approach, wasn't expecting it at all, on that August afternoon in 1984. He'd started 'at a young age tinkering with motor cycles and I had my first bike when I was eleven. I rode it round the fields of Inning [population 3,000, some 37 kilometres south of Munich] and I fell off often, but I wasn't discouraged. I learnt from falling off.'

In time Toni Mang would ride for Kawasaki and remain with them from 1978 until 1982, winning twenty 250 cc races and eight 350 cc races. He took four World Championships but he missed 1983 because of a skiing accident and this year of 1984 was with Yamaha. The approach came from Mr Eistner, racing manager of Honda Germany, initially to do some testing of a prototype 250. Mang was surprised and interested. 'My first reaction was one of interest because the steps Honda were taking in a new technical direction impressed me: different things, like an aluminium frame and a different type of engine construction.'

Mang would contest 1985 on a Honda, but always ran his own team. 'Basically, I was given a budget and I managed the team. It wasn't a Honda operation, not at all. Honda did give advice and they were around, of course, but the mechanics were always German and I was the boss.'

In retrospect, 1984 was a strange year. Lawson took the 500 title for Yamaha but everybody wondered about that. He had 142 points but Randy Mamola, enticed from retirement, joined Honda after the first two races of the season and finished second on 111. If he hadn't missed those two races . . .

Then there was Spencer, fourth behind Raymond Roche on 87 points. His season was haunted by crashes. In practice for the South African Grand Prix his back wheel gave way. 'As I went into the corner the front end just went light, the back collapsed, and the next thing I knew I was sliding into the straw bales.' His ankle was hurt and he left South Africa in a wheelchair. He crashed again in the Trans-Atlantic Trophy at Donington. He crashed again at Laguna Seca. If he hadn't . . .

A montage of Jarama, 1985.
Above *Ron Haslam on the 500.*

Wayne Gardner on the 500.

Randy Mamola, who fell off the 500.

Two studies of Freddie Spencer who won on the 500.

Here he is to prove it.

Stuart Hall, one half of the double act.

BBC
Manchester

Then there was young Gardner, struggling with (or rather without) sponsorship. He would finish seventh in the table on 33 points, having missed half the season.

In retrospect, too, the end of 1984 was more significant than the racing itself. Talks were going on between Honda and Rothmans which, when they came to fruition, created a partnership of mutual expertise akin to Formula One car racing. Honda knew all about racing bikes, Rothmans knew all about salesmanship, press relations, publicity, image building, and so forth. Amongst other things an invasion of pretty girls in Rothmans uniforms was happily on the way.

Spencer tested Honda's 250 in the autumn. (The last time Honda had contested a 250 race was at Fuji on 14 October 1967 when Ralph Bryans won.) Spencer liked the 250 and the idea of 'variety'—namely, contesting the 250 and 500—and what they'd do was very simple: keep the 500 championship as the priority and see how it went. 'When I realized that Freddie was in the 250 class I was very surprised,' Mang says, 'negatively surprised because I didn't know that he was going to ride. Basically, nobody knew. There had been a lot of rumours, but I was only 100 per cent sure when they unpacked Spencer's 250 at Kyalami for the first race of the season.' Mang, the 250 specialist, would otherwise have been very short odds indeed to take the title himself. 'My relationship with him? First, there was a sponsorship difference. I had Marlboro and he had Rothmans. Second, Freddie was the official factory rider. The contact between us was minimal; we hardly ever saw each other and there was a little bit of jealousy because I suddenly realized that Freddie was getting all the good bits. That was the relationship we had that year. No, I don't know him. Spencer doesn't give you a chance to get to know him. He is very elusive. It wasn't a difficult situation because I never really had a chance to beat him. The most time I saw him was when we stood on the podium next to each other.'

Spencer himself, excited by extensive testing at Daytona in March on the 250, was becoming more and more intrigued by the double—this double which, the historians kept insisting, had never been done, not even by Hailwood or, more recently, by Roberts. Nor had any rider won the 250 and 500 at the same Grand Prix for twelve years; the tragic Finn Jarno Saarinen had done the double at Ricard and the Salzburgring in 1973 and had won the 250 at Hockenheim but was halted in the 500 by a broken chain and then killed at Monza in the fourth race of the season.

Spencer rightly saw the double as a personal challenge and after he had won Daytona on 8 March on the new works Honda RS 250-RW he sensed it was possible. He'd been pondering it since the previous autumn. 'We talked about it in 1984 when Honda brought out their 250 cc production racer and as the year went on we talked about it more and more. I rode the 250 for the first time at Suzuka in early September and it wasn't a bad little machine. I tested it again in Australia and then raced it for the first time at Daytona, together with the new NSR 500 and I knew from that moment that the double was possible.' There would, of course, be problems. The 'mental aspect' was the hardest of them because Spencer had to 'separate' the two classes in his mind at each meeting, absorbing information on the 250, forgetting all about it when he got onto the 500, and 'then afterwards remember all the details about both'.

Spencer took the 250 from Mang at Kyalami but Lawson kept him in second place in the 500. He took the 500 in Spain and was leading the 250 when the exhaust pipe split. In that 500 Gardner went off the track, returned, and finished a brave fourth. Nearly a thousand miles away in a very unglamorous BBC studio Stuart Hall was presenting his Sunday afternoon radio programme. This was several hours of a quirky mixture: in-jokes, hard-nosed reporting of live sporting events, all leavened by middle-of-the-road music. Hall knew that Gardner had gone in to the race with an arm injury and was so impressed by his fourth place that, on an impulse, he asked Nick Harris, who was at Jarama covering the race for the BBC, to try and get Gardner to a microphone. Harris, well known to all the riders, obliged. After a few minutes Hall heard Gardner's Australian drawl-growl echoing down the line from Spain.

Hall began professionally, flattering Gardner—a total stranger to him—in order to draw him out. 'Look,' Hall said, 'this is an amazing story . . .'

'It was nothing.'

'So I said: "Tell me the story"—anticipating that if he was a lesser sportsman he'd probably fabricate some story of how he'd twisted all his ligaments doing something heroic on the bike. Gardner replied: "I did it arm-wrestling with the mechanics."

'Then he told me how he chewed suppositories to make him race faster. He was obviously prepared to tell you the truth. I said: "You're my adopted son, I shall follow your career with interest and eventually you'll be World Champion. We are discovering you as of today." '

And so an amazing relationship was born, or rather a great double-act: Gardner and Hall, entertainers. 'It took off and people with no interest in

A montage of Austria, 1985.
Ron Haslam in action.

motor cycling whatsoever were swept up into the vortex of it. He used to come on and tell me his escapades. Anybody can tell you the story of a race but it was what went on away from the circuit which really fascinated me. His character was emerging. They couldn't get over it at the BBC because they said: "You're not interviewing Wayne Gardner, it's like telephone conversations to which we are eavesdropping." I'd say to him: "How did you get on in France?" He'd say: "Well, you know, we had a beano (party) with a few bimbos (female company) and me and Christian Sarron got drunk and we got this dog drunk as well." Then there were the brushes with the law—he was always in trouble . . .'

Spencer was second in both the 250 and 500 at Hockenheim, and then they all went to Mugello. The meeting was called the Nations Grand Prix, which is a more expansive way of saying the Italian Grand Prix. Honda (reportedly) exercised pressure on the organizers to alter the running

Takazuni Katayama in action.

Spencer moves ahead of Toni Mang in the 250.

Spencer moves ahead of them all to win the 500.

Spencer looks mildly stunned.

order so that the 250 followed the 500, emphasizing clearly where their priorities still lay. Spencer himself was unconcerned. He was, as he said, perfectly fit and two races in the one afternoon was fine with him in whichever order they came. This was an echo of childhood and the astonishing variety of machines Spencer had ridden then. As so often happens, adolescence is spent absorbing experiences which, though you have no way of knowing it at the time, are directly applicable in adulthood.

Spencer *was* an elusive recluse. Access to the motor-home was not conducted on a free-and-easy 'hello-how-are-you? basis. Right of entry was rationed or denied. Spencer reasonably pleaded that he had a mind-expanding amount of information to disseminate and what he didn't need was to transmit information to endless journalists. It's unfair in the circumstances, but you have to compare this silence from the citadel of the motor-home with Gardner confessing all live on national BBC radio to Hall. It is fairer to say that in 1985 Spencer was the best rider in the world and one of the best riders the world had ever seen, and he was under unusual if self-imposed pressure. Gardner was moving towards the same sort of excellence but from a wildly differing direction.

The 500 did precede the 250 on 26 May 1985. Spencer was quickest in qualifying for the 500 (2 minutes 01.49 seconds, next Roche 2 minutes 01.67), but only second quickest in the 250 (Martin Wimmer, German, Yamaha, 2 minutes 04.60; Spencer 2 minutes 04.96).

In the 500 race Spencer was positive and prudent, a devastating combination. Ron Haslam on another Honda set off like the furies, but Spencer bided his time, went serenely by on lap two and stayed there, holding a 6-second lead over Lawson for large tracts of the race. When Lawson accepted that he simply couldn't catch Spencer that gap widened towards 10 seconds. It also widened the points gap to 7—Spencer 54, Lawson 47.

Thirty minutes later Spencer was in the 250, positive and prudent again. Wimmer burnt his clutch before the start and went only as far as lap two. Spencer started slowly and came on like a tide. He was up to second behind the Venezuelan Carlos Lavado by lap thirteen out of twenty-two, was past Lavado three laps later, and, despite a slide, was not seen again. He finished 2.80 seconds in front of Lavado and said in his cryptic way that the two races hadn't been a problem, only the rostrum had—a 'mob scene'. To an ascetic man and a recluse we can imagine how

After the crash at Assen. Spencer can only watch.

ungratifying that might have been. The true gratification was having won both races.

Amazingly, Spencer did it all again a week later at the Salzburgring, and this time totally: pole and victory in the 250, pole and victory in the 500. Actually, it was closer than this suggests, although Spencer won the 250 comfortably enough, 5.58 seconds in front of Mang. But the 500 . . . Spencer bided his time again, seventh after the opening lap, third on the third, in the lead on the fourth. He stayed there but with twelve laps left rain fell, as Spencer kept (literally) pointing out with his gloved hand each time he crossed the line. They stopped the race on lap eighteen with Spencer holding a lead of 2.18 seconds over Lawson. Then—chaos. The rain stopped and no one was sure which tyres to fit for the remaining seven laps. Slicks? Wets? Some changed and changed again and the chaos increased. After an hour the race was restarted and would be run over a further fourteen laps. Lawson knew, of course, that he had to beat Spencer by more than the 2.18 seconds to win it overall and he took the lead on lap nine. He squeezed out a gap, Spencer responded, and as they crossed the line into the final lap nervous hands flicked stopwatches. The gap was 1.9 seconds. Lawson went for it and at the last corner had reduced the gap to 2.5 seconds—just enough to give him the race—but as Lawson tried to cut past Takazumi Katayama—on a Honda—the Japanese inadvertently blocked him. Lawson did get through but he'd lost a flickering millisecond. He crossed the line 2.15 seconds ahead of Spencer and it was 0.03 too little. Spencer still led both championships.

At Rijeka, Spencer won the 250 but, trying to overtake Haslam in the 500, his knee struck a straw bale. It almost pitched him off. The pain was so intense that as he tracked Lawson, who was in the lead, he thought several times that he was going to faint. He was sure bones were broken. He did finish, 21.76 seconds behind Lawson, slowed the bike, and collapsed. He sat beside it on the tarmac while team members took his helmet off and unzipped his leathers. He looked stunned. He limped as he was helped away, supported on either side, and his face contorted in agony. He was immediately X-rayed, but no bones were broken. He headed for Shreveport and rest before Assen, only two weeks away. (On a lighter note, Gardner had what was described as an 'aerodynamic back pad'—a sort of fin—strapped to him in practice so that as he crouched behind the faring it would make the air flow smoothly over him. I won't report what Gardner thought of it, but he didn't wear it in the race . . .')

At Assen, Spencer took the 250 comfortably again. The 500 was run in heavy rain and midway round the opening lap the bunch arranged themselves for a right-hander. Haslam was in the lead, taking the right-hander wide; Didier de Radigues was just behind him; Spencer was fractionally further back but on the inside. Spencer, thinking clinically amidst all the churning spray, could have taken de Radigues—for an instant he had a wheel in front—but that would leave him nowhere to go because Haslam himself would be turning into the corner. Spencer braked and began to turn in to the corner. He did not—and could not—see Christian Sarron (Yamaha) coming hard behind him; too hard. But the crowd saw it, this packed, sombre crowd huddled under umbrellas. They saw Sarron's front wheel already off line, pointed towards the grass of the infield of the corner.

A montage of Mamola at Misano. Cranking it over ...

... and cranking it even further over.

Sarron lost it. The bike twisted sideways as it fell, shedding Sarron in front of it and they both careened into Spencer, striking him exactly as he had the Honda banked over at the apex of the corner. The Honda was knocked from him and now it careened away, draping Spencer over the Yamaha; and the Yamaha still slid forward. Spencer got a free ride to the muddy grass of the outfield. He clambered to his feet, took the few steps to where the Honda lay, but couldn't restart it. The bike was stuck in gear.

At Spa a week later the sun shone, Mamola took the lead in the 500, and Spencer swept imperiously by, beating Lawson by 6 seconds. It was not so tight in the 250, in which he beat Lavado by over 12 seconds. At Le Mans he took the 250 from Mang by 9.82 seconds and had some genuine good fortune in the 500. Lawson's Yamaha didn't fire on the start line and he had to push it. When it did fire the leaders were long gone, although Spencer found himself under a sustained attack from Gardner and Christian Sarron (Yamaha). Gardner's tyre broke up on lap fourteen of the twenty-nine and he was out of it, but Sarron set fastest lap and on lap sixteen was poised to take Spencer. Spencer flowed smoothly past a back marker, Neil Robinson (Suzuki), but at a right-hander Sarron, doing the same, went slightly wide and the bike slithered from him. Spencer won

Gardner: a victory salute at Assen in 1986

Raymond Roche, sixth.

the race from Raymond Roche.

At Silverstone, Gardner and Hall finally met. 'He offered me a ride round the track on his bike,' says Hall. 'I thought: It's slightly unconventional but I'll accept. Unfortunately, there was something wrong with the bike and we couldn't do it.'

The race, run in a storm, gave Spencer the chance of becoming 250 champion. All he needed was fourth place; but Silverstone in a storm is a place for extreme circumspection because it is such a fast track and grey water gathers unseen in pools and puddles. Spencer decided to run a hard compound rear rain tyre which didn't give him perfect grip—from time to time the bike wobbled alarmingly. He rode a lonely race to be sure that people ahead didn't fall and take him with them. He finished fourth, 34.06 seconds behind the winner, Mang. Spencer judged the conditions to have been the worst he had ever known. He said candidly that he hadn't enjoyed the race: 'I wanted to go slower but knew I had to finish fourth to win the title.' In points that sodden afternoon it was like this: Spencer 127, Mang 97, Wimmer 69, Lavado 67.

Spencer changed into dry leathers and got on the 500. It was still raining hard. Spencer was on pole, Lawson immediately alongside him. At Copse Corner Spencer was already in the lead and never lost it. He demonstrated absolute mastery, his handling of the bike having an almost uncanny certainty to it. Lawson urged himself up to second place but was still 8.32 seconds behind when Spencer took the chequered flag. The points table stood at Spencer 126, Lawson 106, Sarron 72, Gardner 61. Only Anderstorp and Misano remained. At Anderstorp, Spencer would exercise prudence of a different kind by not contesting the 250. There was no need now, and besides all the proving had been done. He had won South Africa, had been leading at Jarama when the exhaust blew, had finished second at Hockenheim, had won Mugello, the Salzburgring, Rijeka, Assen, Spa, and at Le Mans. It was almost complete dominance.

At Anderstorp it rained but stopped before the race started. And now, as the minutes ticked away to the start, a strong wind began to dry the track making it difficult to decide which tyres to use. Spencer went for a harder compound front, speculating that the track would become completely dry; Lawson took the softer route. Haslam seized the lead, Spencer tracked him and, at a left-hander, slipped effortlessly through. That was lap two. Soon enough Lawson was behind him but the softer tyres weren't helping and Spencer pulled away. On lap eighteen Gardner took Lawson but ran out of petrol on the last lap so that Lawson finished second, although a huge 22.80 seconds behind. Spencer had done the double. He said very quietly: 'Now that it's all over it's just a relief.'

It was a relief for Murray Walker, too. 'I got the BBC to televize Anderstorp (they don't usually take bike Grands Prix) and it was the dullest and worst covered race I've ever seen. A *Spanish* production company with *three* cameras—one of them unmanned and permanently fixed. They stayed with Spencer the *whole race*. From the visual point of view no one else was in it.'

The rest was an anti-climax. Spencer didn't go to Misano. At the first race of the next season, Jarama, took pole and was in the lead when he had acute tendinitis in the right wrist. He came into the pits and would only ride once more that season. Of him Gardner says: 'We weren't team-

The British Grand Prix in 1986 was a beast. It rained …

… and rained.

Gardner didn't seem to mind …

... and won it.

A curious Gardner wheelie in France in 1986, where he was only fifth.

The dangerous moments: the start of the Swedish Grand Prix, 1986.

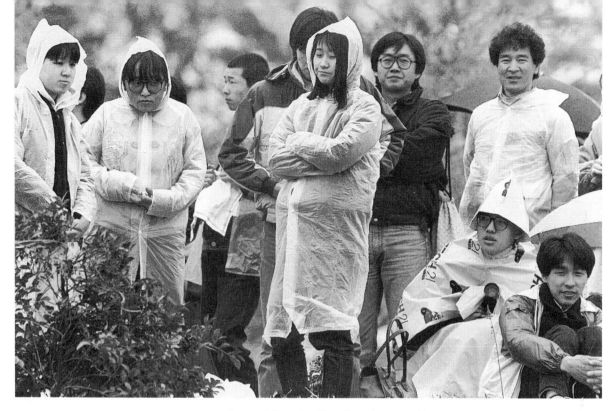

Suzuka 1987 was wet. Some dressed for it ...

... some didn't.

mates. I was riding for Honda Britain and he was a works rider for the factory in Japan. I was trying to make a name for myself and of course he was trying to stop anybody coming along and taking his position, which is normal. Freddie is very . . . I don't know how you'd call it . . . clinical, in everything he says he does, and it's taken out of textbooks, you know. I'm more the opposite. I'm more your general, natural person, I guess. Did I get close to him? No. Nobody gets close to him. Nobody understands him and I think he's got this very aloof image. He hides at the race track, he only talks to some people. I like to enjoy my racing, I like to talk to everybody, just being myself. You could never really talk to him. When you did see him it was just a few words and then off. I don't think he's really like that, I think he's shrouded himself in order to build this image around himself. I don't agree with it but that's maybe the way his personality is.'

Don't expect too much sentiment in motor bike racing.

TWELVE

New Worlds, Old Worlds

I N 1986 Carlos Lavado won the World 250 cc Championship on a Yamaha with four Honda riders—Sito Pons, Dominique Sarron, Toni Mang, and Jean-François Balde—immediately behind him. Yamaha were stronger still in the 500, filling five of the first six places. Only Gardner split them by finishing second to Eddie Lawson. Gardner was now a factory rider and from the moment Spencer pulled into the pits at Jarama was effectively their hope in the 500. He responded by winning that Spanish Grand Prix from Lawson, which brought enormous pressure to bear on him. Honda made deft attempts to calm and reassure him, telling him to ride his own races and not to worry; but Gardner knew full well that 'there are two hundred people at Honda Racing Corporation whose only purpose is to produce a bike that wins the World Championship. All their efforts were riding with me.'

By his very nature Gardner had always been a man likely to respond to pressure by challenging it head on rather than mutely absorbing it. Across 1986 he set himself to do that, finishing in a solid second place behind Lawson at the Nürburgring in May and at the Salzburgring in early June. That Austrian Grand Prix meeting carried within it two other significant developments. Spencer made a brief comeback and was sixteenth, which, if it meant nothing else, confirmed that Gardner was on his own. In practice for the 250, Mang had a crash which broke bones in his foot: 'I was already having problems with my team.' He was not, of course, a Honda works rider and this crash gave Mang time to reflect. The reflection would have direct consequences on 1987.

Gardner continued to hunt Lawson, winning Assen and Silverstone and ending it with 117 points against Lawson's 139. Gardner had handled the pressure well, and had grown in stature. He was now poised to become a force in his own right. Mang, a matured old campaigner whose career had begun in 1978 and who had won four championships for Kawasaki (the 250 in 1980 and 1981, the 350 in 1981 and 1982) decided to make fundamental alterations to his career: 'What I did at the end of 1986 was to change the team around, I sorted it out to suit myself. Technically,

*Steps to Gardner's champion-
ship. Victory in Spain.*

*Victory at Monza (although
here he's behind Eddie
Lawson).*

Victory in Yugoslavia.

I understood the bike because I had the advantage of having ridden it for the two years before, so I was able to set up a team that was motivated and that understood the system I needed. *I* was motivated and it all came together.'

Suzuka was the first Japanese Grand Prix for twenty years, but it rained and the results were misleading. Gardner was second to Mamola (Yamaha) in the 500, Mang eighth in the 250. The meeting was remarkable, and unique, because Masaru Kobayashi, a 27-year old, won the 250—his only World Championship appearance. His mastery of the wet was as remarkable as the result.

This is how the season unfolded after Suzuka: Gardner won in Spain, Mang crashed, Gardner had electrical trouble at Hockenheim and was tenth, Mang won; Gardner and Mang won at Monza and at the Salzburgring; Gardner won at Rijeka, Mang seventh; Gardner was second to Lawson at Assen, Mang won; it rained at Le Mans, where Gardner was fourth and Mang crashed on lap fifteen. It meant that just past the midway point of the season Gardner led the 500 with 93 points from Mamola (81), Lawson (64), Haslam (60), and Mang was second in the 250. That table was Reinhold Roth (Honda) 82, Mang 67, Pons 53, Jacques Cornu (Honda) 42, Dominique Sarron (Honda) 39.

Gardner always did like the British Grand Prix. 'I probably owe more to the British than the Australians. I didn't have any help in Australia at the beginning of my career. I even asked for one of those Government grants for sporting people so I could try and win world championships but I was told: "What's motor cycling? We've got some tennis stars who are more important", and I was only asking for 2,000 dollars for my air ticket to get to Britain. When I did get to Britain the spectators were fantastic, they treated me like one of their own. I've got some wonderfully good memories of England.' That of course brought another dimension of pressure. Donington Park, which had taken the race over from Silverstone, was 'virtually my home Grand Prix'. He was wanted for so many interviews that he found concentrating on the racing extremely difficult; and for the race—again typical of the man—he decided to risk a new 'sticky' Michelin tyre which had been fast in qualifying, where he had taken pole comfortably, but might not last the thirty laps (120.69 kilometres). Gardner's thinking was to get himself a flyer, go off into the dis-

Nearer and nearer in Brazil.

tance and, if necessary, nurse the tyre home towards the end. It went wrong. Gardner started to slip 'n slide and couldn't catch Lawson. Mang won the 250 after a seven-way struggle at the head of the field. In 1987, 250cc racing was like that.

Gardner won Anderstorp and so did Mang; Gardner won Brno and so did Mang; but at Misano Gardner was only third, Mang only sixth. We had better look at the points again. Gardner 145, Mamola 124, Lawson 115, Haslam 69. Mang 117, Roth 91, Pons 75, Sarron 67.

Jarama was hot for the Portuguese Grand Prix, which had been moved to Spain because it would attract a much bigger crowd there. Jarama was also chaotic because 100,000 people descended on the circuit and the

Just before the tears began at Goiania.

organizers were barely able to cope with them. Gardner struggled to finish the 500. The water in the radiator boiled away and being on the bike
was 'like a slow dying process'. He made it fourth, and that was 153 points
against Mamola's 136.

Mang faced something entirely different in the 250. 'Although I didn't
need to win the race to become World Champion I wanted to win it
because that's a nice way of becoming World Champion, and whilst we
still had Brazil and Argentina afterwards I felt a need to win it in Spain. At
overseas Grands Prix you often have to improvise and I wanted to avoid
that. Jarama was extremely hot.' Mang made a decision that is perhaps
typical of him. He did not want to be told by pit board signals where Roth
was in the race. Mang would disregard Roth; he would run his own race,
go for the big win and devil take the hindmost. For that victory he would
be directly challenged by the Spaniard Juan Garriga on a Yamaha and
Garriga would have the full weight of 100,000 spectators behind him. The
temperature reached towards 40 degrees, what Mang describes as
the limit of tolerance. Thirty-six bikes laid their power down through the
heat haze and Roth took the lead. Mang settled himself into fourth place.
He knew there was a long journey ahead, 102.672 kilometres of it. He
took the lead when he was good and ready and tried to pull away, but
Garriga caught him and slipped through on the outside just after the
start-finish line. Mang tracked Garriga and overtook him on the inside at
the same place as they came round again, the Rothmans Honda twitching
as Mang braked for the corner. The corner was a right-handed loop and
within it Garriga darted inside and retook Mang. Somehow it was sym-
bolic of the 250 season, tight, combative, challenging. Mang edged in

front and crossed the line 0.79 seconds ahead. He was utterly exhausted and close to tears.

'Rothmans, my sponsors, gave me an enormous party at an hotel near the airport. It was tremendous. There were tons and tons of people'—among them, inevitably, Gardner. 'I wanted,' Gardner says, 'to do something different so I went and got dressed up as a woman! As usual we were all thrown in the pool. I needed some dry clothes so I borrowed them from one of the Rothmans girls—a skirt and top—and I went to the disco like that. You've got to create fun, huh? It's better than being a boring person. I've got to enjoy myself. In 1987 all I did was have a good time. I was drinking, although not at the races of course, but I was having a few parties during the week, going out and doing crazy things and everyone couldn't believe how I was drinking—but, you see, I wasn't drinking heavily, I was enjoying myself.'

Gardner could take the 500 championship at Goiania, but almost didn't get into the race at all. On the straight in practice he missed his braking point, thundered off and stopped just before the armco. But he took pole and his tactics were the same as Donington: get the flyer, open up a gap, control the race from the front. He was sure the tyres would last this time. He seized the first corner, a right-hander, from Mamola and as he completed the opening lap the pit board told him he had a 1-second lead. 'I can win it from here,' he thought, which was true. Mamola and Lawson, ironically, had tyre troubles themselves.

A montage of Toni Mang as he'll be remembered. The gladiator ...

'I knew I had to finish in front of Randy to win the championship [says Gardner] and I'd set pole, so I was confident; but it was tiring because we'd already had thirteen races and I had to push myself that one more time for that one more hour. I was wound up a lot because the pressure was on me. So I sat alone and tried to think it through and mentally prepare myself. In fact I prepared myself for that race more than I had ever done before, planning it, visualizing what it was going to be like. I imagined different situations and then I tried to put my thoughts into action.

'I could have run around and just finished, but I figured I wouldn't be concentrating as much if I did that as if I was trying. So I set myself a target, which was to win the race. I also wanted to win it in style. I got a good start and left them.

'The last lap was where a dream was going to be fulfilled and I thought: Is it really going to happen? It was like a little childhood dream all the way from when I'd been a kid reading magazines with the great riders on the covers and I'd thought then that maybe it would be me one day. I remember thinking that nothing can happen now . . . I hope. I remember thinking . . . I hope I don't fall off, I hope the bike doesn't seize, doesn't overheat. I was watching the temperature gauge, watching the lap board. The last lap it was especially tense. I tried to nurse the bike home. It seemed to last a long time because I was studying everything so intensely. Everything slowed down. I kept thinking: Am I ever going to finish? I was afraid of doing anything wrong . . . I had visions of falling off . . . or doing something stupid. But it all went perfectly well . . .'

Up there on the rostrum, amid the champagne spray, Gardner was in control of himself until the team manager, Jerry Burgess said: 'Wayne, this is your day.' The tears began and when his girlfriend Donna gave him a hug and a kiss 'the tears just wouldn't stop'.

Gardner gives a fascinating insight into how a man reacts once the

... always ready with a wave ...

... and a familiar presence on the podium.

With wife Collette and Gardner.

The 250 at Assen in 1988.
Dominique Sarron collides
with Sito Pons.

Sarron goes into the barrier.
(He's the helmet on the left,
glimpsed in the dust storm.)

Trying to get the bike upright …

tears have been dried and self-control has been resumed. 'I knew I was World Champion but I couldn't accept it because I'd been chasing this dream since boyhood, chasing, chasing, chasing, and when it happened it was an empty feeling. I thought: "Well, what do I do now? I've come to the end of the dream." So it was a sad feeling in a way, yeah, it was sad because it was over, but in another way of course I was happy and so were the whole team. That night? Oh dear, oh dear. That was a good night. It was still hard to believe I was World Champion. It felt really strange, I still had that empty feeling. We went back to the hotel and there was a big party and we were drinking champagne. There was a big fountain in the hotel so they dumped me in that and I was swimming round and round. We were drinking and drinking and drinking and yelling and screaming and there was water everywhere and it was great.'

This intoxication didn't last far into 1988. Gardner was second at

Suzuka to an American called Kevin Schwantz (Suzuki) after a long and dour struggle that became so intense that near the end Gardner went clean off the circuit and rejoined by way of a helicopter pad. Mang incidentally won the 250. Gardner was second behind Lawson at Laguna Seca, Mang eighth in the 250. Gardner was third at Jarama, Mang crashed.

All this did not prevent Gardner from bubbling down the line to Stuart Hall on BBC Radio from Jarama. 'I've been really busy, it's unbelievable and I think that's part of the problem. We are having a lot of brake problems, inconsistent levers and so on. I got back home at the end of last season and I was very, very lucky because I won the championship at the right time. It was Australia's bicentenary and we had no other world champion. Really, for all the sports presentations and so on the major person I had to contend with was Pat Cash [who had beaten Ivan Lendl in the Wimbledon men's singles final]. I got to meet a lot of people, I got to meet Prince Charles and Lady Di, which was nice, great.

'It was hard work and it's kind of good to get back on the track for a holiday! I never stopped. Everyone was looking at me with big eyes, they were saying: "Oh yes, that's the World Champion". The eyes are on you all right and they're also saying: "He's not allowed to do anything wrong, crash or anything". The other day I went head over heels and landed on my back so I'm glad I've got that out of the way.

'We've just come from America [Laguna Seca] and we had renta-cars and of course everybody knows how you abuse renta-cars—sorry renta-car business. I had a friend, Colin, from Australia there and he was going around with me. I was in one car, he was in another. We pulled up at these traffic lights. I put my car in reverse and of course we touched. I looked across the road and there was a policeman. He said: "Have you got a problem, sir?" I said: "Yes, this guy behind has just crashed into me. I think he's drunk." He said: "Do you know him?" I said: "Yeah, I've seen him at a party and he's following me everywhere." The policeman went back to speak to Colin and I took off like a scared rabbit. Colin followed! The next thing these blue lights are flashing, Colin is still following and he didn't even know what was going on. The policeman pulled him over and said: "What do you think you're doing?" Colin now said: "The guy in front of me has just backed into me. I've seen him at a party and I think he's drunk!" The policeman said: "What are the chances of me finding two Aussies at an intersection in California?" He wasn't impressed at all . . .

'I did break loose this week and had a few beers because I thought it would be good for me but the only thing I got out of that was a headache in the morning.'

The championship was drifting away. The NSR Rothmans Honda was harshly difficult to handle and Gardner could get it no higher than fifth at Jerez. In testing in Yugoslavia he crashed and broke six bones in his foot. Despite this he finished second at Imola but crashed again at the Salzburgring when the rear wheel locked. On a roll he won Assen, Spa, and Rijeka. By now the season was also drifting away from Mang, whose best finishes were a couple of third places. At Rijeka, at the first corner, Donnie McLeod hit him from behind, and that was that: 'I was trying to get between the other bikes because obviously on the first corner there was such a mob. I realized I'd hit the track in an unconcentrated way. I've

Eddie Lawson, new team-member, 1989

had very few injuries: I've broken one thumb, three bones in a foot, and one collar bone. I've never been unconscious. Normally on the first corner I was careful because somebody usually crashes there and, again usually, I was able to get past them if they did. This time it wasn't possible. I didn't think it was a bad injury because I walked away from the accident. But I ran away from the Yugoslavian ambulance man and went straight to the regular doctor in the paddock. I didn't want to end up in a Yugoslavian hospital because I had heard a couple of horror stories about them. I realized it wasn't just a normal fracture when the doctor told me it could take a fair amount of time to recover. My collar bone was fractured so badly that they had to put a plate in.'

For that operation he went to a hospital just outside Munich with his wife Colette. She says: 'It was the doctor and Toni and myself. The doctor looked at the X-rays and I think we knew. It wasn't much of a reaction really. Toni just accepted it. I think he said to himself: "This is part of life, this is what I have been waiting for." After all, he'd had a long and successful career.'

Mang's abiding memory of that career among so many memories was simple: 'My victory in Jarama.'

Of the remaining 500 races, Gardner won Brno and finished the season second to Lawson, 229 points against 252. He rationalizes this in an unexpected way. 'I've got to enjoy myself. In the last couple of years [1988 and 1989] I've tried to concentrate too hard and that shows in my results. In 1987 all I did was have a good time.'

Sito Pons had a good time on the 250 Honda in 1988. He found himself locked into a nationalistic duel with another Spaniard, Garriga, on a Yamaha over the whole season and it captivated Spain. This duel was described as 'bitter' on the track and it could be alarming to watch, neither man backing off. Pons, who was 27 and had studied architecture, constructed this edifice: second at Suzuka (Garriga sixth), second at Laguna Seca (Garriga tenth), victory at Jarama from Garriga, crashed at Jerez, where Garriga won; and as they moved to Imola the points were Pons 54, Garriga 53, Cornu 50. At Imola, Pons was second and Garriga third, a result repeated at the Nürburgring. Pons was fifth at the Salzburgring (Garriga third), and overall Pons couldn't shake him off, 99 points against 98. Garriga won Assen, Pons sixth; Pons won Spa, Garriga sixth, and that was Pons leading it; Pons won Rijeka from Garriga, 129–128. Pons was second at Ricard (Garriga fourth), fourth at Donington (Garriga third), and won Anderstorp from Garriga. Garriga won Brno from Pons and that was Pons leading 216–210. That left Brazil, where Garriga had to win and Pons finish fourth or lower. This shoot-out was flawed because Garriga crashed on the second lap. Lavado (Yamaha) was coming hard up the inside, Wimmer (Yamaha) tried to get out of his way and struck Garriga from the rear. Garriga, churning dust, somehow kept control of the bike but had lost so many places that, despite a prolonged charge, he could get no further than fifth. Pons, flowing comfortably round in third place, had the championship. The final leaderboard read Pons 231, Garriga 221, Cornu third on 166. And that was 1988.

The man climbed easily onto the big bike and a mechanic, dressed in casual blue trousers and a white shirt, pressed both hands against the smooth bodywork behind the seat and shoved. He ran eight steps, pushing hard, and the engine fired. As it did the mechanic peeled away. The engine growled deeper and deeper as Wayne Gardner took the bike along the empty pit lane and out among the barren reaches of the track at Phillip Island, south of Melbourne. Phillip Island is all curves and loops, a graceful, beautiful setting for a man and a machine to blend.

A few moments later there were three bikes out there, Gardner, Eddie Lawson, and Michael Doohan: the Rothmans Honda team for 1989. Lawson, reigning World 500 Champion, had just joined from Yamaha; Doohan, a 23-year-old from Brisbane, was another newcomer. In 1988, on Yamahas, Doohan had won the second leg of the Japanese round of the World Superbike Championship and both legs of the Australian round. It was a useful apprenticeship for Grand Prix racing and now here he was.

That more than a hundred journalists from London, Rome, Paris, Athens, Amsterdam, Lisbon, Dubai and Sydney were able to see it on this February day in 1989 emphasized how professional bike racing had become in the marketing sense. Rothmans had arranged a global pre-season press conference via satellite, and it was live so that the journalists could ask the riders questions. We have come a long way from the van which turned off the main road in Onchan Village and crawled slowly up the drive to the Nursery Hotel in May 1959. It was almost exactly thirty years, but in another sense thirty light years. Moreover, the press conference was not an expensive gimmick, it was extremely useful. Here is the flavour of it.

Question: What's it like, Wayne, having Eddie in the same team as you? You were arch rivals before. 'It's been good actually. We are getting on extremely well. It was the media that caused the problems. It's good to have a Yamaha rider on the machines because we can get a better feedback and produce a much better machine this year.'

Question: It took you seven races to win in 1988. On the evidence of this testing, how advanced do you think the bike is compared to the same stage last season? 'Well, the first thing is that it goes in a straight line.' [It could have been Hailwood himself speaking, circa 1967.]

Lawson now takes the microphone. 'The NSR 88 that I rode in Japan, well, the weather was very very cold so really I couldn't get a good feel for the bike. [Aside from Gardner: 'Come on, tell the truth!'] I think the NSR 89 model has come a long way from that. I know that the bike is very comfortable to ride. I feel right at home on the motor cycle.'

Question: What's your reaction to the Spencer comeback? 'It's a question for you,' Lawson says immediately. 'Nobody wants to answer it,' Gardner says just as fast. Both men grin broadly, then Gardner does answer it. 'I think that it's good to see three World Champions on the grid. Whether or not Freddie is interested enough I don't know because I don't know his complete motive at the moment. He's got the ability if he really puts his head down. Who knows? It's unpredictable.'

Question: There seem to be an awful lot of spills but riders just seem to get up and walk away. Does this mean racing is becoming more or less dangerous? 'Our race tracks are getting safer,' Lawson says. 'That's something the riders are working on with the FIM and I feel we have pretty good equipment, protective gear, good helmets, boots, leathers. The motor cycles are a little easier to ride so all in all I think the sport is getting much safer.'

Question to Lawson: Was it the money which made you move or the professional team quality? 'Well, it certainly wasn't the money. I took less money to do this. I felt that being here on the Rothmans Honda team was where I needed to be.'

Question: Why is the sport growing in popularity? 'You can see the riders,' Gardner says. 'You don't just see helmets as you do in cars, you see close dicing, you can actually see the riders working hard and moving, and of course you see accidents as well.'

Question to Lawson: You have three titles but not the same recognition in America as Wayne has in Australia. 'For me it's nice to go home and not be recognized. The only unfortunate thing is that the sport isn't bigger in the United States. Wayne can't walk down the street and he's kind of hounded whereas I can go home and my next door neighbour doesn't know me.'

Question to Gardner: What are your preferred circuits in Europe? 'The ones I win at.'

Question to Lawson: Do you have team orders? 'We do have some team orders, and that's to win.'

It would be a particularly intriguing season. Lawson and Gardner were now team-mates, Spencer was back and on a Yamaha, Schwantz (Suzuki) and Wayne Rainey (Yamaha) were coming on strong. At Suzuka, Rainey and Schwantz seemed to have set the tone for what was to come, duelling almost desperately, all thrust and counter-thrust, taking and retaking each other so often that the vast crowd lost count. Schwantz won. Gardner meanwhile plunged off the circuit and trapped his left testicle against the petrol tank. In a celebrated comment he said that 'it hurt so bad I could have curled up and died'. He didn't. He finished fourth.

Two weeks later Gardner was back at Phillip Island for the very first Australian Grand Prix. He crashed in practice and so did Lawson, who lay stunned and spread-eagled on the grass for some time. Both were fit for the race. On the second lap Rainey led from Schwantz who, before his tyres were properly heated, felt the bike wobble. It flung him off and he cartwheeled in front of it in a wild, churning moment. The bike reared like an angry horse and spun off by itself. Schwantz rose, fled the track, and lay in deep frustration on the grass. Gardner was fourth at that point. The bunch began to close on Rainey, Gardner up to second and forcing the Honda so hard that momentarily both wheels were off the rim of the track and onto dry, reddish dust. Gardner did take the lead, at the right-left complex, Rainey came back at him and now Christian Sarron took the lead. Gardner bisected Rainey and Sarron and retook the lead himself, holding it to the end.

'That was the best win of my career without a doubt. The motor cycle scene really picked up from when I won the World Championship and that's why we have an Australian Grand Prix. And then of course I went and won it. The World Championship was a different kind of feeling, winning Australia was a home boy's fulfilment. I remember going round when I'd won and I stopped and got an Australian flag off a marshal and all the people came onto the track and left a tunnel for me to ride through. I was trying to hold back the tears and I held them all the way until I got back to the grid. Donna came up and she was crying, all my friends came running up, Alan Jones [former Formula One car World Champion]

Gardner, vintage 1989 ...

... and here in Brazil, now recovered from his crash.

came running up to do a TV interview and I just bawled and Alan Jones started crying. He saw me crying and he started too.

'I was tired because we had been travelling a lot. It's pretty hard to race one weekend in Australia and the following week you're racing in America. It's a strain not only on the riders but on the mechanics as well.' At Laguna Seca, Rainey led from flag to flag, Schwantz second, Lawson third. Gardner crashed on the eleventh lap when his foot caught the kerbing and he felt the bones crunch as he went down. He lay in agony beside some straw bales, hands clutching his leg. 'It was the first major fracture I'd had and the first time I'd missed races in my career. Basically,

the machines arrived late in America and it's a dangerous racetrack. I had a few problems with the machine which cut my practice back even further. I probably tried to push a bit too hard, the machine probably wasn't set up properly enough, and I went into the corner a little bit too hard. The front bounced and I ran wide because I'd missed the apex of the corner. I put my foot down to steady myself, kicked the kerb, and then ran along the dirt and fell over. Unfortunately, the bike fell on my leg and broke it. It meant the end of the championship, which hurt a lot because at that time I was one point behind the leader [Rainey 34, Gardner 33] and I was sure I would have won the championship. The machine was improving the whole time.'

This left Lawson essentially on his own because 1989 would be a learning year for Doohan. Lawson responded by winning Jerez, although Schwantz was leading by 5 seconds with only six laps to go when he crashed in a vast barrel-roll. 'I thought I might have thrown the championship away,' he said. Meanwhile Sito Pons was leading the 250 championship from the Italian Luca Cadalora (Yamaha).

At Misano it rained, the track dried, and they started. It rained again, the riders all came in to the pits and refused to go out again. It was quite naturally a controversial move, but in his phlegmatic way Lawson discussed the reasoning. 'This place is unique in that the surface is very, very slippery. When it has water on it you can't ride on it. All the top riders felt it was too dangerous and so we didn't ride, it's as simple as that. It's one of those things. It's very unfortunate for everyone, the riders, the teams and all the people. I've spent two weeks here so I wanted to race and we go to plenty of racetracks where we test all week in the sunshine. Then it starts to rain, we'll put rain tyres on and we race. This place you can't do that. Regardless of testing, you just can't ride in the wet here. It's just too dangerous.'

At Hockenheim, Schwantz took pole. Rainey fought him for the lead but Lawson took them both, made a mistake, was back to third, retook them, but Rainey got him on the last lap, Doohan third. Going to Austria Rainey had 91 points, Lawson 78. The race encapsulated the season, Schwantz v Lawson v Rainey, and it finished like that. The championship was tightening, Rainey 106, Lawson 95, Sarron 71, Schwantz 57. At Rijeka, Lawson made another mistake, went off, rejoined, and finished third. Gardner came back at Assen, but Rainey took the race, Lawson second. At Spa it rained during the race, although by now Lawson was on the pace. As the rain fell Schwantz and Rainey eased off, Sarron crashed, and the race was stopped after five laps. It was restarted and after another four laps the riders stopped. There was a third leg which amazingly wasn't counted overall, so Lawson won on aggregate. Rainey said: 'It was very dangerous, one of the toughest races I've raced.'

At Le Mans, Lawson took pole, held off Schwantz's prolonged challenge and won. On the eve of the British Grand Prix at Donington, Giacomo Agostini effectively fired Spencer from the Yamaha team and it was scarcely put less diplomatically than that. 'I am not happy,' Agostini said, 'he is not happy and the team is not happy. To compete for eighth or tenth place is not good for Freddie Spencer.' Meanwhile, also on the eve of the meeting, a British rider, Niall Mackenzie, put the season into perspective nicely. 'Rainey has improved a lot this year, he is consistent, doesn't take chances, and is riding within his limits on a reliable Yamaha.

Schwantz is the fastest rider of the season so far but he has made errors and had some bike troubles while Lawson is more aggressive than ever before. He is really trying hard and enjoying it.' In his own way Lawson contented himself with saying that 'it is an important race to me but there are a lot of races to go and I have to keep pushing on'. Schwantz won it, Lawson second, and it may be that the season turned on the next race, Anderstorp, where Rainey was second behind Lawson and the bike bucked, flinging him away. It gave Lawson a 13 1/2 points lead which increased at Brno. He was second to Schwantz.

That left Brazil and now Rainey had to win; Lawson only had to finish in the top eleven. 'I feel I've been beat up by everybody in the world,' Rainey said. Lawson fully intended to win the race, do the thing in the proper manner and he challenged Schwantz for the lead, duelled for 32 laps with Schwantz and Rainey but Rainey—in tyre trouble—drifted back. There was a short, sharp sting in the tail of 1989. Lawson was in second place and had only two laps to go to the championship when a backmarker, Vince Cascino from Chile, lost control and fell almost directly in front of him. Lawson managed to keep his tight line and missed Cascino. He finished comfortably enough behind Schwantz and said this was the best of his championships, an absolute vindication of his decision to join Honda.

Lawson was now one of the greatest riders of all time. He had become the first man since Kenny Roberts (1978, 1979, 1980) to win the 500 Championship in consecutive seasons, the first since Agostini (MV Augusta, Yamaha) to win it on two different makes of bike. Nor, amidst all this, must we forget Pons, who had built another edifice, 262 points

Memories of France, 1962, in the 50 cc: Robb sandwiched between Taveri and Takahashi.

against Roth's 190. Gardner of course was gazing ahead to 1990. 'It's not the money, that's not why I do it. I don't think I have to worry too much about where the next dollar is coming from.' *Question: How can you cope with the life, the danger, the travel, the crashes and fractures, the fame and the rest?* 'That is a good question. What makes me do it? It's a passion for the sport. I enjoy motor cycles, I enjoy being a competitive person. Everyone, I suppose, has different things which drive them on. Mine is just for the love of it, you know. I've enjoyed motorized things since I was a little kid.' That seemed the perfect place to leave it—with a glance into the man and a glance towards the future. But his words were soon to be tested, and tested hard.

The Statement precisely reflected the turbulence of the season, and there had been moments when the turbulence seemed to be overwhelming the season. Lawson had gone back to Yamaha, Gardner was fit again, and as a direct result 1990 seemed to offer even more interesting possibilities than any another year, although inherently they all had to be . . . well, interesting; and yet after only five races Honda found themselves trying to save 500 cc racing while at the same time suggesting forcibly that if their ideas were not adopted they would simply withdraw. That was the essence of The Statement, and we shall come to it all in good time because it's better to start at the beginning and let the several aspects of the turbulence unfold all by themselves. Suzuka and the Japanese Grand Prix was 25 March. In testing two weeks before, Gardner had been going round Suzuka faster than Schwantz's new bike, a revised version of the old one, lighter with a lot of work on the suspen-

Doohan started to establish himself in 1990. Here he leads Gardner during testing in Australia.

sion. It was intended to be more rider-friendly, in the jargon of the age. Immediately before the race Gardner said: 'After breaking my leg last year I wanted lots of practice on the new bike to prepare myself both mentally and physically. Also I wanted to build up a working relationship with my new team manager, Erv Kanemoto. Things could not have gone better between us and it's a privilege to work with somebody who has so much knowledge and commitment to winning. I'm also happy with the progress of the new machine and we are ready to have a real go at winning back that World Championship.'

Doohan, meanwhile, had crashed and broken his left arm in testing before Christmas, had recovered and now said: 'The arm is getting stronger all the time and should be just about right for the race.' Dominique Sarron was eyeing the 250. 'Last year I never had a chance on the 500 because we could not do enough testing. Already this year I have tested the new NSR 250 Honda in Australia, France and Japan. I'm confident about the season and I'm determined to make a good start.'

All these are the sort of prudent words you would expect—although they shouldn't be belittled for that—and if they scarcely presaged what was actually going to happen, forgive the riders. This would be a season which almost defied anticipation.

At least Suzuka demonstrated that Gardner was back on the pace, but Doohan drew sharp words from Yamaha team boss Roberts. Doohan had been having problems with his brakes and on lap five, coming down from 180 mph, he used one finger as usual but the brake lever came all the way back to the bar and sandwiched his other fingers. He extracted them and pulled the lever hard. The bike reared and careened into Lawson, who went down—and out. What, Roberts mused aloud, was Doohan doing if he knew he had that problem?

Gardner finished second behind Rainey and made the encouraging judgement that at one stage 'I was really racing with Schwantz and suddenly I thought I must be back to my old self to be doing that with somebody as fast as him. I'm delighted with the result. The Honda steers so much better than in previous years, although there is still work to be done.' Doohan was candid enough: 'I just ran out of brakes. I'd been having trouble with them since the second lap. By the time I pulled in the lever the second time I was going too fast and lost the front end. The worst thing was that I also took out Eddie Lawson and I'm so pleased he was not badly hurt.' In the 250 Sarron led briefly. 'I made a good start then a small mistake and dropped back. I got among the leaders again and took the lead but my wrist kept pumping up.'

Somehow Doohan's crash had set a tone, although again that only became clear in retrospect, and anyway worse, far worse was to come at Laguna Seca, which Gardner approached with 'caution' after his crash of '89 ... well, not too much caution. He'd already tested there during the winter so that any psychological barriers had gone. This United States Grand Prix meeting would achieve notoriety, no less, bringing into questions the whole future of the track as a venue for bikes. Lawson damaged a foot in practice and missed the race; Kevin Magee (Suzuki) fell on lap two in the race—a 'high-sided' accident—and went into a coma after emergency surgery; three other riders were injured and Gardner crashed twice. He was not hurt.

All this was bad enough, but simultaneously another factor was com-

Gardner at Laguna Seca. Whatever memories he had of the track, he didn't back off.

Doohan was one of the few to leave Laguna Seca with something pleasant to remember— second place.

ing into play: a deep and growing concern about the size of the grids. In California it was a mere 15, the lowest since the late 1970s, and this, too, would be a potent factor in prompting The Statement. Of the Honda team only Doohan, second to Rainey, left with any sense of satisfaction. 'This is my best-ever Grand Prix result. The bike was fine throughout and my only worry came when Wayne crashed right in front of me on the second lap.'

There was an aftermath because Laguna Seca, an unloved and distrusted circuit, had brought what was happening into the sharpest focus. Joe Zegwaard, road race President of the FIM, announced publicly that measures were needed to slow the bikes because they were getting more and more difficult—and by definition more and more dangerous—to ride. He likened the 175 bhp that the bikes were now generating as being excellent to pull a truck. In brief, his initial thinking was to limit carburet-

Right *Spain was good for Doohan—pole position and fourth in the race.*

Right and below *Spain wasn't good for Domique Sarron. He crashed on lap ten.*

tor bores, use a maximum of 98 octane fuel and raise the minimum weight of a bike to 135 kg. Honda had already made noises about reducing the whole 500 class to 375 cc and within weeks that would lead to controversy, acrimony and The Statement . . .

The race after Laguna Seca was Jerez, where Gardner would say: 'I think all riders look forward to getting into Europe and settling into a regular pattern. I won here in 1987 and it's a very hard track both for rider and machine. Although Rainey leads me by 23 points in the Championship the title race is far from over.' Gardner proved that. It was hot, the crowd was estimated at substantially more than 150,000 (Formula One car racing please note) and Gardner tracked Rainey, Rainey responded, Gardner tracked him again and outbraked him on lap nineteen. He won by a clear 7 seconds, his first since Australia the year before. 'It was easy,' Gardner said. 'Once I had caught Rainey it was just a matter of getting past him, and once I'd done that I could pull away easily. I'm really pleased for the team—they have been working really hard for me. It helps to make up for my crash at Laguna Seca.' The season seemed to be coming alive, albeit it that Rainey had 57 points and Gardner 37. There was, after all, a long way to go.

And they went to Misano, where there was a great deal more than a race. Honda met the FIM and, exploring the background to that, Zegwaard would say: 'The accidents were happening almost daily. It is the "high-sided" ones which are dangerous most of the time. The rider is flying through the air followed by his motor bike. If you crash in a slide, in the old-fashioned way, you slide along the tarmac and if you don't hit anything you don't hurt yourself very much—but a "high-sided" accident means that you may land on a shoulder or your head.

'It is a surplus of power in the lower rev region. A four-cylinder two-stroke 500 starts to develop power rather suddenly at 9,000 to 9,500 revs and stops somewhere near 13,500. Most of the accidents are happening at relatively low speeds. Opening the throttle makes the power come in too rapidly, it makes the rear wheel tend to spin and a rider's natural reaction is to close the throttle. At that point the spin stops, the tyre gets grip again, it turns the bike over and you are thrown off as you would be from a horse. In a nutshell, that is what is happening. Honda brought the proof on paper to Misano. They were very, very worried about it.' Steve Whitelock, a consultant to the Honda road race team, says crisply: 'We made an offer to the FIM at the race at Misano and then they came back with what they had decided to do.' He added: 'Considering the number of accidents we have had this year, we see it in a couple of different ways: the power the machines are making and the power-to-weight ratio. We think there are maybe only five or six guys in the world who can really ride these things the way they should be ridden, and even they are having accidents.'

This did not break as a news story until the following race, at the Nürburgring, but when it did it was a very big story indeed.

On the track at Misano Gardner judged that 'I must keep on winning', while Doohan said of his fourth place at Jerez: 'I think I proved to myself just what I can do when I am in pole position (at Jerez). Both Wayne and myself know we must finish in front of Rainey during the next few Grands Prix if we are going to overtake him in the Championship. It rained so hard at Misano last year that I never really got the chance to learn the circuit.' In the 250, Sarron—who had broken a bone in his foot crashing at Jerez—said: 'I hope it will not cause me many problems. I like the track very much at Misano and I must score some points.'

Now during practice Gardner crashed and cracked two ribs when Christian Sarron on a 500 Yamaha went down in front of him and Gardner had nowhere to go. 'At some stage I thought it was impossible that I was going to ride in the race but they did a lot of work on me in the warm-up. It was very painful without pain-killing drugs [at one point Gardner was observed to be in tears] so Dr Claudio Costa—the Grand Prix doctor—filled me up with some.' The race ought to have been 36 laps but was stopped after 24 when rain began—the correct decision, Rainey would say, because 'we've got enough guys hurt already'. Schwantz was leading Doohan and, as Gardner said, 'I was catching Mick and I wish it had gone the extra laps because I'm pretty sure I would have caught him. Then the race was stopped. When it was re-started as the twelve-lapper I finished second to Schwantz. I probably rode a bit better because I was a bit more in tune and more motivated, I was a bit more confident in my ability by then. Also I got a better start and went with the leaders. It's one of those week-ends—I suppose it's good but it's also very, very painful.' Gardner described this as like having a knife stuck in the ribs. Overall Rainey won, then Schwantz, Doohan and Gardner.

By now Zegwaard was becoming more and more concerned. 'We had the accident at Misano. Sarron came off and he hurt not only himself but Gardner also. Gardner crashed after two laps of practice because, according to his own words, his ribs were hurting so much that he couldn't master the motorbike. This is what we faced.' Zegwaard expands on that. 'People are talking very, very proudly of having twelve pain-killing injections before they go to the starting line.' (He is clearly not referring to Gardner, who is matter-of-fact about these things but never particularly proud). 'What I saw in Misano was absolutely disgusting: a rider of world class level being taken from a mini-bike by his wife and a mechanic and put on the racing bike because he couldn't stand on his feet. How can we defend that? I saw one rider, I spoke to him at the start and he didn't recognize me. He was looking at me as if he was sleeping with his eyes open.'

You can argue the case that bike riders have always been macho, always ridden in pain, always accepted the risks or what would they be doing there in the first place? But this was becoming, had become, something else and it was grouped around a growing awareness of safety—hence the riders' refusal to race in the rain at Misano in '89—awkwardly balanced against the pressures of how much money was now involved, how there were professional expectations on the riders. (This money, incidentally, was not enough to give the leading riders their own jet aeroplanes or helicopters like the Formula One car drivers, true, but was still serious money. Interestingly, Honda never allowed such pressures to go near their riders as we shall see in this chapter and the next, and presumably neither did the other teams. The pressures were external.)

So they went to the Nürburgring for the fifth race of the season, this unloved new Nürburgring which was by no means distrusted. Constructed after lengthy work on computers, the possibility of silly risks had simply been designed out of it.

Gardner had been told by Dr Costa that the pain would be even greater in Germany, 'but I'm prepared to ride through it. I've just got to keep going.' He was pitched off in practice and broke nine toes. 'You know what it's like when you crack your knuckles. Well, it sounded like that.' He found another evocative phrase, like crunching a packet of crisps. The same afternoon Sarron fell off the 250 and broke three bones in his right foot. Of the Rothmans Honda team that left only Doohan, who was on his first visit to the track. He qualified second behind Schwantz, and if you want it in time, only two-tenths of a second slower. In this qualifying Rainey had his first crash of the season. He was going 140 mph in the chicane, the rear wheel flicked up, he hurt his head and dislocated a finger. For a moment it looked a very bad one.

In the race Doohan took the lead but on lap two Schwantz took it from him and began to ease away. On lap three Doohan was still second, the Italian Pier-Francisco Chili (also on a Honda) third, when both moved into the fast right-hander behind the pits too fast and it was almost balletic: both their rear wheels lost traction at the same moment, both were pitched sideways, both regained traction at the same instant, both were pitched into the air and both landed at the same instant. Doohan had a sore shoulder ('I put it out') and a cracked toe.

(More happily, Dutchman Wilco Zeelenberg won the 250 on a Honda, their first of the season, and Carlos Cardus of Spain came second, so Honda had one-two, after a typically hectic race.)

And now we come to The Statement, which was released at the Nürburgring. It said that Honda were proposing the 500 cc class to become multi-category embracing two-stroke, four-stroke and rotary engines based on 375 cc.

'If the proposal is accepted we are prepared to manufacture a highly competitive production racer at a relatively low price, one 375 cc triple for approximately £38,000.

'If Honda's proposal is not accepted we consider the future of the 500 class to be in imminent danger of collapse. There would be no participants outside factory-supported riders and no private teams. In these circumstances Honda would have to consider withdrawal from the 500 class.

'We at Honda would like to see a definite decision reached before the end of June 1990 in order to allow sufficient time for the development of the 1991 machines.'

It was a revolution, no less, and it needs some expansion. Steve Whitelock: 'Honda were looking for a commitment from the FIM that they would change the rules for 1991 and if they did then Honda would produce a fair few machines for the racing customer. I think reports of $1 million to lease one of our present machines is a little inflated—it's between $400,000 and $500,000, although that package includes quite a bit of technology and spare parts; and at different times of the year your engines are sent back to Japan for total re-conditioning. It sounds expensive if you write it on a page, but in fact it's a pretty competitive price.

'On the grid the level of professionalism has come to such a state now that young kids who want to try 500 realize that their chances of being in a competitive team are pretty slim so they have chosen to go off and ride superbikes or another class of motor cycling—which is not a bad thing because it does give us a place to hunt for talent. But on the other hand we feel that if we can build a machine that we can sell to them at a very competitive price they will come and take the chance with a budget which is probably 50 per cent lower than they have now. To find half a million dollars is very difficult but our projected price for one of our packages for a team is between $200,000 and $250,000. That includes two machines and spare parts to run them both. It makes it much more feasible and we feel it would solve the problem of low numbers on the grid.

'Since Honda can see that the idea of 375 cc is not possible immediately [more of this in a moment] they are going to re-study and maybe offer 500s for sale. We want to stay in the class, we don't want it to die. It's the best thing that motor cycle racing has to offer. One of the reasons Honda allowed me to go public with all the information at the Nürburgring was to try and see if there was going to be some interest among importers and riders. If you do market research, our importers in all the different countries have shown little interest in selling them. Now perhaps they will show that interest and say "yes, we want to buy it". This is the only way to go. We have to get back into the business of selling racing bikes.'

So, amid this turbulent season, Honda's reasoning was two-fold: to make it safer and more competitive. Of the crashes, Whitelock said: 'I think we are getting so much horsepower out of the engine that we are a little bit behind a chassis design. We are looking at everything. We are not happy with a situation where Mr Gardner falls off and injures himself pretty good, Doohan coming off in the race in Germany. If you watch it, it is almost unexplainable the way he and Chili both crashed in the same place. When I talked to Doohan in the hospital he said he had no idea what had happened. He hadn't even got onto full power—he was a long way from full power.

'In the 250 race there is an instructive shot of Luca Cadalora falling off but he is falling off in the typically safe way. He loses the front end and it slides out—what we call a "low-sided" crash. It just slides out, nothing happens—in fact he gets up, remounts and continues. But all the big crashes in the 500, and they are also showing up in the 250, are "high-sided" crashes where the rider is basically ejected off the seat. The wheel is already spinning, then it's suddenly completely free, grip is lost, the rider closes the throttle and it seems he gets traction again and it ejects the rider over the handlebars. Then he's totally airborne and the bike goes on its merry way.

'We are looking at some ideas on how to reduce that kind of power but the Yamaha people don't agree with it, the Suzuki people have spent a lot of time on their four-cylinder development and a lot of the teams feel it would downgrade the class. So we are up against a lot of people who are against the idea. Even some of the traditionalists in our company feel it would damage the class. We have that problem also.' *Question from me: But not damage the class as much as a big, possibly fatal, accident would?* 'Yes, yeah. I have said that several times. We feel that we have seen the warning signs. That was the thing that prompted the paper that was written, and there was also a lot of technical data what was passed on to the FIM: it was the reasoning for suggesting this. It came from Honda in Tokyo.'

There are all manner of ironies in this. Honda had been competing in the 500 class since Redman and Hailwood, had known those great days when the eyes of the world were so firmly riveted upon them as they

Gardner defies the pain of a practice crash at Misano. Here he leads Wayne Rainey and Doohan.

challenged Agostini, had known the strange hypnotism of the Isle of Man and Hailwood forcing that big, big bike round as no other man on earth could have done; and now, however you care to read The Statement, they were proposing in the most sober and reasoned way the destruction—or rather substitution—of it because technology had outgrown it. There is an analogy with motor car racing here, and it was never very far away from the thoughts of the people struggling with the problem, as they kept saying.The Formula One cars had skirts which were banned and turbo engines which were banned, circuits were altered to become more difficult to slow the cars but the cars still got faster, led, incidentally, by Honda in the Marlboro McLaren; but that was to miss the point. Skirts were frightening because they gave such adhesion that drivers simply pointed the cars into a corner and hoped to God they stuck. Turbos were frightening because of how much they cost. In the background, however, technology worked to make the structure of the cars fantastically strong, and I use the word fantastically in its proper sense. The material kevlar would absorb impacts, the three sets of safety belts, each so strong that you could lift the whole car with a crane by using only one, held the driver so rigid that if he wasn't wearing them he risked breaking his rib-cage under the G-forces; self-sealing fuel tanks minimized the chance of fire; and so it became possible to survive moments which would have had lethal consequences a decade before. But the objective was that you stayed within the carefully constructed cocoon of the car and rode out the storm there.

Bikes remained true to the fundamental that the tarmac was flowing just there beneath your elbow and in a crash you needed to shed the bike, throw it from you and, just as dear old Ralph Bryans used to do, steer yourself down the road using your elbows. Or, as Joe Zagwaard said in 1990, if you get off and slide and don't hit anything, there's a favourable chance you'll be OK. Gravity would stop you eventually and gravity hadn't changed. What had changed was the power, the power which it seemed a bike could almost exert by itself, and that had a wider, more representative application: technocrats, working within a defined space, could produce amazing progress, could make engines which would generate a performance which no engines had generated before. And still, as there had always been, a fallible human being sat astride it, master or servant of it. The sharp edge of what Zegwaard was saying became almost a hymn: too many of the riders are servants and perhaps any day now all will become servant—or, in the terminology of motor sport, passengers.

Of course the 500 class had accelerated under the heat of competition and that was intrinsically understandable, in a sense necessary, the way to go and the only way to go. Progress, you know, just like every other branch of motor sport. Honda stood back for several reasons, each compelling.

Zegwaard points to one. 'Honda were saying their main worry was no longer winning Grand Prix races but to try and get rid of this bad image, because that image at the moment is connected to bandages and ambulences and hospitals and maybe worse. It will not only affect their racing bikes but street bikes and cars. They all bear the name of Honda.' This is not a callous judgement and must not be seen as such. As Gardner will say, Mr Honda wants riders to enjoy racing, savour the sport.

Quite naturally Honda also want to be seen to win and are prepared to take the risk of losing to achieve that. They do not want, and have never wanted, it to be anything but that; they certainly do not want to compete openly in a sport and then discover that their very name is associated with bandages and ambulances and hospitals. Would you?

'I had a meeting with the Director of Development and Planning of Honda Racing at Misano,' Zegwaard will say, 'and he presented me with a hell of a list of documentation and analyses, including a computer chart detailing laps round various circuits. They were so vivid you could almost feel yourself on the bike. One of these analyses contained the points of accidents like the one Wayne Gardner had at Laguna Seca.' Mr Zegwaard remains disconcerted by that—disconcerted by what Honda call the 'A' zone, the 'A' meaning 'accident' of course. The zone is generally as a rider emerges from a corner with less than half the throttle in play and the rev counter flickering at 10,000 revs or slightly more. In other words, above the 9,500 where things start happening but far below the gut-busting 13,500 maximum.

Summer '90 and it had come to this, come to it all the way from the van which inched its way so nervously up the drive to the Nursery Hotel, Onchan Village; not the Clypse Course with Hunt in his spaceman helmet being bounced around the uneven road surfaces, but space age technology and all its inherently awesome possibilities. Perhaps it was always going to come to this, but that is not significant. It had reached it.

'I spoke to Wayne Gardner on the Sunday night at the Nürburgring and mentally he was in a terrible mood. He said "I really cannot think how I could be so stupid as to do that." Eddie Lawson is one of the classic examples of the way it should be done. He says: "I can walk now after my injury but I don't want to be at race meetings, I don't want all that fuss. The moment I know I am fit and I can do a job for my team I will start again but I won't be around in plaster until then."

'I have spoken strongly to the President of the Medical Committee and I said: "Please listen, because I have witnessed these things week by week and if we wait until it really does go fundamentally wrong we will be made responsible and I just don't want to be part of it." The doctor at the Nürburgring admitted after the race that half of the riders were not fit enough to be in it. I am asking myself the question: How come then that they are racing? Are we kidding the spectators? Are we kidding the sponsors? Or are we kidding ourselves? If people want to risk their own lives they can do so, but if you are in a race with more than one competitor then the lives of others are in jeopardy as well.'

We have not, however, discussed whatever happened when Honda approached the FIM at Misano armed with all the data and made The Proposals. They were turned down, although not finitely. Zegwaard explained in this way: 'The reduction in capacity was rejected by the Management Council because the majority opinion was that the 500 class must remain. You cannot sell (in marketing terms, to sponsors, spectators and the television audience) the 500 as being something else. Having said that, Honda's idea of lowering the capacity to prevent these accidents is only one of the solutions. We should not react in the way of panic. People tried to make me look ridiculous when we had a meeting with the industry one year ago at Assen [1989] and I said the same. I told the Press then that it's not only my opinion—various members of the manufacturers have the same opinion.'

Panic? There was some of that in the air, mixed with the nasty spectres, the reality of too many crashes and the nearly grotesque spectacle of the tiny grids made worse by the crashes, so that if 15 riders set off and five crashed only ten were running at the end. At the Nürburgring, as someone observed, it was neither a spectacle nor a procession; it was almost nothing, a few strung out churning their way home. And as someone else observed—actually it was Gardner's manager, Harris Barnett—there was a time when spectators drank their beer and ate their sandwiches during the 125 and the 250 races and then went to watch the 500s; now it had become the reverse. And Barnett is one of those people who is both an acute observer and a well-wisher. Moreover, Barnett pointed out, all the teams were testing a great deal more often than they ever did before, testing in fact in much the same way as the Formula One car people did, and this had two immediate implications: statistically, the more often you were on the bike the more chance you had of crashing and, with another race or test session looming, the less chance to recover as fully as you might wish if you happened to be injured. And this did not include the cumulative physical and mental strain of actually being on a bike so much, manhandling it round and round.

Because Honda cannot be isolated from the overall picture, and because the overall picture was not of such importance, we must, and I insist upon the royal we, look at the list of walking wounded after only the five races:

Japanese Grand Prix, Suzuka, 25 March: Mick Doohan and Eddie Lawson crash, Lawson breaking his foot.

US Grand Prix, Laguna Seca, 8 April: Lawson crashes in practice; in the race Kevin Magee falls, is very badly concussed, taken for emergency surgery, his family around his bedside; Schwantz and Randy Mamola break wrists; Tadahiko Tairo cuts a deep gash into his hand; Gardner crashes twice—and this is where he shattered his leg the year before.

Spanish Grand Prix, Jerez, 6 May: Alexandre Barros pitched clean over the handlebars in what was truly a 'high-sided' crash.

Italian Grand Prix, Misano, 20 May: Pier-Francesco Chili and Barros crash; Gardner breaks two ribs.

West German Grand Prix, Nürburgring, 27 May: Gardner breaks his foot in nine places in practice; Doohan and Sarron crash; and so does Rainey in practice. The rear wheel flicked up.

Put it together and you have a lot of different people in various stages of recovery and the words of the German doctor come back: 50 per cent should not have been racing. There are of course those people we've mentioned before who object to all this, who see the sport as something you do because you want to and you know the risks, and the risks make it what it is anyway; but they are invariably elderly and equally invariably not riders.

Honda's Statement provoked very mixed reactions. Kenny Roberts said emphatically that he didn't 'bitch' when Honda were winning, and by implication wondered why they were bitching now. That was the hard edge of it: you don't cancel a whole class of racing, you learn to ride the bikes just the way people always have. But the big question remained. The bikes are subject to the laws of progress and can take a rider to places he can't always control; or, paraphrasing Zegwaard, once upon a time the rider controlled the bike, now the bike was starting to control the rider. A chilling thought, and much more chilling because there was hard evidence for it every place they went. You only had to ask the walking wounded, and they were not hard to find. And the big question: what to do about it?

The FIM rejected the Honda Proposals but they decided to seek a meeting in Japan with the manufacturers to talk it over, sound it out, seek opinions, form a communal judgement. Not that that was going to be easy. Zegwaard: 'As you will appreciate, the Japanese manufacturers regard it as a very delicate thing. It's not only technical, it's a little bit mixed with politics [explanation, if I may: politics means image, reputation, high-selling, integrity and the global mega-bucks you've invested] and we cannot avoid that. We will have a meeting in Japan to show that we are interested in finding a solution. We have been asked to wait a little while until all the Japanese personnel who are in Europe for the races are back in Japan. It is no use talking to the teams separately because a solution has to come from everybody together.'

This was at least pragmatic. As Zegwaard was speaking these words to me, Gardner was in his apartment in Monte Carlo making his own balance: ordering every satellite dish he could lay hands on to watch the races, to obey the habits of a lifetime, but not yet in a fit and proper frame of mind to give interviews, which he had also done all his life. It had cut too deep. He—of all people—needed rest, perhaps solitude. Whatever, he had earned it.

The beautifully simple thing, man, machine, Mother tarmacadam, had passed into another dimension. No matter, really, that it had acquired the trappings of the hard–sell, market–research, pretty girls hired to show a leg (but don't touch), advertising budgets, Press Conferences where everybody got the Party Line; I mean, this was the way the world went, wasn't it, went in a whirlwind and don't you know what progress is about?

Before Misano Honda said no, this was not what progress was about.

They found a deep echo, which no doubt they perfectly understood, from Zegwaard himself. You must hear his rich guttural Dutch tones chewing the words, and although he is speaking quickly he is still measuring out the words, an interesting form of balance. 'Listen, I'm in this game from my schooldays on—I stopped road racing before 80 per cent of the riders on a grid today were even born, I've been in it 40 years—but I have always had the luck [he chews that very hard] to be able to adapt myself to developments and new mentalities. But one of the disadvantages of being around for so many years, with people saying I'm on the other side of 50 years of age, is that they ask "What can he know about it?"' The irony does not necessarily offend him. Older people know better, and when I mention that most of the Prime Ministers of the world are over 50 he chuckles in affirmation. 'If you talk about sport, people laugh at you. They say: "We are professionals, don't talk about sport." Once it has got that far we are already on the downhill road.'

Honda, meanwhile, had taken the pressure completely off Gardner. They told him to 'rest, watch the satellites if that's what you want, come back only when you are ready. You judge the time and we are content to wait.' I am not being idyllic: it is what they said.

Japan-America-Spain-Italy-Germany, the rat-a-tat of a season—they had come round quick enough and some good men stayed on the bikes, some good men fell off. This is what it meant: the fundamentals were harder to cope with.

THIRTEEN

The Timeless Machine

T HE formal interview is over and Stuart Graham sits in a corner of an English pub similar, no doubt, to the saloon bar of the Nursery Hotel, but this one is in Cheshire, England, not Onchan Village on the Isle of Man. And it's now the end of the '80s, not '66. He sips coffee and eats a cheese salad deftly, the way a businessman with catholic tastes would do. He retired from bike racing long ago but was lured to the TT a couple of years later. The bike—it wasn't a Honda—he considered to be unsuitable and he didn't enter the race at all and caught the plane home instead. In the corner of the pub, two decades later, he's still searching somewhere within himself for an answer to whether it was braver to do that than race, and he remains unsure. But he dwells on it and just for a moment his eyes meet your eyes to try and divine what your judgement is. Not that it matters, except to him. He runs a Honda dealership, 22 employees, turnover £3 million. He doesn't sell bikes. He sensed cars were the future.

Kikue Carran was invited to Tokyo by Honda in 1987 for a reunion. It was the first time she had been back since 1953 and she found Japan had changed.'So many houses, so many people.' She went to the factory and met eight of the riders: 'They had all grown bigger! Some of them cried because they suddenly realized it was all thirty years ago. Every time they came they stayed at the Nursery Hotel and some of the riders used to visit my house to see me. The whole family made a friend of Taniguchi and he wrote to us, telling us about his wife and children.' I interviewed her by 'phone on the Isle of Man. Her son Arthur forewarned me that she still had a strong accent and hoped I'd be able to understand what she said: when she did speak a lovely, lilting laugh came cascading down the 'phone. The words were fine, too, and better because they came from the heart.

Derek Minter runs a haulage business. He has hair which is clerical-collar white now, and is virtually teetotal ('I only drink to be sociable'); as he speaks he uses his hands a great deal for emphasis. The third finger,

Memories of Holland: Redman leading McIntyre.

left hand, is foreshortened into a half-length stub. That was Ulster 1962 and the crash he still can't remember. 'I make deliveries all over the UK, up to Manchester three times a week. I thoroughly enjoy it. The only trouble is to me the truck doesn't go quick enough.' This statement is followed by a deep reverberating chuckle. We move into the front room of his house to examine the trophy cabinet standing against one wall. His daughter and her boyfriend are on a sofa poring over an illustrated history of the twentieth century, arranged day by day. I wonder if Derek Minter is in there, just a line covering the Isle of Man, 4 June 1962, but it's not the sort of question you ask.

Murray Walker sits in his minor chateau in Hampshire. His study, painted an immaculate white, is a library of motor sport, wall-to-wall books and bound magazines, videos, records he and his father made of the Isle of Man with gutteral gurgles of passing engines as a backdrop. 'My own view of the TT, where they've had a hundred and odd casualties, is that since the races began in 1907 they've ridden millions of miles—when you talk of a week of practising and a week of racing for 100 people in each of four events. If you express the deaths as a percentage I imagine it's a lot less than on ordinary roads. But I'm not denying it's a frightening prospect to go round it. It's bloody dangerous, oh yes, but then all racing is dangerous . . .'

Bill Smith sits in a functional office in Chester and beyond it, through an open door, Honda bikes can be seen arranged across the sales area. 'Crazy as it seems, at 53 I am still racing. I had a bad accident five years ago on the Isle of Man and I smashed nearly every bone in my body. On the last lap going into Ballaugh Bridge the gearbox nicked up and it chucked me over the top. I was in intensive care for three weeks. Broke both my legs, both arms, elbows, pelvis, but I still raced a 750 there this year [1988] and I still lapped at 104 miles an hour.' He is a formidable man, affable but strong, grown slightly portly but his presence somehow intensified by that. 'I was', he will say, 'the first Honda dealer in western Europe.' Only recently did he lose the franchise. He has a workforce of

Redman in full flow.

30, a turnover of £3 or £4 million, and could have a comfortable middle-age. But still crazy after all these years? Nothing fundamental changed.

Ralph Bryans has a single picture high on the wall of his office outside Ayr, a sepia-cum-crayon drawing of a motor bike overtaking another motor bike, the overtaking rider glancing down at his prey. There is no caption and I wonder which rider depicts him, but again it's not the sort of question you necessarily need to ask. 'I like good food, just about anything will do, and I like Japanese food. Once I invited all the Honda personnel to come and stay with us between Grands Prix. We went shooting and fishing. One evening my wife and I were going out and we left the mechanics in the house with a lot of fish we had just caught. My wife was a bit concerned that they were going to make a mess of the kitchen. When we returned everything was spick and span. There wasn't a smell of cooked fish anywhere. We discovered that they had just sliced the fish and eaten the whole lot raw. "Delicious," they said.' He's chairman of a company making body panels, 173 employees, turnover £6 million. He rests muscular hands on the desk ('When you've spent as many years as I have pulling levers you do end up with a very strong grip') and drifts gently into memory. 'You put your own pressure on, Honda don't, because you know that if you're not producing the goods the bottom line is that they'll hire somebody else.' He pauses. 'Even in Grands Prix I was never of a nervous disposition, but a rider gets nervous when he is expected to win. It might sound strange, that.'

Tommy Robb has just had hard, heated words with his staff in his show-room in Warrington—somewhere out there where Honda bikes and other bikes stand displayed in rows. He comes bustling into his office, a partitioned room, and switches into a calmer mood. He has pictures on the wall, some trophies on shelves, but they are not flaunted. 'I retired officially in 1971 but kept on a bit. If I woke up in the morning and felt like going racing I went racing, it was that simple, and I was paying my own entrance fee. I went to a race at an old disused airfield and I always made sure I arrived a few hours early to walk the circuit, every circuit. Because I had established a reputation young riders would follow me trying to learn something. At the right-hander at the end of a straight there was cow dung all round the corner and it was 3, 4 inches deep. We went to a local farmer, borrowed shovels, and I recruited these lads. We were standing shovelling it away and I suddenly thought: after twenty years of battling with Italian officials, Germans, the French, the Finns, and the rest of them over start money, and here I am, I've paid £3.50 of my own money and I'm shovelling cow dung and I'm enjoying every minute of it.' Pause. 'I went out and won two classes.' He has a workforce of nine and is trading profitably. Like Smith and Minter and Bryans his hands are chunky from the pulling of the levers but, also like them, the handshake doesn't hurt at all. His muscular control remains as sensitive as that.

He still gets strangers coming into his shop because they've noticed his name up there outside it and they say: 'I saw you race so many times but I didn't have a chance to speak to you then.' Tommy Robb is always delighted to meet them. He still gets fan mail. He shows me one from East Germany which says: 'You gave me so much pleasure at the Sachsenring but I didn't have the chance to get your autograph, please may I have it now for my album? If you have any stickers for my son I would be very grateful. I wish you and your family a happy New Year. Sorry I cannot obtain the postage stampes here so you can send the autograph back to me.' It touched Robb a great deal because, truth to tell, it's only when the noise of battle has died and you're not longer a celebrity that you have time to reflect on what you meant to so many strangers.

Jim Redman still goes riding but it's horses now. He's a breeder in South Africa and has, in equine terminology, 'a good one'. It's winning a lot. And his life in Durban? 'It's been like *Dallas* down here for me.'

John Dee is a snooker journalist. The peace of snooker, where even coughing among spectators is actively discouraged, is about as far removed from the Island as you can get, aside from a monastery. He has a military moustache, a dry wit and a way of nursing his memories so that he can conjure up events as if they were only yesterday. Well, the day before yesterday. 'Hailwood was the greatest rider I ever saw. I spoke to

Memories of the days before armco. Taveri at La Source hairpin, Belgium 1962, on the 50 cc.

It rained even in those days. The start of the French 125 cc race. Taveri (22).

a chap once who had tuned Norton engines and he said Ubbiali was the greatest because he'd raced nearer the lap record in the rain—which Spencer does now—but you know for me it was . . . Hailwood.'

Ken Sprayson is a small, strong man and if you want the measure of him, he came to see me for the interview when convention demands that it should be the other way round. He was happy to do so. He's that kind of bloke. He had brought some photocopies of newspaper and magazine articles for me and, because photocopying isn't easy if you're trying to arrange two or three cuttings at a time, some of it was indistinct. Wherever this happened, he had laboriously written in biro in capital letters (for legibility) what was missing so that I could read it. I don't know whether he is a genius but I do know the definition of genius: the ability to take infinite care. We are in the foyer of an outrageously expensive hotel at the National Exhibition Centre, Birmingham and he, like Minter, is all but teetotal. He sips an orange juice and when the resident pianist begins he automatically raises his voice into my tape recorder. He, like the riders, has short, strong fingers and they bear the encrusted oil-stains of a doer, not just a thinker.

'I've kept mentioning,' he will say as the piano plods through neutered transatlantic tunes, 'about how friendly everybody was. Well, it went even further than that. Norton arrived at Monza in 1952 or 1953 and they'd got hopelessly the wrong gearing. Norton's opposition are the Italian Gilera but the Gilera tool room made them a set of gears for the race. You can't imagine that now. When Reynolds started at the Isle of Man there was no other source for welding. If they wanted that they came to me—works bikes, private owners, anything. Nowadays the teams have pantechnicons, totally mobile workshops. Honda came to me a year or two ago and said: "We've got it, come and use it if you want." They were offering me the facility.

'But mostly the teams have gone into their own shells now, they all do their own thing. You know: don't let the others know what we're doing.' Still the pianist rambles on and in this foyer, almost exclusively populated by businessmen, Ken Sprayson with his mild-mannered Birmingham accent might be out of place. But he isn't. Like all people close to bike racing for a long time he's been to too many places, seen too much to be intimidated by anything so harmless as a frosty waiter.

'I mean, there was no money in it in the 1950s. Jim Redman did very well out of it and that's why he kept quiet, kept himself to himself. Hailwood was the first one who started to cash in on his talent and people were talking about £30,000 retainer. You take John Surtees and MV. His retainer was £5,000. John Hartle as the second-string was on £3,000.' Ken Sprayson pauses again. He saw the end of the lovely, innocent days when, in the garage next to his welding unit, teams were run by a handful of all-purpose people; and then the Japanese came to the garage next door and 'we found every bike had its own mechanic who worked in meticulous white linen gloves, and there were designers, race managers, publicity personnel and the place was crowded with people.' At this moment Sprayson has raised his voice high above the pianist as if he needed to dismiss any false notions about his role in it all. 'You talk to someone like Bill Smith, you're getting the inside story. I was just one of the hangers-on, if you like. I wasn't involved in the way that a contract rider would be.'

The man who comes to Zurich Airport to meet me is called Peter Johnson. He's an American conducting a love affair with old Honda racing bikes, of which he owns several. He telephoned Luigi Taveri one day—a cold call, as they say, one stranger speaking to another—and a friendship was born. Johnson travels annually from Redwood City, California, to spend a holiday with Taveri and they talk and talk and talk. We are moving smoothly away from the airport towards the autobahn and the 30-odd kilometres to the hamlet where Taveri lives. Johnson says that Taveri is one of the warmest people he's ever met but warns me I'll come across two key words in any extended interview: Top Secret. Honda didn't tell Taveri everything, and they didn't tell anybody else everything either.

To illustrate this, Johnson recounts an anecdote of his own. Johnson knows another man who is having the same love affair with old Honda racing machines, who also has some of the bikes. In order to restore one, he wanted original drawings from the factory. It was a very innocent request. The man got only one drawing, and it had to be smuggled out of the factory. 'I can't divulge any more,' Johnson says—we're on the autobahn now, well on the way to Taveri's home—'because a lot of people would get into trouble. But don't forget it was a *27-year-old drawing* . . .'

Taveri's home is on a gentle slope. Meadows fall away towards the lake which goes all the way back to Zurich and on this February evening the wind presses and moans against the window-panes. Snow, turning to rain, is driven on the wind. The door opens, Luigi Taveri is a small, impish, jolly man and you know even as the door opens that his house is your house and it doesn't matter that you're a stranger. He wants you here. He likes the bustle of people around him but is reluctant to take centre stage for himself. He is self-effacing. In the hall stands a wide cabinet built into the wall and on three shelves sixty-four trophies are arranged. It is a magnificent sweep of a collection and, instructively, Taveri does not even point it out. Instead he leads me into a lounge and we sit, although, from time to time, he rises to supervise the evening meal which is being cooked on a grill on the open log fire, apologizing each time he does so.

On a shelf a small, wooden-framed photograph is tilted at an angle and the familiar face of Mike Hailwood gazes down. (At no stage in the interview, which lasted, I suppose, three hours, did Taveri refer to Hailwood as Hailwood; only Mike, as if, a quarter of a century later, the name is enough to tell you who he's talking about.) Soon enough Taveri produces a broad, deep photo album. It is an amazing thing: it was sent to him by Honda and contains, page by page, handwritten messages from the team personnel of so long ago, and with each message photographs of wives and children. It is a family album, no mistake, but an album of a vast family—which is clearly how all the members of it saw themselves. Taveri's eyes dance from page to page, his large hands turn the pages with great delicacy, just the way he rode Honda bikes. 'For me,' he will say, 'it was always necessary to compete with a big heart. Winning is not everything, to do your best is everything.' And as the words tumble from him his hand has left the album and is spread tight across his chest over his heart.

Today he has a panel-beating business, fifteen employees, a turnover of 1.25 million Swiss francs, and a holiday villa in Spain. He still rides bikes but at bicycle races so that a Press photographer on the passenger seat can take pictures. He was invited to Japan in 1988 by Honda to meet all the people he'd known all those years before. He had a meeting with Mr Honda, who had told his chauffeur: 'Today you will have a very nice day because you will see Mr Taveri.'

Taveri also rode a lap of honour at Suzuka during the Grand Prix meeting that year. This is what the caption to a photograph taken at the Grand Prix says: 'The man in the black riding suit and a bowl-shaped helmet is Luigi Taveri, Honda works rider in the 1960s. However, the photograph was not taken some twenty years ago but on March 27 this year. The machine Taveri is riding is the original RC 149 that won the World Championship in 1966. Honda spent as much as two million yen to bring this machine back to life. It had been fast asleep in a warehouse. Looking very pleased, the 59-year old Taveri made a lap of the circuit, the engine making an ear-piercing noise. He was well received by applauding spectators most of whom were younger than the machine.'

Lawson in 1989. 'That's the problem with you, Stuart. You're an amateur and we're professionals.'

Mick Grant, who is still actively involved in motor cycle racing as a team manager, is also one of those rare people who have a rounded view of a competitive career. 'Some riotous and hilarious things happened to me,' he says, and deep within his Yorkshire accent there is warmth and humour. It does not stop him from adding: 'Virtually every Honda racing bike in private hands has been "nicked" [linguistic note: a softer meaning than stolen; but only just]. I think only Hailwood was ever given one by the factory. You do hear dark tales of Honda loading a boat with bikes, taking it out to the Irish Sea, and throwing them overboard.' As good a way as any to let the bikes guard their secrets.

Kenny Roberts owns the Lucky Strike motor bike team and plays golf whenever he can. 'My handicap is ten. I'm not bad, considering, but really I just do it for fun.' Is it true that golf is so elusive to master, so frustrating that it can drive you mad? 'It's trying to . . .'

There is another question, a much larger question. Tell me about Freddie Spencer. 'I knew him as well as anyone. No one really knows him. He was very religious—I don't know if he still is—and he was very . . . oh, I'm not sure how to say it, he was very unpredictable, although not on the track.' Except, it must be stated, that August afternoon in 1983 at Anderstorp, Sweden when they both went for the final corner together. 'He just wanted to win, but I didn't think he wanted it that badly.'

The letter comes from Durban and is covered in stamps: four are postage, one to say it is airmail, one to say it is express. The envelope bears the stamp of the Royal Hotel, St Peter Port, Guernsey, but don't be confused by that. People who travel acquire stationery as they move along and use it wherever they happen to be. Inside the envelope there is a charming note and then twelve large pages of a letter written in careful handwriting. Several words have been crossed out, which suggests that the writer has not only read it through carefully but wishes to make sure the words are exactly right. Few men on earth understand attention to detail like Nobby Clark.

'When I lived in Japan I read a lot about their customs and cultural habits. I was interested to know how their writing originated. Studying it was very interesting but I cannot write it. I was very fortunate because the Japanese mechanics taught me correct Japanese and I used to get up early in the morning and listen to the US Forces radio. They had a phrase of the day which I wrote down and this helped me an awful lot' [attention to detail again]. 'I liked going in to Tokyo by myself and exploring the city armed with a small pocket dictionary. This did not please some of the bosses, who thought it was dangerous, but I never had any problems.

'The one year I was in Japan Christmas Day fell on a week-day and they asked me if I would like to take it off. Christmas is not really celebrated there but I'd walked along the Ginza a few days before and you could have been forgiven for thinking that it was—they had everything from Father Christmas to reindeers. The day after Christmas it was all gone. It had simply disappeared overnight.

'I met Mr Honda at the Research and Development Centre in 1964. I had only been there a few days. He came in to our section one morning and was very surprised to see me. He asked who I was. Our chief mechanic, Aika San, told him I was Jim Redman's mechanic. He shook

Memories of Gardner in 1988.

And here at Suzuka.

hands with me and said: "My name is Honda." That was all. I met him in Spain twenty-one years later, he shook hands with me and said: "My name is Honda." '.

Mike Hailwood was taking his daughter Michelle, nine, and son David, six, to buy some fish and chips one Saturday night in March 1981. Fish and chips were, and perhaps still are, Britain's very own contribution to fast food. In a small place called Portway, in the countryside just south of Birmingham, his 3.5 Rover was 'in collision' with a lorry. Michelle was killed, David injured. Hailwood died in hospital. There is too much pathos as well as tragedy to comprehend it, even all these years later.

Stuart Hall is sitting in his small dressing-room at the BBC studios in

A classic picture of men and machines.

Manchester. Words flow easily from him. 'Ford asked me to drive a Fiesta in a race at Oulton Park against thirty professionals. I qualified well and they didn't like that. In the race I was shoved off at the first bend by the pros and that made me angry. I thought, "Sod you lot" and I had a go, I had a real go, I went motor racing. I can't remember where I finished but afterwards somebody said: "We'll give you a car next year and you'll win the Fiesta Championship." At my age, I was very excited to be made an offer like that. I went to Silverstone the following day for the British bike Grand Prix and those guys were ripping round at horrendous speeds on a track which wasn't fit to be ridden on because of the weather. In fact I was due to fly to Silverstone but the conditions were so bad that I couldn't. The cloud base was down to 500 feet.

'The winds were gusting across the track at 55 knots, there were rivers of water and flooding through Woodcote, and these guys were ripping round. I talked afterwards to Wayne and Freddie Spencer and Eddie Lawson and Randy Mamola—they were sitting in a semi-circle in their leathers sipping Coca Cola and they were so laid back. I was saying: "You know, you're going out there risking your lives on a millimetre of rubber, you make one mistake and crash, I'm still on a high from finishing a motor race yesterday, my adrenalin is still coursing through my body" and Lawson said [Hall mimicking a slow, deliberate American drawl]: "That's the problem with you, Stuart. You're a good amateur and we're professionals." He was right. Calm it all down, stay laid back, keep your nerves icy. They had a round robin to see whether they should race and the four of them said: "We have to." They are peerless, those guys, a race apart.' The pun was entirely unintentional.

Wayne Gardner has hobbled into the garden of his agent, Harris Barnett, in deepest Hertfordshire. It is a couple of weeks after his crash at Laguna Seca in April 1989. He positions himself on a chair and words simply bubble out of him. 'The danger is there, but it's as if something is satisfying you. You risk something, you go out there and beat it. There is something there to be done and you can either walk away from it or attack it. I'm frightened like normal people. I always think of Assen, and I think, "Well, it's dangerous" but you can also ride within your own limits and eliminate a lot of danger. It's the old story of what you understand. People ask me what it's like and I say it's like when you first go to drive a car, you're really worried, you're nervous about it, but when you do it more, when you start to understand the basics of it, you get more confident and you think: this is easy. That's exactly what it is racing. You begin, you're a little bit frightened of it, you get confident, you might have an accident or two, you analyse the whole situation, and it sort of comes naturally then.' He pauses briefly. 'I have lived life to the full, yeah. I've been in a lot of scrapes but I think that's my personality. I'm a reasonably flamboyant person who just wants to go and do things and have fun. I've never been in any serious trouble. The good thing about motor cycles is that it's given me a hobby.'

Every now and then Gardner alters the position of his body for comfort. Soft sunlight is falling on the lawn and the noise and bustle of racing a ferocious bike seem utterly remote at this moment. 'Always funny things happen. As I say, I could be a dull person like Freddie Spencer and hide away in my motor home but I prefer entertaining my friends and having good clean fun. There's nothing wrong with that.' Now he alters the position of his leg again. 'Honda have said it's up to me when I get back on a bike. They've been very good, they haven't pushed me. They said "When your leg is ready we'll go back racing." Even though it's a business, Honda's main idea is that we must still enjoy it. That's come from Mr Honda. He loves the racing . . . I've worked hard at my image in Japan but, for example, Freddie charged people for interviews in Japan—he was charging journalists like 10,000 dollars an hour. Honda were very, very mad at that. What does it take to just sit down and talk with some people? There was big trouble over it.

'I've had a really good insight into my future with this broken leg. In one way I haven't enjoyed it but it's been a blessing in disguise because its made me realize that I shouldn't retire and just sit around . . . My heart was bleeding when the others were riding—because I race from my heart, you know. I realized that I can't stop just yet. Everyone was sending me Fax messages saying "Hurry up and come back, we miss you."

'I was curious to know how I'd react to not going to the races, curious to see whether I'd be missed, to see if I'd miss it. My team were sending through Faxes during the practice sessions and races and I'd sit in Monaco reading all the timesheets. I had to be involved someway or other. One race day I went for a drive with some people. All day I was edgy. I couldn't stop wanting to know what had happened. We were sitting having lunch and I was looking at my watch. I was saying "They're half way through let's go home, let's go home to see what the results are."'

It could have been any of them saying it, all the way from Taniguchi at Governor's Bridge so long, long ago to Minter and Redman, little Luigi Taveri, Robb and Bryans and Hailwood and Mang and Pons and Lawson and Gardner himself.

Nothing fundamental changed.

Index